Comparing Cultures *and* Religions *in a* Postmodern World

Joseph Ki-Zerbo Versus Jacques Maritain

To Mr Arin Janderman,

With compliments from

the author!

(Blessings!

BASILE SEDE NOUJIO

PAGE PUBLISHING, INC.
Conneaut Lake, PA

First originally published by Page Publishing 2021

ISBN 978-1-6624-2564-6 (pbk)
ISBN 978-1-6624-2565-3 (digital)

Printed in the United States of America

With gratitude

to my elder brothers,
Rogers Sede and Vincent Ngwanyia

CONTENTS

FOREWORD

This work is rooted in the previous publication of the same author on Hegel's philosophy of history which is, in fact, a challenge to every African thinker and to anybody who dearly desires authentic knowledge about world civilization. Father Basile, in his first work, took a major step in steering the *academic* back on the course of truth in this exhaustive study, confronting the Hegelian ideas concerning Africa and the concrete African reality as represented by the highly celebrated thinker and politician of African origin, Leopold S. Senghor.

In this present work, he highlights many other conceptions of history and goes on in his normal comparative style to confront the African thinking to the Thomistic Christian approach, using Joseph Ki-Zerbo and Jacques Maritain to epitomize the African and the Thomistic ideas, respectively. It is a study that is long overdue in that it goes directly to the source of the misdirection concerning Africa. Such luminaries as George Wilhelm Fredrick Hegel, Arnold Toynbee, David Hume, Albert Sweitzer, and George Carrier may have earned a position of honor and respect in other areas of the academic. However, when one turns to the history and achievements of Africa and its people globally, these savants have done the academic and Western scholarship a tremendous disservice in their complete and utter defamation and misconceptions of the latter.

As a result of the Hegelian influence on the intellectual world, one rarely, if ever, hears the words *African* and *philosophy* (African philosophy) or *African* and *history* (African history) but together in

11

a phrase. In all areas of philosophy, basic and derivative, Africa is peculiar, if not absent. From this picture, one can only conclude that Africans either have no philosophy or that nothing that Africans have to say is of any philosophical significance. The same is true in the field of history. Again, one can only conclude that Africa has no history but only the history of others (Europeans and Asians) in Africa.

These mischaracterizations have kept the academic off course for too long. However, for the person of African descent who must chart a course of study through Western scholarship and institutions, it is virtually fatal. As W. E. B. DuBois said, "One must look at oneself through the eyes of the 'other' and consequently look to the other for enlightenment, completely unaware of the historical and philosophical significance of his own community." This is where the comparative approach used in this work is valuable, especially in this postmodern era.

There are such brilliant African minds and diasporic luminaries as Check Anta Diop, Theohille Obenga, Chancellor Williams, Eric Williams, Frank Fanaon, C. L. R. James, Molefi Asante, Náim Akbar, John Henrik Clarke, Léopold Senghor, and many others. One must also mention the brilliant Africans who provided the intellectual basis for Christianity (Catholicism): Origin, Tertullian, Cyprian, Athanasius, Augustine, Anthony, among others. It is to them that one owes the creeds, doctrines, and many of the hymns with which one is familiar.

Hegel and his companions' mischaracterization of African people furnished a much-needed justification for their enslavement since, according to them, Africans were already enslaved by darkness and barbarity. African enslavement, according to Hegelian thought, brought them in to contact with the more advanced species of humanity.

This work—with the use of the ideas of the African historian, Joseph Ki-Zerbo, and the Thomistic Christian ideas of Jacques Maritain—fills us with hope in a world that culture, history, and, consequently, human value seem to be relegated to an insignificant level in the name of postmodernism.

Hopefully, Fr. Basile's writing, with its analytic and comparative approach, will be the first of many to help right a wayward academic and steer it back on a course for truth.

Dr. Winston A. Bell
Prof. Emeritus, Winston Salem State University,
North Carolina and Livingston College, Salisbury, NC, USA

PREFACE

AFRICA, BEING THE human cradle of civilization with archaeological and fossil records dating back millions of years and predating other records from other countries, does not sit well with some past and present-day scholars. It is our responsibility to debunk the myths about Africa, and it must start with rewriting history and acknowledgment of the misinformation that helped spread the virus of racism, discrimination, and ignoramus misconceptions about a continent that is rich in culture, religions, languages, natural resources, etc.

European colonization had its hand in robbing, pillaging, and raping mother Africa and exploiting the continent for personal gain and greed, all while instituting Eurocentric point of views via language, customs, and culture. The media has also had its fair share of spreading falsities about Africa in cartoon images and representations, such as that of George of the Jungle and the movie *Cleopatra* starring Elizabeth Taylor, a White American actress. Over time, the misconceptions somehow became an embodiment of facts in the lecture halls of academia and scholarly writings.

Comparing Cultures and Religions in a Postmodern World seeks to debunk Hegel's declaration that Africa did not contribute anything to the history of the world and gives Africa its proper place is the canon of history, culture, and religions.

The concept of racism as deeply rooted in the history of the Africans, specifically the African Americans, is also highlighted in this publication, and the author also sees justification to the extensive Black Lives Matter protests going on in the world today. We subscribe to his inference that the future of mankind will be truly meaningful if, at all levels, the intrinsic value of each human person is rightly considered, irrespective of race, color, or religion. This is the meaning of true humanism.

Marco R. Morris
Liberal Studies Instructor
Department of Liberal Studies
NCA&T State University
Greensboro, NC 27411

ACKNOWLEDGMENTS

SOME MAY INTERPRET it as a guise of escapism or as a way of endorsing minimalism, yet for me, it is the most practical representation of human ingenuity that "nothing would be done at all if one waited until one could do it so well that no one could find fault with it." This phrase by John Henry Newman has always inspired me, granted that there is always room for improvement.

Considering that this work is an adaptation of my PhD thesis, I must start by expressing sincere gratitude to my teachers, professors, and benefactors. Many of my friends have always encouraged me to write, including Rev. Frs. Denning Achidi, George Nkeze, Peter Nouck, Felix Nkafu, Henry Tutuwan, Moses Njoh, Aloysius Ndifor, Giles Ngwa, Earnest Tubuo, Ernest Neba, Melchizedek Yemu, Innocent Amasiorah, and Michel Nganchop. I thank my mother, Odette Sede, my brothers Vincent, Rogers, and Dr. Eric; my sisters Victorine, Nicole, Adeline, Rosemary, Doreen, Comfort, Jusline, Imelda Ngwanyia, Simen Solange, Ines Meyoupo Sime Chunang; my secretaries Beth Pisano and Colleen Kudela. Special appreciation to my friend and colleague, Dr. Christian Mbock and his wife (my sister), Miriam Bih, and to Ekwoge Nadedge, Gladys Mbonifor, Tinzim Fon-Ndikum, Eugene and Favour Nkede, Mr. Nelson Kamga, Lambert Mbom, Mesembe Brian, Nzeme Hope A., Ekenyia Juliette, Nkie Veronica, Killa Forbi, Derick Nkeng, Seraphim Bama, Frank Sadat, Tina Yong, Phino Diangang, Elvis Eseh, Barbara Kaya, Dr. Agbor Ebot, Bestos Fongo, Dr. Prisco and Mabel Nkembeng, Dr. Roger Nkwadi, Wilson Esua, and many others.

Mr. Mue-Nkeme Basile, Dr. Pius Mosima, and Mrs. Clotilde Randa proofread this work. I am thankful to Bishop Peter Jugis, bishop of Charlotte; the Very Rev. Mgr. Patrick Winslow, chancellor and vicar general; Rev. Frs. John Putman, Pat Cay, Richard Sutter, Mgr. Mauricio West, and other priests of this diocese. I am indebted to the Christians of Our Lady of Consolation Church and the other parishes that I have served. Thanks to Mr. Robert Gallagher, Rick Rotondi, Raphael and Odilia Epingo and family, Patience Ewang and family, Michael Lawson, Ivo Ndime, Stephane Nwatchou, Ernest Etchope, Dr. Collins Ibeto, Peter and Agnes Ngoh, Jules Teta Bua Chapnda Nya Iglo, Yomba Ngassa, Flora Asongwe, Richard and Rose Mabo, Julius and Kelah Tar, Earnest and Bih Ita, Terence Ndiangang, Yvonne and Ngale Mongoh, Ferdinand and Shirly Ngimndo, Angela and Tom Matacoins, Mary and Wade Sample, Kevin and Elizabeth Keating, Chip and Maryfaith Stone, Ed and Gladys Hood, Delores Aklassou. Tovia Burroughs-Christian and Jeroneshe McMahon, Russell Martins, Bartina Edwards, Caro Elad, Benjamin Elad, Judith Fang and Kizito and Fidelia Kaba, Naomi Byrd, Lambert and Maryline Obenson, Alvin and Deborah Bond, Henry Wallace, Denise Duliepre, Toni Tupponce, Zeta Kenner, Dr. Bertrand and Laura Fote, Sam Cooper, Dr. Clarence Coutts, Chanele Jackson, Fomanka Basil, Joseph Nkeze, Innocent Lah, Greg Camp, Deacon Todd, Willis and Mary Joe, Bill Albertson, Mamun Kuna Gasper Cletus and Sally Fotibu, and Steve Crump. I appreciate the financial support of Andrew Habine and Stan Fri, and I am enormously grateful to Humpy and Patricia Wheeler for sponsoring this publication. My bishops, Immanuel Bushu (emeritus) and Michael Bibi, have been greatly supportive.

Due to human frailty, I must have omitted the names of many wonderful persons who have been of enormous assistance to me. You are all in my heart and prayers. Please accept my earnest gratitude.

May God bless you all in space and time and, finally, in eternity.

Basile Sede Noujio, PhD

GENERAL INTRODUCTION

Culture and religion form the major elements that constitute the history of a people. Philosophy of history is concerned with the examination of the cultural and religious elements that constitute the worldview of a defined group of people. After obtaining my PhD in philosophy from the Pontifical Lateran University (PUL), Rome, all my professors encourage me to open my thesis to the world. The question was, how do I do this? Then I thought of making a two-volume publication so that the world may discover not only this new perspective in philosophy of history, presented in two volumes, but also the richness of multiculturalism and the danger of postmodern thinking. My first publication, *Hegel's Philosophy of History, a Challenge to the African Thinker (Compliments to Léopold S. Senghore)*, forms a good background in appreciating this present publication that deals with cultural and religious diversity in a multicultural and postmodern world.

We can rightly understand the culture and religion of a people, especially in the comparative sense that we are to use in this work if we examine them from the perspective of history, precisely, philosophy of history. The *New Encyclopedia Britannica* explains that the term *history* can be employed in two senses: (1) the events and actors that, together, make up the human past or (2) the accounts given of that past as the modes of investigation, whereby they are arrived at or constructed. In the first sense, the word refers to what as a matter of fact happened while, in the second sense, it refers to the study and description of those happenings.[1] In the perspective philosophy of history, the question is about the significance, if there is any, in human history. Reflecting further on the basic implication of history, Daniel Little indicates that the significance of history rests basically on the fact that as a discipline, it suggests the possibility of better understanding ourselves in the present by understanding the forces, choices, and circumstances that brought us to our current situation.[2] This is where religion and culture emanate as constitutive elements in the study and evaluation of history, and it is along this consideration that we are in this work, presenting some major world conceptions of history in a comparative manner.

Though we shall mostly be talking about history or philosophy of history in this work, the core concepts are culture and religion. Philosophy of history explains that every history is an embodiment of cultural and religious values. In this regard, John Henrik Clarke explains that "history is a clock that people use to tell their political and cultural time of the day; it is also a compass that people use to find themselves on the map of human geography... The most important role that history plays is telling a people where they still must go and what they still must be."[3]

Hegel, the philosopher, has much to do with the Western mode of thinking in his philosophy of history. Other versions of history, originating from the West will also be considered. Furthermore, are to examine the Christian religion and culture as Western, considering that they originated from the West. The Eastern worldview as represented by some major Eastern religions, the African American conception as well as the traditional African culture and religion will be effectively discussed. Our main emphasis, however, would be on the African and the Thomistic conceptions. This is because all major civilizations, to a greater extent, sprang from Africa. Equally, it is

---

[1.] Cfr. W. BENTON, ed., *New Encyclopaedia Britannica* (London: Encyclopaedia Britannica Inc., 1977), 961.

[2.] Cfr. D. LITTLE, *Philosophy of History*, in URL: < http://plato.stanford.edu/entries/history > (accessed on the June 20, 2013).

[3.] J. H. CLARK, *African World Revolution* (New Jersey: African World Press, 1996), 406.

generally considered that devoid of a history of Africa, the history of the world would remain vague in many respects. Similarly, we are considering the influence and prominence of Christianity in the world. The African conception would be represented typically by the ideas of Joseph Ki-Zerbo[4] while the ideas of Jacques Maritain would be used to portray the Thomistic-Christian conception of history. This explains why their names are used in our subtopic as an indication that we are using a comparative approach in this work.

The brutal killing of George Floyd is certainly very significant in the evolution of world history. This happened at this time when the global COVID-19 pandemic is affecting the entire world. The transition from the quarantine state of home confinement into the spontaneous rioting along the streets of various cities in the world, especially in the United States of America, is eminent at this historical epoch. This is very significant in the philosophy of history of every continent and culture, especially the African Americans. This is because, at this time, human beings in every part of the world are

---

[4.] (Joseph Ki-Zerbo (1922-2006) was born in Toma (Haute-Volta, now named Burkina Faso). He is recognized as one of Africa's foremost thinkers, with a special interest in African history and politics. He started his education in his home country in the missionary schools in Toma. He later studied in Faladie (Mali) and, later, in the famous Sorbonne University in France. After getting his aggregation degree in history, he returned to Africa and got actively involved in the politics of his country, Burkina Faso. From 1972 to 1978, he was professor of African history at the University of Ouagadougou, yet for political reasons, he was forced into exile in 1983 and was only able to return in 1992. He is also considered as an ardent humanist, ceaselessly fighting for the respect of human and universal values. As a committed African historian and intellectual, he fervently promoted Pan-Africanism, endogenous development, social justice, and peace in Africa. As a professor, he dedicated his life to education by serving as director of national education, and secretary-general of the African and Malgache Council for Higher Education [CAMES]. He was also a member of the UNESCO executive board. Professor Ki-Zerbo is known and appreciated as an eminent, highly cultivated scientist and specialist of African history in which, having written so many books and articles, he has become a solid authority. He stands as a symbolic figure of contemporary Black African struggles.) Cfr. E. K. AKYEAMPONG et al., eds., *Dictionary of African Biography* (Oxford: Oxford University Press, 2012), 401-402.

becoming conscious of the fact that racism is like a virus, historically proven to be more dangerous than the coronavirus. Consequently, in this era of multiculturalism and globalization each person's worldview, despite his or her culture or religion, is influenced by a deeper understanding of the true meaning and value of the human person. This is why the African conception of history, as represented by Joseph Ki-Zerbo and the Thomistic-Christian conception, typified by Jacques Maritain, is most relevant and highly recommended at the end of this work. The inference is that life should revolve around genuine humanism.

Our major reason for using Africa as our point of departure is not only justified by the fact that Africa is the springboard of civilization but also because this continent remains controversial in many regards. There is still much misunderstanding about the African people and their activities. As John Parker and Richard Rathbone remark, the African concept of history, just as African history itself, "has been so controversial and contested."[5] Therefore, this work is also intended to make some basic clarifications not only for the service of the Africans themselves but also for the totality of humanity, considering the ever-growing globalization or sociocultural interdependence.

To analyze a people's conception of history is to analyze their religion, beliefs, or culture; it is to analyze their world and their destiny. Therefore, as implied in any genuine epistemology, we shall not only recount the aspects that constitute the concept of history (culture and religion) for the African and the other Western, Eastern, and Christian cultures, but we shall also attempt to make them understandable. This is where practice goes with rationality or thought, justifying what Kwame Nkrumah once said that "practice without thought is blind."[6] In the same perspective, with specific reference to Africa, we shall be considering seriously the words of the one-

---

[5.] J. PARKER and R. RATHBONE, *African History, a Very Short Introduction* (Oxford: Oxford University Press, 2007), 2.

[6.] K. NKRUMAH, *Conscientism: Philosophy and Ideology for Decolonisation and Development with Particular Reference to the African Revolution* (London: Panaf Books, 1970), 78.

time prime minister of Congo, Patrice Lumumba, as quoted by Ki-Zerbo himself that "un giorno, la storia dirà...l'Africa scriverà la propria storia."[7] Joseph Ki-Zerbo, we shall come to discover as this work unfolds, is one of the most significant figures in the annals of African historiography. He does not only write and defend the true African history, as well as the authentic African conception of history, but he also equally discusses in a very profound and convincing manner the immense importance of African past with regard to the rest of the world. In this regard, Ki-Zerbo reiterates that "l'Afrique, et son nom méritent d'être retenus par l'histoire universelle. »[8]This work is our humble attempt toward this recommendation, especially if we consider the harm that philosophers like Hegel have done to the Africans. Considering Hegel's ideas and influence, therefore, Ki-Zerbo remarks as follows:

> Hegel (1770-1831) had no hesitation in stating in his Philosophy of History that Africa 'is not a historical continent; it shows neither change nor development' and that the black peoples were "capable of neither development nor education. As we see them today, so have they always been." This preposterous view of Africa persisted into the twentieth century, when an Oxford professor could be heard to say: "Perhaps in the future, there will be some African history to teach. But at present there is none: there is only the history of the Europeans in Africa. The rest is darkness... and darkness is not a subject of history."[9]

---

7. J. KI-ZERBO, *Storia Dell'Africa Nera*, Un Continente fra la Preistoria e il Futuro, Giulio Einaudi Editore, Torino 1977, 3. "One day, the history would be told... Africa would write its proper history" (the translation is ours).

8. J. KI-ZERBO, *Histoire de l'Afrique Noire* (Paris: Hatier, 1972), 360. "Africa and her name deserve to be retained in universal history" (the translation is ours).

9. J. KI-ZERBO, ed., *General History of Africa*, vol. 1, *Methodology and African Pre-History* (Oxford: James Currey Publishers, 1990), 12.

You can consult our previous publication, *Hegel's Philosophy of History, a Challenge to the African Thinker.*

Henry Odera Oruka, having considered that in the contemporary world, assimilation is an illusion, considering that people have become very conscious of their personality and that, at the same time, independence is a hallucination in a world where the interdependence of peoples announces itself so clearly, insists that the African researcher is challenged to investigate and unearth the principles that surround their conception of reality; that is, their culture and their religion as embedded in their history. According to him, "This is necessary for posterity and for the development of a national culture. This investigation should be part of the national program in every African state."[10]

Considering the reality of multiculturalism and interculturalism, our interest is also to discover the liaison, if any, between the African worldview and other religions and cultures as embedded in their own conceptions of history. In this regard, we shall discuss the cyclical version of history, as well as the spiritual, the material, the Eastern, Western, and the African American conceptions of history. However, we shall elaborate more on the Christian-Thomistic conception typified by Jacques Maritain.

Our comparative approach is meant to project more the values imbedded in history in order to come out with a world culture that can work for the whole of mankind plagued by the vices of postmodernism. This approach is essential, considering that philosophy of history is integrally linked to the field of virtue, ethics. Maritain, like Ki-Zerbo, sponsors a notion of history that is basically founded on humanism or personalism. This again gives us a good ground to compare both thinkers, bearing in mind the important lessons eminent in any healthy comparative analysis.

Like Ki-Zerbo, Maritain reflects on history as based on the human person in all facets. As a typical Thomist, he presents his

---

[10.] H. O. ORUKA, *The Philosophical Roots of Culture in Kenya* (unpublished research proposal presented to the Minister of Culture and Social Services, Government of Kenya, 1976), 8.

version of history, culture, and politics with a strong accent on the paramount value of the human person as implied in Christian personalism. Joseph Evans, Maritain's devoted editor, confirms that his philosophy is principally centered on an "authentically Christian politics" and that his effort was to establish, in light of a philosophy of history and of culture, the nature of a new humanism.[11] Yet in the last chapter of this work, we shall realize that many other forms of humanism prevail in the world today, which contradict the Christian/African humanism, propagated by the postmodern thinkers.

[11.] Cfr. J. EVANS, *Integral Humanism: Temporal and Spiritual Problems of a New Christendom* (Paris: Notre Dame University Press, 1973), v.

CHAPTER ONE

An Explication of the Concept of History in the Light of Joseph Ki-Zerbo

LIKE MOST OF the intellectuals of his generation, Joseph Ki-Zerbo was not only a politician but also a fervent advocate of African history. He did not only assume invariably bold positions concerning some fundamental issues about his continent and his country but equally also did a lot of research to secure the historical reality of the African continent. In this regard, Ki-Zerbo had certain categories that he used in defining and presenting history. Basically, he does not limit his perception of history to an impersonal manifestation of a certain force or spirit; neither does he look at it in terms of great and, perhaps, recorded spectacular events. Rather, history for him revolves around the concrete expression of the lives of a people. History revolves around culture and religion as on the title of this work. This is precisely the focus of any genuine philosophy of history.

Another striking conviction of Ki-Zerbo is that Africa is, in fact, the cradle of humanity and has produced, over long periods of time, the first major inventions of the human mind.[12] Yet he is also quite aware of the writings of philosophers like Hegel who drastically castigate the African continent as unhistorical. Such Hegelian lectures

---

12. Cfr. J. KI-ZERBO, *International Bureau of Education* (1999) UNESCO, vol. XXIX, n. 4, 615–627.

on history within the context of a philosophy of history that dehumanizes Africa were of great inspiration to his approach to history, and they also inspired his preference to study history in an interdisciplinary form. He also laments the injustice done to history by those who limit it merely to written documents. Such approach, for him, is being treacherous to natural events and even to the actual value of history.[13]

While insinuating that the study of history as a discipline must uncompromisingly be viewed from an inner perspective and must unquestionably be the history of the people concerned, Ki-Zerbo also suggests that such a study must avoid being too narrative but rather, even in an interdisciplinary manner, should be tangible and systematic.[14] It must be studied as a natural heritage of a people which has to be given flesh.

In this historical epoch, the fact that the African, and we include the African American, is as rational as every other human person is obvious for those who have genuinely overcome racism and ignorance. There is equally no doubt that Africa does not only have a history but also a conception of history which, in the Western sense, can also be termed a philosophy of history and can be put at par with the philosophy of history of other cultures or nations. Yet the primordial questions we are asking ourselves are like those asked by many other persons, as presented by John Parker and Richard Rathbone framed as follows:

> Is African history in its essence the same as that of other peoples or parts of the world, subject to the same "universal truths" and amendable to the same methods of scholarly analysis? Or does the particularity of Africa demand that its past be studied according to its own logic, or even to the diverse logics of its myriad constituent

---

[13]. Cfr. J. KI-ZERBO, ed., *General History of Africa*, vol. 1, 12-13.
[14]. Ibid., 16-22.

parts? How "African," in other words, is African history?[15]

The above questions form a major problematic in this work as they still reveal how controversial the whole concept of history is, especially as regards the African continent. Consequently, with the above questions in mind, we are not only attempting a geographic and historical analysis of Africa but, more intently, we are also presenting the notion of history for the Africans in the perspective of the historian Joseph Ki-Zerbo.

History is enormously important in every society considering that it projects the originality of the culture. This is more important for the Africans who have been humiliated, crushed, and even converted by Western acidic conceptions that turn to devalue and neutralize their history. History must be the grounds on which to stand in order to reclaim and celebrate such a lost dignity. Ki-Zerbo insists, therefore, that life must start with history and end with history. Accordingly, only by remaining true to her identity can Africa achieve development and find a role to play in a world of multiculturalism. This is the only means by which Africans can become subjects and masters of their own identity and destiny. The inference at this level is that history functions as an identity provider. Every society has a history, and history elevates and humiliates a people and a community.

If Europe and America, for example, consider their history as their identity stamp, then they will do all it takes to encourage and support other nations and people who struggle. An authentic study and fidelity to history will easily provide conscientious solutions to the issue of immigration and racism which seem to dominate world politics today, especially in the United States of America. This great nation, the United States of America, that is founded on immigrants and built by immigrants should practically be humbled by her history and, in this way, respect and support healthy immigration procedures as well as vigorous policies that would accommodate people

---

[15.] J. PARKER and R. RATHBONE, eds., *African History, a Very Short Introduction*, 3.

of all race and colors. Until this is done, the random killing, hate, stress, and insecurity will continue to persist, and these flaws defeat a genuine perception of development. As a result, we dare to ask: are the so-called developed nations really developed? Such a question stems from our submission to the conviction of Léopold Senghor that development should not be considered solely in terms of structures and machines. Rather, development must start with a heart-to-heart contact between peoples, and this alone can make the future of mankind a valuable possibility.[16]

Ki-Zerbo explains that the concept of history must be linked to that of development. For him, these two concepts must, of necessity, go together and may also include the concepts of liberty and finality. History goes with relevant choices that are also conditioned by nature since nature is the ambient that embraces and conditions the demographic and scientific endeavors as well as the balance of power in the religious, cultural, and political spheres.[17] This is because amid the geographic and cultural realities, "man certainly adapted at a very early stage to well-defined habits, each with its own peculiar climate...sometimes with certain features in common, but also displaying regional and even local variations."[18] By implication, the human person is identified as the most crucial element in Ki-Zerbo's categorization of history. He considers the human person as both the principal subject and the irreplaceable object of history. Thus, history operates within the ambient of the sociocultural realities within which man finds himself and operates as the principal agent. A person is fully a person if he lives in complete community awareness as history unfolds. Even though the forces of nature, both the irresistible and the adaptable, play an integral role in the unfolding

---

[16.] Cf. W. KLUBACK, *Léopold Sédar Senghor, From Politics to Poetry* (New York: Peter Lang Publishers, 1997), pp. 10-11.

[17.] Cfr. J. KI-ZERBO, *Punti Fermi Sull'Africa*, M. HOYET, trans., (Bologna: EMI, 2011), 13.

[18.] J. KI-ZERBO, ed., *La natte des autres*, 233

of history, the human person is the chief instrument. Accordingly, Ki-Zerbo declares,

> In this "history of nature," man stands out, because he unites all the realm—animal, vegetable and mineral—because he was made up of a fragment of everything that exists before him, and also because he has been crowned with speech and is consequently the companion of God and the guardian of nature. The complexity of man is expressed in the maxim: "There are many persons in the person of every person."[19]

From the above, we can understand why he links up his study of history essentially with the study of the human person. Consequently, he considers that in the study of history, all other broad categories can only be regarded as extremely relative and provisional. To this, he regrets that "for many years, Central African prehistory consisted only of typology and chronology and very little attention was paid to man." Though he accepted that there was not really a well-defined culture in this area, his still made his conviction clear that culture, or rather man as a cultural being, remains a major category in the study of history.[20]

Ki-Zerbo, in the above consideration, links history to the study of reality, a reality as lived concretely by a people. This is, therefore, the most significant element in Ki-Zerbo's conception of history. Unlike some thinkers in the caliber of Hegel who concentrate on the phenomenology of the spirit, Ki-Zerbo, like Senghor and other twentieth-century phenomenologists, brings us to the concrete existence, to the living community; it is the cultural identity of a people in the past, the present, and the future, considering that culture in itself is history that is moving. This implies the dynamism evident in his conception of history, bearing in mind that history is not static,

---

[19] J. KI-ZERBO, ed., *General History of Africa*, vol. 1, 65.
[20] Cfr. Ibid., 233.

and neither is it out of the human domain of existence. In this regard, he makes the following declaration:

> Innanzitutto, l'identità culturale non è una struttura fossile o statica; non è neppure un concetto astratto o un'etichetta incollata dal di fuori. L'identità culturale è un processo che ingloba il passato e il presente ma anche, potenzialmente, il futuro, perchè la cultura è la storia in cammino. L'identità culturare è la vita.[21]

It is with reference to the above characteristic which he attributes to history that Ki-Zerbo castigates the idea of people locking themselves into the static and straitjacket of Kant's logical egoism. In his account, therefore, history is truth that must be verifiable in one way or another. Accordingly, Ki-Zerbo recommends historians to always come into contact with others and compare their views, not only for the fact of arriving at truth but also to arrive at truths that contribute to their own critical reflection and their own development or the development of their country.[22] The study of history, therefore in his vision, is not for the sake of keeping records but for the development or well-being of humankind, that is, of the human person to amend or purify the nasty cultures sponsored by some history while upholding the reputable features.

It is equally the firm conviction of Ki-Zerbo that history should not be limited to narratives, focusing on the great battles and exploits of outstanding figures, as some thinkers have stressed, but rather, it should deal with the principal or basic sociocultural and political performances. History is authentic existence; it is life as it is lived

---

[21.] (First of all, cultural identity is not a fossil or static structure; it is not even an abstract concept or a label glued from the outside. Cultural identity is a process that incorporates not only the past and the present but also, potentially, the future because culture is the story on its way. Cultural identity is life.) J. Ki-Zerbo, *Punti Fermi Sull'Africa*, 14.

[22.] Cfr. J. Ki-Zerbo, in *International Bureau of Education* (1999), UNESCO, vol. XXIX, n. 4.

by a community, and living without a history is like being a piece of flotsam or like a tree that has been felled and seeks to form a link with foreign roots.[23] His recommendation, therefore, is that in an authentic history as typified in his research on Africa, "we must consider the vitally important elements in the recognition of the African heritage and should bring out the factors making for unity in the continent."[24]

Thus, the definition of history in the very words of Joseph Ki-Zerbo is as follows:

> The fundamentals of civilizations, institutions, structures, techniques and social, political, cultural and religious practices. In conclusion...the methodology used for this history will make an invariable scientific contribution to historiography in general, especially as far as the interdisciplinary approach is concerned.[25]

To better understand this definition, we shall identify education and tradition as two basic arms or categories of history.

1.1 History and Education

The most profound regret that Ki-Zerbo has is based on the fact that "for a long time now, all kinds of myths and prejudices concealed the true history of Africa from the world at large."[26] In the midst of all controversies surrounding African history in particular and the perception of history for the Africans in general, Ki-Zerbo builds his conviction and his research on the simple sociocultural facts binding the African people with a stiff certainty that Africans are like other people but have been shaped by different people in different

---

[23.] Cfr. J. Ki-Zerbo (ed.), *General History of Africa*, vol. 1, 9.

[24.] Ibid., xiii.

[25.] Ibid., 9.

[26.] Ibid., vii.

context.[27] Accordingly, Africa has to master her story; Africans have to study the reality of their history as vested in the cultural heritage inherited from their forefathers in order to develop. In this regard, he perceives history as a very necessary tool for development that must be taken seriously as we read from his recommendation below:

> Teams must be mobilized to save as many vestiges of the past as possible, and museums must be opened to preserve these vestiges. Legislation must be passed to defend them, scholarships granted for training specialists, syllabuses and degree courses recast in an African perspective.[28]

The importance of the study of history, which implies culture and religion, is for the growth of the African nation. This is to assist most African young people, especially those in the diaspora, more especially their children who are considered lost. Therefore, with the use of an African proverb, Ki-Zerbo reminds us that he who is lost does not know where he comes from; neither does he know where he is going.[29]

Africans must study African history as embedded in the African cultural heritage with pride and with an intercultural humility in recognition of the existence of other cultures and of the need to live a balanced life with people from other continents. Though our intercultural study in this work is to tie with the Thomistic culture as presented by Jacques Maritain, Ki-Zerbo, in his recommendation of an intercultural study, looks more on the countries that have strong ties with Africa, especially the United States of America. To this, he

---

[27.] Cf. Ibid., 5.
[28.] Ibid., 9.
[29.] Cfr. A. NIANG, "Joseph Ki-Zerbo: The History and His Struggle."

makes the following declaration in his introduction to the *General History of Africa*:

> The *General History* sheds light both on the historical unity of Africa and on its relations with the other continents, particularly the Americans and the Caribbean. For a long time, the creative manifestations of the descendants of Africa in the Americas were lumped together by some historians as a heterogeneous collection of *Africanisms*... The cultural inheritance of Africa is visible everywhere, from the southern United States to northern Brazil, across the Caribbean and on the Pacific seaboard. In certain places, it even underpins the cultural identity of some of the most important elements of the population.[30]

We can see in this direction that the epistemological benchmarks of Professor Ki-Zerbo's thought are based on self-knowledge, thinking by oneself for oneself, a sound understanding of otherness, critical reference to the past, and the irreplaceable importance of research based on popular African wisdom. This is where he situates the importance of education, insinuating that the key factors of African promotion are education and training and African unity.[31]

While emphasizing the importance of education, Ki-Zerbo also insinuates that education based on history must be perceived as a means, a working tool (both theoretical and practical), rather than as an end. This, in his consideration, would provide the answer to the question that he certainly considers most crucial: how can one be born again? The question may sound absurd, yet it portrays certain nostalgia for the past; it is an existential question about the causes of the present situation of the continent that was once the cradle of humanity but is now lagging behind for want of science, technology,

---

30. J. KI-ZERBO (ed.), *General History of Africa*, vol. 1, x.
31. Cfr. J. KI-ZERBO, *Histoire de l'Afrique Noire*, 632.

and knowledge.[32] Accordingly, in his book *Histoire de l'Afrique Noire* (The History of Black Africa), which became a reference text for African history and struggle, he made the following declaration:

> It's high time Africans liberate themselves from cultural asphyxiation; it is high time they went in search of what it is to be African, to draw the necessary lessons from their own traditional history in order to apprehend the future with confidence. The approach will consist, for Africa, in re-conquering its confiscated identity for without identity, we are just a mere object of history, a prop in the play of globalization, an instrument used by the others—a utensil.[33]

In his address to the Conference of African States on the Development of Education in Addis Ababa, on May 15, 1961, Ki-Zerbo highlighted the importance of studying the aspects that constitute African history as a condition for any real development in Africa. He insisted that "education in Africa must be African; that is, it must rest on specifically African culture and be based on the special requirements of African progress in all fields."[34] Such a recommendation is grounded on his firmly held conviction that African thinking does exist, which is peculiar to Africa. "African ethics, metaphysics and sociology do exist... African teachers must be mainly responsible for carrying out fuller research and making better use of these philosophical resources of Africa."[35] It is in this connection that he describes history as the main foundation of the national conscious-

---

[32.] Cfr. J. KI-ZERBO and M. IZARD, "Du Niger à la Volta" in B. A. OGOT, ed., *General History of Africa*, vol. 5 (Berkeley: University of California Press, 1992), 327-267.

[33.] J. Ki-Zerbo, *Histoire de l'Afrique Noire*, 632.

[34.] J. KI-ZERBO, "The Concept of Education in Africa," in *United Nations Scientific and Cultural Organization* (1961) UNESCO/EDAF/S/5, Paris, of 10 April 1961, 1.

[35.] Ibid., 1.

ness and goes on to regret that its prime of place has not yet been fully situated within the African continent, as we read from the following declaration:

> History must take a prominent place in the reform of the curriculum, since it is one of the main foundations of the national consciousness. In many French-speaking African States, however, the national history is never taught at all in the secondary school, although many people today admit that Africa has a history. In fact, it can easily be shown that African history exists, that it can be written and that it has, several times, played a decisive part in world history.[36]

Consequently, as he identifies the human person who needs to be genuinely educated as the principal agent of history, he also insists that education, in this regard, must be given "its proper function as a catalyst, consolidating African national values, which, though not expressed in the same manner as in Europe or elsewhere, nonetheless exist."[37] Therefore, irrespective of the ills of colonization that destroyed some of the values of Africa, some are still rooted in the African system that can complement the good aspects in colonization for a better Africa. Consequently, we need a transformation of our educational system to be adequately fitted into the complex world of today. This is a kind of complementarity that recognizes the absolute importance of a people's culture as Ki-Zerbo intimates as follows:

> Il est évident que l'éducation était un sous-système plus important que d'autres. Aujourd'hui, peut-être, certains éléments ont disparu ou se sont repliés dans l'anonymat...je suis convaincu que l'éducation doit être transformée pour que la

---

[36.] Ibid., 2.
[37.] Idem.

société soit transformée. Nous avons affaire à une
sorte de rapport dialectique positif.[38]

Ki-Zerbo is fully convinced that the concept of history must
line up with the anthropological model of structuralism in view of
the fact that structuralism considers that the key to understanding
lies in the structures which, consciously or otherwise, are the logical
mechanisms triggering off the actions of human groups.[39] He generally considers that man is a historical animal; he lives in history and
must naturally and necessarily remain grafted to history even without an attachment to the chronological aspect of history. It is for this
reason that he castigates any consideration that places chronology as
a sine qua non condition for a definition of history. Consequently,
he declares that "there is no reason to make a cult of chronology,
however great its importance as the backbone of history, and whatever efforts we make to base it on solid foundations. Dates are means
rather than end in themselves."[40]

Even though Ki-Zerbo does not look at chronology as an
absolutely necessary category for the consideration of history in the
African sagacity, he does not imply that chronology did not exist
in African history or that it is unnecessary in the conception of
history according to the Africans. His discoveries show that there
exist at least some chronicles in Africa before the ninth century of
the Christian era although there is one exception that was virtually
unknown until quite recently. To this effect, he mentions the *Ta'rikh*
of *Khalifa b. khayyt*, one of the oldest Arabic annals, which contains
necessary information on the conquest of the Maghrib. It is also vital
to note that *Al-Tabari* reproduces in his *Ta'rihk* one of the oldest
Arabic explanations of the Black world in the shape of the testimony

---

[38.] (It is obvious that education was a larger subsystem than others. Today,
perhaps, some elements have disappeared or fallen back into anonymity... I
am convinced that education must be transformed in order for society to be
transformed. We are dealing with a kind of positive dialectical relationship). J.
Ki-Zerbo, *À Quand L'Afrique?*, 201.

[39.] Cfr. Ibid., 6.

[40.] *Ibid*, 7.

of the historiographer Umar B. Shabba. This is mostly about the revolt of the Sudan at Medina in AD 145 + 762. It also bears witness to the substantial presence of Africans at the height of the period. Reference is also made to a collection of legal traditions assembled by Ibn 'Abd al-Hakam, as these also contain historical information.[41]

The inference we can draw at this point is that history, in the conception of Ki-Zerbo, is not only a matter of cultural heritage but also a cultural heritage in motion that is clothed in life, that is enrobed in the actual activity of the people. Typically, he insists that this cultural heritage needs to be studied for a better life in the present and for posterity.

Ki-Zerbo embarks much on the concept of education as a necessary ally to history in the sense that since history is embedded in traditional or cultural values, these values must not only be handed down but must also be studied as they are acquired. Values and beliefs are not to be blindly handed down, and when they are well studied, they also become helpful to the development of a nation. Hence, we cannot talk about history without talking about education. The African nation, as he said, would grow faster if historical values are well studied and are placed as the foundations of other forms of innovations and even inventions. This idea is generally accepted by most African political authorities, even at the level of the United Nations. It is recorded that in 1961, there was a conference of African ministers of education held in Addis Ababa, convened by UNESCO, in cooperation with the former colonial powers. This conference reflected on strategies for the development of education in Africa based on the peculiarities of the African system of life as entrenched in the African culture. The conference also adapted a long-term plan for universal education which is African-based by the year 2000.[42]

[41.] Cfr. J. KI-ZERBO, *À Quand L'Afrique?*, 40.

[42.] Cfr. 1961 Conference Addis Ababa which was based on decolonization of school as a motor for development; 1964: Conference of Abidjan (pedagogical concerns); 1968: Nairobi Conference (system crisis education); 1976 Lagos Conference (basic education, education crisis); 1982: Conference Harare (the illusion maintained between the school and its funding); 1991 Dakar Conference (eradicate illiteracy); 1998 Durban Conference (the weight of the

By and large, the focal point remains as Ki-Zerbo inscribes that there is a crisis in the educational system of Africa which must be redressed to accommodate the essence of the African culture for a better Africa, and he was not alone in this school of thought. He was a member of the said conference and had the same line of reasoning with other African educational analysts, including Hilaire Sikounmo and Joseph Brandolin who were all interested in letting Africa out of the crisis of education by emphasizing on ideas of democratization and Africanization of the school no matter how revolutionary this process may be.[43]

Hilaire Sikounmo, for example, insists that even teachers of schools must be insiders, with a good knowledge of the traditional system so that at the very initial state of education, these values must be initiated into the people. Therefore, the traditional African adults must play their role as initiators for the younger. Hilaire, in 1992, with his teaching quality, identified so many evils such as individualism, greed, and cultural nonchalance that are creeping into Africa. He requests, in the light of Ki-Zerbo, that a system be put in place where the African traditional cultural values such as community lifestyle, hard work, creativity, dedication to the God of our ancestors are preciously valued. For him, therefore, it is only with such an African-oriented education that Africa can be liberated from the poor style of individualism and a craving for personal success and respect for elders, as well as for community goods and values.[44] Sikounmo is very convinced from his survey of young people that the consolidation of customs and traditions in African schools is urgent. This, he considers, is a remediation work which would root more students deeply into the African society proper and into the ancestral culture. In this regard, social ties, long broken, would be restored. Accordingly, to get out of the crisis, it is necessary to "canaliser le

---

technocracy international), see also World Conferences on Education; 1990: Conference World in Jomtien (Education for All by the Year 2000); 2000 World Conference in Dakar (reduce poverty worldwide through education).

[43]. Cfr. J. KI-ZERBO, *Eduquer ou périr,* 87.

[44]. Cfr. H. SIKOUNMO, *L'école du sous-développement. Gros plan sur l'enseignement secondaire en Afrique* (Paris: Karthala, 1992), 234.

trop-plein d'énergie de la jeunesse vers les activités de production, de meilleure organisation de la vie collective"[45] (to channel the overflow of youthful energy to the activities of production, and of better organization of collective life).

Along the same vein of African-centered education, Charles Hadji talks of African humanistic values, insisting that this should be the backbone of the education of children in Africa today.[46] Joseph Brandolin knows the African education system, thanks to his long experience in several African countries for French support for various ministries of education. He questions the relevance of many colonial aspects enforced in the educational system of Africa, and at the same time, he agreed with Joseph Ki-Zerbo and Hilaire Sikounmo concerning the need for a revolution in education in Africa. For him, these proposals must not only be initiated at the level of the ministry of education but also at various grassroots levels. In fact, considerations must start from the base.[47]

Joseph Brandolin, in the above light, perceives it more as a fight to be carried on between formal and nonformal education, considering formal education as more of developing separate schooling, literacy, education, and training schools for employment. For him, this is where the crisis lies, that is, if it is not done alongside informal education. The informal sector is the nonformal training on some basic works of arts and architecture. The informal sector implies the very important aspect of teaming with all contexts of life. In this regard, he makes the following assertion:

> L'éducation formelle est en crise, les formations non formelles bricolent, le secteur informel grouille de vie, mais on ne cherche pas à les mettre en relation pour réinventer un système éducatif

---

[45] H. SIKOUNMO, *Jeunesse et éducation en Afrique noire* (Paris: L'Harmattan, 1995), 160.

[46] Cfr. C. HADJI, *Penser et agir l'éducation* (Paris: Coll. ESF éditeur, 1992), 130.

[47] Cfr. J. BRANDOLIN, *Réinventer l'éducation en Afrique, 2ème tirage, Serres/Cap* (Paris: Editions Afrique, 1996), 85–87.

qui sauverait la vieille institution morbide tout
en réalisant le rêve d'éducation pour tous.[48]

1.2 History, Culture, and Tradition

Tradition and culture, as already explained in this work, go
hand in glove. All key areas of cultural heritage that imply history as
identified by Ki-Zerbo are verifiable both in the domain of space and
time, as well as in the traditional African social, political, and religious aspects that constitute and sustain their history. History, in the
strict African consideration, is transmitted mainly by oral tradition
and by other traditional means, such as music, dance, craft, and other
cultural elements. Here lies the reason why his definition of history
is extended to the memory of the human person. Considering that
memory is a human faculty, he insinuates that history fundamentally
rests in the collective memory of a people, and it must serve "not only
as a mirror in which we recognize our own reflection, but as a driving
force that will propel us on the road to progress."[49] This explains why
he considers factors such as traditional religion, rules for the good
of the community, government, and good fortune as paramount in
every human conception of history.[50]

Even though he insists on tradition or cultural heritage as the
foundation of the African conception of history, Ki-Zerbo wants us
to avoid the temptation of thinking that Africans, in their history,
are only copying the deeds of their ancestors as some people seem to
think. In an interview by Bahgat Elnadi and Adel Rifaat, he clarifies
this misconception as he recalls that "it has often been said that the
African only repeats what his ancestors did. This is one principle,
but it is not the only one. It is reductionist to limit Africans to this

---

[48.] (Formal education is in crisis, nonformal training is tinkering, the informal
sector is teeming with life, but we are not trying to put them in contact to
reinvent an education system that would save the old morbid institution while
fulfilling the dream of education for everyone). Ibid., 121.

[49.] Ibid., 9.

[50.] Cfr. Ibid., 9-21.

dimension. In Africa there has been change as well as continuity."[51] This explains why Ki-Zerbo always highlights the importance of the past, the present, and the future in explaining his conception of history and development with due consideration that for the Africans, the past is always animated by myths.

As he developed his conception of history with his African background, Ki-Zerbo was thinking of other handed-down factors that affected such a conception. In this regard, he referred to the art of writing, the spread of Christianity and Islam, as well as the introduction of the Africans into the world of profit. He, however, saw these factors as part and parcel of the African identity. Therefore, he insists that any authentic conception of African history must bear this reality in mind as he inscribes the following:

> Three factors, however, had an impact on the quality of the Africans' conception of history. The first of these was the spread of writing, which helped in quantifying and measuring, and hence organizing the passage of time. The second was the introduction of the major religions of Islam and Christianity, with their roots in a given historical tradition. By a sort of contagion, African converts managed to incorporate their own local history into the overall picture of the history of their religion. Lastly, the Africans' entry into the world of profit and the measuring of money weaned them from their own conceptions and subjected them to those of the economically powerful nations, which set their pace and their rules. The wristwatch worn by African workers or businessmen is a symbol of the new demands made on them.[52]

[51.] J. Ki-Zerbo, in *UNESCO Courier*, 10.
[52.] J. Ki-Zerbo (ed.), *General History of Africa*, vol. 1, 22.

The fact remains that writing, even though not initially common, was not entirely absent in representing African traditional values. Yet considering that contexts and societies are different in approach, Ki-Zerbo subscribes to the veracity that everything vital to the proper workings of a society is transmitted by means of written documents in societies with writing and by means of tradition in oral societies. Far from being merely entertainment or folklore, tradition is vested with the essential mission of social reproduction. In this regard, with concrete reference to some African nations, he seems to perceive a distinction between traditional societies that had the system of a state and those that were ordinarily traditional. The fact, as he sees it, is that the seemingly institutionalized system represented as *state* systems are complementary to the traditional systems, inasmuch as tradition is to be understood as handed-down values and systems of behavior.[53]

Traditions, Ki-Zerbo continues to explain, have a host of social meanings, and these meanings or functions affect their content. He goes on to differentiate between official and private traditions.

Official traditions, as he explains, include not only genealogies, king lists, and accounts of the origins of dynasties and privileges of chiefdoms but also encompass land-right charters and legal customs regarding water, animals, trees, foreigners, and other social concerns and practices. Private traditions, on the other hand, are connected with restricted groups, such as families, people with interest in the same cult, craftsmen's guilds, and other small groups. These are often less well-preserved. Nevertheless, they are also true and, like other traditional issues, are, in a larger or lesser scale, handed down as valid traditions, considering also that they are likely to be true to fact and can be used to cross-check the reliability of official traditions.[54]

Certainly, some oral traditions have been subjected to distortion, but as Ki-Zerbo intimates, it is possible to draw up a catalogue of the different types of oral testimony and of the distortions to which each category has probably been subjected to, for instance,

---

[53.] Cfr. Ibid., 58.
[54.] Cfr. J. KI-ZERBO (ed.), *General History of Africa*, vol. 1, 58.

by taking the brief answers given to such question as "How did we start growing maize?" "Where did this dancer's mask come from?" and so on. The emphasis he makes in this regard is that the value of a tradition cannot be dismissed without proof that distortion occurred or that the probability of its having occurred is very great. Thus, the collective memory exists, and in almost every traditional society, there are people specializing in crafts, politics, the law or theology, who know many things of which their contemporaries are totally unaware. With facts and conviction, he explains that every ethnic group has its thinkers and goes on to make some practical examples as in the passage that follows:

> Among the Kuba of Zaire, for example, we know of three men who, on the basis of the same system of symbols, had worked out three very different philosophies. Among many peoples, the secret traditions are the privilege of very restricted groups forming secret societies. The Asante royal family knew a tradition about their origins of which the general public was ignorant. In Rwanda, only the Biiru specialists knew the royal rituals, and even then, they only knew them all when they were all together, since each group of Biiru knew only part of them. Secret practices and traditions are found in almost all the rituals for the enthronement of kings throughout Africa. Each tradition has its own social surface, which has to be identified precisely, if the text is to be interpreted properly.[55]

We must always bear in mind that Ki-Zerbo gives chronology the importance it deserves in the construction of any conception of history. He makes it very clear that without chronology, there can be no history since it would not be possible to distinguish what pro-

---

[55.] Ibid., 56-57.

ceeds from what follows. Yet he also insinuates both as a challenge and as an alteration to those who think oral tradition has no value that oral tradition always gives a relative chronology, expressed in the form of lists of leading figures or generations. There are no numerical dates, yet they form a chronology in their own way. These, therefore, are the relative chronologies which have to be linked together and an attempt could be made, if necessary, to work out numerical dates.[56]

Ki-Zerbo, while praising the art of writing, also affirms that whenever an oral source has been well tested, it can be considered as valid as a written source. The written quantitative information, he continues to say, can be more reliable because it is more consistent to the time kept and more faithful to the source. On the other hand, he gives additional credit to explanatory information because it involves psychological and sociological motivations. This, he reminds us, often emerges more clearly from oral traditions.[57] Whatever the case, he reminds us that the collection of traditions calls for a great deal of time and patience. There have also been occasions when a process of contamination has resulted in *traditional* informants passing on written or broadcast information with which they have been in contact. This, too, is a problem for historians to guard against. Ki-Zerbo regrets that patience is sometimes lacking which should be the strong point of the historian. Finally, he affirms that unless the work is published, it cannot be made available to the world of scholars. This is still a challenge to the African students at all levels.[58]

From the perspective of cultural anthropology, it is generally agreed that there are many diverse definitions of culture. Yet those that are objectively momentous, as recorded by David Levinson and Marvin Ember, point to the idea that "cultures are like fabrics, interwoven with patterning of ideas and meaning that individuals lived and expressed in values, attitudes, goals, beliefs, customs, ceremonies, material objectives and Social ranking."[59] This is where each cultural element or value is often treated as traditional since it entails

---

[56]. Cfr. J. KI-ZERBO (ed.), *General History of Africa*, vol. 1, 59.

[57]. Cfr. Idem.

[58]. Cfr. Idem.

[59]. D. LEVINSON and M. EMBER, eds., *Encyclopedia of Cultural Anthropology*, 574.

a pattern of life or a value attached to something that has to flow from one generation to the next. Thus, as a tradition, such a configuration of ideas, feelings, and activities in a culture depend for its continuity on conditioning individuals to adhere unconsciously to ideal patterns regulating behavior.[60] It is, therefore, plausible that in the African conception of history, the cultural is often treated as the traditional. In this perspective, Martin Nkafu Nkemnkia places absolute importance on tradition as an embodiment of history. Accordingly, Nkemnkia upholds thus:

> Tradition is something real and tangible. All events contributing to the formation of history of a people were originally understood (and still are) as tradition. For example, a religious practice continues because it has been handed on by previous generations to the future ones through customs, rites and cult. It is known that all human races have their own custom, their own fashions, their own way of interpreting reality, of acting in their community...their own tradition.[61]

Culture is an important component of development in an authentic nation building, considering that the building of a nation can never be accomplished without being adapted or founded on a culture that is imbedded in history. This is why Wim van Binsbergen, in his work *Intercultural Encounters: African and Anthropological Lessons towards a Philosophy of Interculturality*, emphasises that the concept of culture, embedded in a people's history, offers a contemporary solution for the perennial problem of society; it defines how to negotiate the tension between the individual and the community. Thus, his accent is like that of Ki-Zerbo. Effectively, Wim Van Binsbergen maintains that culture is one of the principal empowering concepts at the disposal of political actors in the local, national, and global

---

60. Cfr. Ibid., 45.
61. M. N. NKEMNKIA, in *Aquinas* (1999), vol. 10/LIII/2-3, 493.

arenas of our time.[62] He explains further that the concept of culture may deal with social contradictions, yet its importance in nation building, especially as it is an embodiment of history, can never be downplayed, considering that culture is man's deepest essence. This is well expressed in the following inscription:

> It (culture) offers the possibility of defining a central identity within which a person's many identities as the player of many social roles can be rearranged within a hierarchical framework... This identity is supposed to define, not just a partial aspect of an individual's life, not one specific role, but a total life-world, whose parts hang together meaningfully and organically, have their place within the ensemble—resulting in a situation where the subject can confront the world as if that subject were a monolithic whole, and can find meaning and order in that world.[63]

John S. Mbiti, after a keen study of African culture, intimates that for the Africans, history is practically conceived and expressed in terms of some obvious cultural events, verging on an interplay of some basic elements: God who is the ultimate, spirits (made up of superhuman spirits as well as spirits of ancestors), man (human beings who are alive and those to be born), animals and birds, as well as phenomena and objects without biological life.[64]

[62.] Cfr. W. V. BINSBERGEN, *Intercultural Encounters: African and Anthropological Lessons towards a Philosophy of Interculturality* (London: New Brunswick, 2003), 48.

[63.] Ibid., 48.

[64.] Cfr. J. S. MBITI, *African Religion and Philosophy* (London: Heinemann, 1975), 16.

Conclusion

It is a consensus that looking at Africa, the aspects which unite her as a continent are more than those that divide. It is but normal that differences must abound, considering that each group of people are united as a region, clan, or nation with distinct peculiarities. Though it is of different parts, segments, or nations, yet as a continent, their history runs along the same direction and with similar sociocultural and religious characteristics. Africa has always been renowned for animal rearing, organized farming, trading, and arts. Arts were used for aesthetic, social, cultural, and religious motives. Ki-Zerbo is convinced that Africa is one of the richest continents in rock art. Peter Hunziker affirms that African arts "reflects but also stimulates action and these prehistoric carvings and paintings proclaim the relentless struggle of the African man to dominate nature and also to add to his own nature through the divine joy of creation."[65]

It is worthy of note that the Nile is the cradle of one of the most astonishing and enduring civilizations; it is and has always been an immense legacy to Africa and the world. Ancient Egypt was an African civilization, and the history of Africa can never be written appropriately without it being connected to the history of Egypt. Any historian who evades this problem is either oblivious, fainthearted, or a neurotic. The moral fruit of this civilization is intertwined with the cultural, ethical, and theocentric values embedded in the African tradition in general. Considering that our work is basically on culture, as sustained in history, which operates on the plane of time and space, we can only understand better the concept of history with a clear knowledge of the concept of space and time in the African perspective.

---

[65] P. HUNZIKER, ed., *The Story of Africa* (London: K Gygax, 2005), 21.

CHAPTER TWO

The African Notion of Space and Time

2.1. Some Preliminary Considerations of Space and Time

IT IS COMMONLY testified that every history, every civilization, and every cultural study involves a conception of space and time, taking into consideration that nothing operates in a vacuum. Related to this ontological truth is the conviction of David Masolo that the mode or level of existence of living humans is directly related to the concept of space and time.[66] It is a typical African belief that "man is part of a whole and he must always be considered in relation to other human beings and in an immediate relationship with his natural environment, thus nature and the world."[67] Such a relationship cannot be conceived or practiced outside the categories of space and time—two concepts that are often expressed interchangeably.

As John Mbiti explains, in the reasoning of the traditional African, "space and time are closely linked, and often, the same word is used for both."[68] Mario Brdar endorses Heinz Kronas-ser, who, as if to justify this assertion, draws attention to our everyday life in

---

[66.] Cfr. D. A. MASOLO, *African Philosophy in Search of Identity* (London: Edinburgh University Press, 1994), 110.

[67.] M. N. NKEMNKIA, *African Vitalogy*, 71.

[68.] J. S. MBITI, *African Religions and Philosophy* (London: Heinemann Educational Books Ltd., 1969), 27.

which we cannot have an experience of space without time or an experience of time without space.[69] Thus, Martin Nkafu's assertion is justified that every history implied a notion of space and time and the subject of time is impressed deeply in the issue of being, which belongs to an ontological nature.[70] In the same scheme or reasoning, Joseph Ki-Zerbo insists that "per conoscere veramente l'identità totale di un'individuo o di un paese, occorre prendere in considerazione le influenze veicolate dello spazio o attraverso il tempio" (to truly understand the true identity of an individual or a nation, it is necessary to take into account the influences conveyed by space and through time).[71]

Ki-Zerbo is fully aware that for a valid notion of history, the questions must be asked concerning how a people conceive ideas such as time, space, causality, and historical truth.[72] His peculiar touch is that he makes a concrete and remarkable liaison between the concept of time and space to the concept of myth, insinuating that for the African people, the theme of space and time often involves a significant direction in which its origins tend to be sustained.[73]

From a very practical perspective, he explains that for the Africans, rivers often represent the fixed axis of the cardinal point and often form part of the myths. In African antiquity, "myth governed history and was at the same time responsible for justifying it."[74] Time in mythical history is best described thus as suspended time. In this kind of suspended time, the present may even act on what is regarded as the past but, in fact, remains contemporary. Therefore, primarily, "some accounts attribute to a mythical past advances that were made in historical time; as the latter is not perceived as such by each individual, it is taken over by the none-historical group mem-

---

[69] Cfr. M. BRDAR et al., ed., *Space and Time in Language* (Frankfurt: Peter Lang, 2011), 1.

[70] M. N. NKEMNKIA, *African Vitalogy*, 71.

[71] J. KI-ZERBO, *Punti Fermi Sull'Africa*, 105.

[72] Cfr. J. KI-ZERBO, ed., *General History of Africa*, vol. 1, 58.

[73] Cfr. Idem.

[74] J. KI-ZERBO, ed., *General History of Africa*, vol. 1, 16.

ory."[75] It is in this regard that he defines myth as the nonrational representation of the past, and in explaining its relation to time and the concept of history at a wide-ranging perspective in the traditional African society, he declares the following:

> Myth, or in other words, the non-rational representation of the past, used to occupy an important place in the African approach to society. Customs were often imposed on those who had roles to play in society: all of them, from the ruler downwards, had to model their slightest acts and gestures on those of an exemplary prototype whose origins were shrouded in the mists of time… Two characteristics emerge from this type of historical thinking: its timelessness and its essentially social dimension.[76]

Consequent upon the above citation is the fact that mythical and collective conception of history makes time an attribute of sovereignty, especially when linked to the person of the ruler of the community. To demonstrate this conviction, Ki-Zerbo cites, as an example, the *Shilluk* king in Sudan, saying that "the *Shilluk* king is the mortal repository of the immortal power, for he combines in his own person, both mythical time (he is an incarnation of the founding hero) and social time, regarded as the source of the group's vitality."[77] In almost all of Africa, the chief is the main stay of collective time. The death of the king is a break in time, which halts activity and social order and all expressions of life from laughter to agriculture. This is a clear example of a part representing a whole.

Whatever the case, we must understand that in mythical thinking, the passage of time in the ordinary sense is only one aspect of another time, expressed by other dimensions of the individual. This

---

[75.] J. KI-ZERBO, ed., *General History of Africa*, vol. 1, 16-17.

[76.] Ibid., 16.

[77.] Ibid., 17.

is because social time is expressed by a group, especially with respect to the handing down of power, which goes with some symbolic objects that express the transmission of power from one generation to the next, say from a king to his successors. This may be a golden ball, a war drum, a chain, or a part of an animal.[78] This, however, as Ki-Zerbo indicates, does not mean that the Africans have a conception of a "historical process that is static, repetitive and sterile, and that myth is the motive force behind a history that is merely marking time."[79] Rather, the point that he is stressing is that the African conception of time is never interpreted solely from one perspective. He is also convinced that the mythical dimension of history is common to all cultures and religions and in some cases (as exemplified in the case of the Nazis in Germany); the mythical current overwhelms the nation's attitudes, opinions, and ideology.[80]

John Mbiti seems to have envisioned the possibility of the drive from ontology to epistemology. He attempts to construct a critical African perspective on empirical knowledge in his account of an African conception of time. For him, time is "an ontological phenomenon that pertains to the question of existence or being."[81] Thus, Kwasi Wiredu is correct in his claim that John Samuel Mbiti uses his thesis on the African concept of time to "explain belief, attitude, practices and general ways of life of African peoples, not only of the traditional set-up, but also of the modern situation (whether in political, economic, educational or church life)."[82]

John Mbiti explains that for the African, time is equivalent to and can only consist of actual events, implying events that have just occurred, events that are taking place now, or events that will likely occur very shortly. What has not taken place or the things that are likely not to occur immediately are classified in the level of no time, whereas the things that are likely or certain to occur are classified

---

[78]. Cfr. Idem.

[79]. Ibid., 18.

[80]. Cfr. J. KI-ZERBO, ed., *General History of Africa*, vol. 1, 18.

[81]. J. S. MBITI, *African Religions and Philosophy*, 15.

[82]. K. WIREDU, *Cultural Universals and Particulars: An African Perspective* (Indianapolis: Indiana University Press, 1996), 83.

under potential time. This also involves things that fall under the natural rhythm of events, that is, natural phenomena. Actual time is what is present and what is past. It moves backward rather than forward. Concentration is not on future things but on practical events since future events are yet to be realized.[83]

This time, analysis is explained by Mbiti with a case study of the *Akamba* and the *Gikuyu* people of Kenya, East Africa. He implores their time terminologies, identifying the time dimensions as the *Sasa* period, which encompasses the recent past, the present, and the very immediate future, and the *Zamani* period, which corresponds with a deeper, more infinite past.[84] The *Sasa* generally binds individuals and their immediate environment together. It is the period of conscious living. On the other hand, *Zamani* is the period of the myth, giving a sense of foundation or security to the *Sasa* period and binding together all created things.[85]

Traditionally, Africans are most concerned with what is near; therefore, the *Sasa* is the period of the most consequence because it is where or when they actually exist. The *Sasa* of the African slaves would have included the following events: "I was home. I was taken from my home. I have lost my ancestors and my village. My village and my ancestors have lost me. We are lost." Another important point to understand, according to Mbiti, is that the community is also bound by these same temporal views: The community also has its own *Sasa*, which is greater than that of the individual. Yet both for the community and the individual, the now point is most relevant.[86]

For the Africans, names are mostly given to newborn children as a way of immortalizing certain historical moments—events that happen in time. Hence, Henry Odera Oruka cites the *Luo* people of Uganda who, in their oral history, use certain phenomena, such as famine, which might have occurred at a certain point to mark the

---

[83.] Cfr. J. S. MBITI, *African Religions and Philosophy*, 17.
[84.] Cfr. Ibid., 17-19.
[85.] Cfr. Idem.
[86.] Cfr. Idem.

point in time when, for example, children were born. Such children were given specific traditional names that marked this period.[87]

2.2. Some Basic Differences between the Western and African Conception of Space and Time

Considering the vital importance of space and time in the conception of history, we dare to state at this point that, pedagogically speaking, a concept is better understood within a particular culture if it is placed within the background of another. To Westerners, time could be considered as a set of stripes drawn on the tarmac, that is, on the road on which we drive. Time is like a commodity that is precious, bought and paid for, and must be delivered in a particular system and format, whereas for Africans, time, just like space, though also precious, is a flexible ontological reality that depends intrinsically, and not extrinsically, on the people and events that are at work. Time goes with a deep degree of understanding within situations on which it is employed, with a valuable effect on the persons or community involved. It is the quality of time, that is, what is achieved at the time that matters and not the time as a concept. The analysis inferred from the presentation above is well summarized by Orville Boyd Jenkins in the following words:

> In the European view, the movement of time would be forward, coming from behind us. Europeans have the idea that time exists as an entity in itself, and it moves. We speak of time travel in science fiction in the terms of forward in time or backward in time. In the Western view, an event is a component of time. As time moves, you must use it or lose it. If you do not use it, it is gone. In the African view of time one might say that time flows backwards. It flows toward you from the future, and the more or faster the

---

[87]. Cfr. H. O. ORUKA, *Sage Philosophy* (Nairobi: Acts Press, 1991), 118.

activity, the faster time flows. Time is created, in a sense. Time is not something in itself. Life is made up of events, defined by relationships. Time is a component of the event. Your activity really determines the amount of time that passes. Thus, the faster you work, the more time you use, because more activity is occurring, more energy is being used. If you are sitting and resting, you are conserving time. Time is not actually passing; it is simply waiting for you.[88]

I have a practical example to buttress the above difference between time for the Westerners and for the Africans. This happened in Rome in July 2012 on a very hot afternoon. I was in a bus, and I felt a strong and sharp pain in my heart apparently because of the heat. I was really very thirsty, and I felt the need to drink some water to get myself back to normal. Immediately, the bus stopped. I jumped out, and fortunately for me, there was a shop just around the bus stop. This was a few minutes after 1:00 p.m. I immediately rushed into the shop, slammed some euros on the counter, and asked for a bottle of water. The vendor was on his way out. He immediately pointed at the notice on his door indicating that he was on break from 1:00 to 3:30 p.m. This was a few minutes after 1:00 p.m. The more I insisted to him that I was desperately in need of the water, the more he reminded me that he was on his way out and, at the same time, struggling to push or force me out of his shop.

Worse of all, the passersby who stopped briefly to intervene could not understand the point of a dying man in need of water. Instead, some asked if I was mad or out of senses. They could not understand why I could not read on the wall that it was break time. I also could not understand why water could be available but could not be sold because of out of time or inappropriate time or break time, especially in a situation that someone was in a grave need.

[88.] O. B. JENKINS, "Time, a Cultural Concept," in *Focus on Communication Effectiveness* (1998), of February 1998.

Seldom could I understand that we were operating on two different epistemologies of time, with each person trying to defend his. The final extreme I took was to shout out violently as my situation deteriorated. Someone had to call the police who came and immediately took the water from the shop himself to give me, and that was the end of the struggle. Similarly, I found myself inside a Food Lion Supermarket in the United States after the closing hour, 10:00 p.m. The vendor was willing to assist me, but the machines could not work; they had been programmed to shot down at a certain time. The inference is that in the West, time controls human activities, and consequently, the human being is controlled by time. On the contrary, the African controls time and puts it under his activities.

Certainly, that which Mbiti wants us to understand more is that the traditional African is not a slave to time. He places his interest on life, on the practical events, that is, on the practical happenings here and now for the interest of a person or, most of all, of the community. As to when something happens or, worse of all, as to when something is to happen is a secondary consideration, coming only after the practical has been taken care of.

In line with the above experiences, we can infer that a technological approach to time is implemented in the West while the Africans follow but a relational African approach. For the Westerners, time is principally seen like a commodity or a product which must be utilized, sold, and bought; otherwise, one misses it. Whereas in the traditional African approach, time is perceived more as an ontological reality that could be created and produced. Therefore, the actual human interaction in the understanding of time takes preference over the mathematical conceptions of the West. As Mbiti explains, in Africa, one makes as much time as one wants.[89]

In contrast to the Europeans or the Westerners in general, when Africans reckon time, it is for a specific purpose, in relation to events and not just for the sake of some mathematical classifications of issues. Time is reckoned to serve a purpose that satisfies people. It is the purpose, that is, the service rendered or the service to be

---

[89.] Cfr. J. S. Mbiti, *African Religions and Philosophy*, 19-20

rendered that makes the time relevant. Therefore, their stress is on phenomenon calendars and not on numerical calendars, considering that "the day, the month, the year, one's life time or human history are all divided up or reckoned according to their specific events, for it is these that make them meaningful."[90] In a bid to demonstrate this point, Mbiti makes the following assertion:

> The rising of the sun is an event which is recognized by the whole community. It does not matter, therefore, whether the sun rises at 5 a.m. or 7 a.m., so long as it rises. When a person says that he will meet another at sunrise, it does not matter whether the meeting takes place at 5 a.m. or 7 a.m., so long as it is during the general period of sunrise. Likewise, it does not matter whether people go to bed at 9 p.m. or at 12 midnight; the important thing is the event of going to bed, and it is immaterial whether in one night it takes place at 10 p.m. while in another it takes place at midnight. For the people concerned, time is meaningful at the point of the event and not at the mathematical moments.[91]

Time, for the Africans, was simply a composition of events which had occurred, those which were taking place now and those which would occur in the immediate future. Time had no academic concern. What had not been realized and did not have an actual possibility of happening could not enter their concept of time. In African thinking, there was no concept of history moving toward a future climax or toward an end of the world, not concept of a messianic fulfillment. Neither life nor history could be destroyed, and

---

[90] Ibid., 19.
[91] Ibid., 106

life was an eternal cycle from birth to life after death and a constant communion with the ancestors and the company of the spirits.[92]

Nkafu passionately insists on the social aspect of time in the African culture. In a work edited by A. Tymeiniegka, he gives the following explanation in relation to time:

> In the African way of thinking, there has never been a moment that time was not linked to relationship between man and the rest of the universe, and to life in its multiple forms. Therefore, it is impossible to speak of time as of an entity by itself that can condition and make someone lose something absolutely... Since African time is present moment, we cannot but say that it is a predicate of reality itself.[93]

In the above context, Nkafu explains that time is not to be understood as a commodity or as money that is possessed and spent. One cannot say, for example, that one has lost or spent too much time. Time is a fundamental element of reality itself so that one lives with time in its eternity in the present moment.[94] Consequently,

> one can understand that "time is expensive" but would dispute the fact that there is an urgency to finish a certain job just because it was foreseen. When an African makes an appointment at 2 p.m., one must bear in mind that all the afternoon could be taken up with that appointment. This does not mean that the African does not have a sense of time. The main motive that

---

[92.] Cfr. M. N. Nkemnkia, *African Vitalogy*, 74.

[93.] M. N. Nkemnkia, "The Notion of 'Eleng,' That Is of Time in African Original Experience: The Vitalogical Dimension" in A. Tymieniecka, ed., *Analytica Husserliana, the Yearbook of Phenomenological Research*, vol. LIX (London: Kluwer Academic Publications, 1999), 118.

[94.] Cfr. M. N. Nkemnkia, *African Vitalogy*, 120.

we can imagine is found in the relationship that is lived with the other. It is finally in being at the disposal of others that reality of time can be defined. It is expensive because it enables one to be consumed by others…time belongs to life and life belongs to God… Thus what has been said of time can be applied totally to *Aliuh*, to space. Space is in fact a dimension of time.[95]

Time, therefore, is always conceived as an essential measure of the living reality.[96] Therefore, events, names, and time are often put together.

Conclusion

William Kluback, in this regard, explains that the African thinker, Léopold Senghor, as he endorses Jacques Maritain's approach to reality, explains that life must be lived in the concrete, in the ambient of space and time, and it is within this reality that civilization and history are to be discussed. According to him, as Kluback cites, "we are men because we converse with each other and can transcend the spatial and the temporal. We need our ancestors. We need to transform the present into visions of the future."[97] Even Hegel, who happens to be one of the champions of panlogism (a theory that places the reality of life and history only at the level of the logical), still could not help accepting the importance of space and time as he intimated that nature is the manifestation of the idea in space while history is the manifestation of the spirit in time. Thus, anybody reflecting on history cannot escape the twin concept of space and time.

The Africans, however, traditionally invest more in the emotional marks of time, not only on things that are past but also on the importance of the things happening now in space. Their interest

---

[95.] M. N. Nkemnkia, *African Vitalogy*, 126-127.

[96.] M. N. Nkemnkia, *African Vitalogy*, 126.

[97.] W. Kluback, *Léopold Sédar Senghor, from Politics to Poetry*, 7.

is not on numerical dates and chronology or on time as a boundary for events. This is where we situated historical time. Yet as far as the future is concerned, these emotional marks of time are still to be made though the typical African would consider his or her impact on that as meager. That which is also striking in this section is our brief juxtaposition between the African and the Western conceptions of space and time. Here, someone may deduce that the Africans do not have a sense of time considering that, often, coming late to events, for them, may be perceived as normal, if not circumstantial.

The practical reality is that when the traditional African makes an appointment at 4:00 p.m., he does not look at it as a mathematical 4:00 p.m.; he intends the entire afternoon. For him, this is not an abuse of the concept of time. He may not have the facilities that can make him fulfill the time to the letter. Accordingly, coming late does not mean that he does not have a sense of time. His interest is in the person he is to meet or the mission he is to fulfill. The primary motive is thus found in the relationship that is lived with the other, the life that his presence is to touch, the achievement of something that would, in turn, satisfy the common good. Paradoxically, this traditional outlook of time has extended into the modern age to the extent that people talk of Black man time which is often misconceived and abused. We shall now have a close look at Africa as a continent and examine the concept of history.

CHAPTER THREE

Ki-Zerbo's Presentation of Africa as a Continent

IT IS STRIKING to note that, thanks to archaeology, it is now acknowledged that Africa was very probably the cradle of mankind and the scene of the Neolithic period.[98] It is generally affirmed that Egypt was the setting for one of the most brilliant ancient civilizations of the world.[99] Yet Ki-Zerbo regrets the attempts that have been made to split Africa. This is explained by the citation below:

> The continent of Africa was hardly looked upon
> as a historical entity. On the contrary, emphasis

[98.] This period is otherwise known as the New Stone Age. It was a period in the development of human technology that is traditionally the last part of the Stone Age. The name Neolithic was invented by John Lubbock in 1865 as a refinement of the three-age system of stone, bronze, and iron ages. It can be roughly dated from about 9000 BCE to 3000 BCE. However, the term *Neolithic* does not refer, rigorously speaking, to a specific chronological period, but rather to a suite of behavioral and cultural characteristics, including the use of both wild and domestic crops and the use of domesticated animals. Some archaeologists prefer to refer to this period as the period of Early Village Communities. Life, as we know it today, began to take shape during this period, commonly referred to as prehistoric, a term that refers to the lack of written documents. However, this word *Neolithic* has often generated a bedevilled connotation because of its ambiguity of meaning. Ki-Zerbo suggests that in Africa, it is better avoided whenever possible and certainly in the case of sub-Saharan Africa.

[99.] Cfr. J. KI-ZERBO, ed., *General History of Africa*, vol. 1, xi.

was laid on the things that divided north "White Africa" from "black Africa." The Sahara was often presented as an impenetrable space preventing any intermingling of ethnic groups and peoples or any exchange of goods, customs and ideas between the societies that had grown up on either side of the desert. Hermetic frontiers were drawn between the civilization of ancient Egypt and Nubia and those of the people south of the Sahara.[100]

In this connection, in describing the book *General History of Africa*, of which he is the principal editor, Ki-Zerbo makes one fundamental declaration: "Africa is presented in this work as a totality. The aim is to show the historical relationship between the various parts of the continent, too frequently sub-divided by works published to date."[101] Therefore, as he focused on African history as well as the notion of history for the Africans, he also brings out the contribution of Africa or the Africans to the history of mankind, insisting that "without a history of Africa, the history of the world would remain obscure in many respects."[102]

3.1 Presentation of the Historical and Geographic Identity of Africa

3.1.1 Historical Identity

Joseph Ki-Zerbo bitterly regrets the fact that most of those who claimed that Africa is an *unhistorical* continent, including Hegel and G. P. Murdock, author of the book *Africa: Its People and their Culture History*, published in 1959, worked mainly on prejudice. They never set foot on Africa. He goes on to explain that African local history,

---

[100.] J. Ki-Zerbo, ed., *General History of Africa*, vol. 1, vii.
[101.] Ibid., xiii.
[102.] Ibid., 9.

which was taught in school, was only intended and twisted to serve the interest of the colonial masters. Hence, what was more important was the history of their colonizers.[103] His conviction, in view of all this, is of a radical rediscovery of African history, a discovery that would also actualize a better improvement of the African continent, considering the fact that to understand one's history, as well as the elements and events that constitute this history, brings one to a brighter consciousness of oneself and of one's environment. It is in this connection that Ki-Zerbo makes the following appraisal of history as a concept:

> Nous avons affirmé la nécessité de refonder l'histoire à partir de la matrice africaine. Le système colonial se prolongeait jusque dans la sphère de la recherche... La recherche était un des instruments de la colonisation à un point tel que la recherche en histoire avait décidé qu'il n'y avait pas d'histoire africaine et que les Africains colonisés étaient purement et simplement condamnés à endosser l'histoire du colonisateur. C'est pourquoi nous nous sommes dit que nous devons partir de nous-mêmes pour arriver à nous-mêmes.[104]

From the above citation, we can comprehend why Ki-Zerbo frowns at colonization, just like the era of the slave trade, considering them as the two unfortunate periods in African history. Accordingly, as we read from an interview that he presented in *UNESCO Courier* magazine on September 1, 1993, he decries as follows:

> I think the period of the slave trade can be considered as a hemorrhage which undermined and exhausted the biological and social forces of Africa. But the fundamental change was colo-

---

[103.] Cfr. Ibid., 12-14.
[104.] J. Ki-Zerbo, *À Quand L'Afrique?*, 12-13.

nization. Colonization was a major amputation. It was a brutal separation that cut its victims off from many essential things, it was an enforced divorce from their own history, the social structure they knew, their organized civic identity: the society's peculiar way of organizing space, the use of its language in the main public places... in short an ethnocide punctuated by occasional genocides...but Africa did not lose their creativity under colonization, whatever some colonial historians might have claimed—hence the importance of an African history viewed from within.[105]

Africans can now tell their story and reflect on historical facts about the reality of humans on earth, fitting it authentically into the general portrait of the history of the world. Ki-Zerbo articulates the historical and philosophical principles that must critically monitor any authentic study or writing of African history. In his account, history is an indispensable concept in the building of a nation and the security of a people. With specific reference to the African people, he recounts that the history of Africa, like the history of mankind, is really the story of an awakening. The history of Africa needs to be reworked, for up till now, it has often been masked, faked, distorted, mutilated by force of circumstance, i.e., through the ignorance and, in some cases, self-interest of those who claimed to have written it. The history of Africa or even the concept of history by the Africans has been crushed by centuries of oppression. Africa has seen generations of travelers, slave traders, explorers, missionaries, governors, and scholars of all kinds, painting its image as one of nothing but poverty, barbarism, irresponsibility, and chaos. And this image has

---

[105.] B. Elnadi and A. Rifaat, "Interview with Joseph Ki-Zerbo," *UNESCO Courier* (1993), of September 1993, 13.

been projected and extrapolated indefinitely in time as a justification of both the present and the future.[106]

It is in the above perspective that Joseph Ki-Zerbo describes the immense difficulties that are often attained once a person attempts to write a history of Africa, especially in the perspective of a cultural heritage. In addition to these difficulties, he considers the nature of the physical geography of the continent, the severe demographic drain caused by the slave trade, and the very vastness of the continent itself.[107] The above difficulties, notwithstanding, he is comforted by three main sources which could be of absolute importance in any approach to history, especially the African history. These sources are written documents, archaeology, and oral tradition.[108] With these complications, as well as the available possible solution from the perspective of sources, African historiography would be propelled toward new and better frontiers research.

Ki-Zerbo is aware of the research findings of Charles Darwin which point to Africa as the home of man as explained in his modern theory of evolution and the origins of man. This theory, which has stood unchallenged in the past hundred years, is also used by Ki-Zerbo to explain not only the historical situation of Africa but also the importance of African history to the development of the human species.[109] He goes on to insinuate that Africa is the cradle of mankind, explaining that "although the evidence of Man's development in Africa is incomplete, but over the past decade, material has been gathered suggesting that Africa was the continent on which the hominids first made their appearance."[110] He proceeds to explain, in a bid to justify this position, that the very scale of Africa accounts for a wide variety of climates which has always offered a suitable habitat for man who could move about, along both latitudes and longitudes.[111]

[106.] Cfr. J. Ki-Zerbo, ed., *General History of Africa*, vol. 1, 2.

[107.] Cfr. Ibid., 5.

[108.] Cfr. Ibid., 5-16.

[109.] Cfr. Ibid., 189.

[110.] Idem.

[111.] Cfr. Ibid., 191.

There are three periods that characterize the history of Africa which can approximately be dated as follows:

- The Early Stone Age or Old Stone Age (from 3 million to about 100,000 years ago)
- Middle Stone Age (from around100,000 to 15,000 years ago)
- Late Stone Age (from about 15,000 years ago until the beginning of the Iron Age, some 2,000 years ago)[112]

Irrespective of the above classification, we shall, in this section, discuss African history in a general form, with more emphasis on the prehistoric era, considering that African history has its foundation practically in this era. The fact is that the transition from one period to another is complex to analyze, yet development took place within each of the three periods as well as from one period to another.[113]

In the prehistoric era, Ki-Zerbo explains, there was also good rainfall in Africa and the availability of water. The action of the wind and water eroded the topsoil, especially in areas in East Africa. This made it easier to discover the fossils of Hominidae. In the *Omo* valley in Ethiopia, sedimentary beds of 1,000 meters thick were observed as having lasted for a period ranging from 4.5 to 1 million years ago.[114]

In the account of Ki-Zerbo, the history of Africa north of the Sahara has been more closely linked with that of the Mediterranean basin than has the history of sub-Saharan Africa, yet he wants us to understand that Africa remains a single continent and that, generally, it is widely recognized that the various civilizations of the African continent, for all their differing languages and cultures, represent, to a greater or lesser degree, the historical offshoot of a set of peoples and societies united by bonds that are centuries old.[115] Therefore, in this part of our work, we shall look at Africa in its entirety. Therefore,

---

[112.] Cfr. J. Ki-Zerbo, ed., *General History of Africa*, vol. 1, 196.
[113.] Cfr. Idem.
[114.] Cfr. Idem.
[115.] Cfr. Ibid., vii–viii.

writing about the historical and geographic peculiarity of Africa, Ki-Zerbo explains thus:

> It must be the history of the peoples of the African continent as a whole, and that continent includes both islands such as Madagascar and the North African regions, with which the lands to the south of the Sahara have had close and often beneficial relations for long... Even the most absolute kings and chiefs were bound by customs, and hence by a form of law laid down by established authorities such as councils, priests, seers and so on... Thus, from prehistoric times, there have been not only wars, but also social cross-currents, cultural and religious borrowings, and countless permutations that are reflected in the intricacies of the map of Africa.[116]

According to Ki-Zerbo, therefore, the fact is that the first scientific techniques were brought to the world from the African cradle. Egypt, he states, was the teacher of Greece and the entire Mediterranean basin. This historical fact should form an integral part of the educational program of schools in Africa. Africans must be educated to uphold the authentic historic and geographic realities of Africa.[117]

Working from the findings of archaeologists, Ki-Zerbo recounts that although Africa is quite sparsely populated, it accounts for 20 percent of the world's total land surface but only 10 percent of the population. It is also evident that, in general, Africa displays a greater degree of linguistic complexity than all the other continents. There are about 1,500 African languages and 1,000 or 66 percent of them exist alongside one another.[118] Hence, talking about the linguistic

---

[116.] J. Ki-Zerbo, ed., *General History of Africa*, vol. 1, 8.

[117.] Cfr. J. KI-ZERBO, *l'Afrique Noire* ; *D'hier à Demain* (Paris: Librairie A. Hatier, 1978), 642.

[118.] Cfr. J. KI-ZERBO (ed.), *General History of Africa*, vol. 1, 19.

connectivity or similarity of the African languages, Ki-Zerbo cited the Cairo Conference of 1974 which insisted that "the Egyptian language could not be isolated from its African context and its origin could not be fully explained in terms of Semitic. It was quite normal to expect to find related languages in Africa."[119]

3.1.2 Geographic Identity

From the geographic perspective, Ki-Zerbo documents the following facts peculiar to Africa as a continent:

> Africa is a gigantic immerged landmass stretching over a distance of 8,000 kilometers from Bizerta, in Tunisia, to Cape Agulhas, and 75,000 kilometers from Cape Verde to Cape Gardafui. Throughout this vast expanse, there are very few breaks in continuity or openings. It is like a great fortified bastion, with a scarcely indented coastline, unlike Europe, Central America or South-East Asia. Since the marine deeps start very close offshore, there are very few islands.[120]

In the central areas of Africa are great plateaus and rift valleys, especially in the Democratic Republic of Congo, stretching 4.000 kilometers from Mozambique to the Red Sea. The features of this area include many other undulating hills and gigantic furrows running north to south, the volcanic summits of Mounts Kenya and Kilimanjaro, which are considered as the root of Africa, culminating at an elevation of 6,000 meters.[121]

Unlike what some critics think, Ki-Zerbo observes that Africa has always been a part of the world though her contacts or commu-

---

[119.] Ibid, 31.

[120.] Ibid., 124.

[121.] Cfr. J. KI-ZERBO, ed., *General History of Africa*, vol. 1, 122-124.

nication with the world was conspicuously weak. He, therefore, uses the following words to explain his convictions:

> Africa has never been completely cut off from the outside world. However, the absence of extensive plains as in Asia and North America prevented internal liaison and population concentration, while the obstacles round the edges, such as deserts and mountain ranges, inhibited external communication. The Atlantic Ocean was very little used. Until the fifteenth century of the Christian era, when it began to be frequented by explorers and slave-traders, it was barred to sea-farers, who were unable to go beyond the Sahara coasts, since their sailing vessels could not negotiate the return journey on account of the constantly southward-blowing trade winds.[122]

Ki-Zerbo also explains that Africa was somehow isolated from the other parts of the world because of her lack of good natural sites for ports; even the African coast of the Red Sea, the Mozambique Channel, and the eastern shoreline of Madagascar are fringed by coral surf, in which the waves break in rollers against underwater sand ridges.[123] Ki-Zerbo, however, is quick to intimate, after presenting some of these difficulties to establish physical contact with Africa, that these difficulties should not be exaggerated because there are many magnificent harbors and roadsteads that have made it possible for Africa to take part in the history of the Mediterranean people since earliest antiquity. In the same vein, there were several unexploited port sites which existed along the Atlantic and India Ocean seaboards.[124]

[122.] Ibid., 125–126.
[123.] Cfr. Idem.
[124.] Cfr. Ibid., 125-126.

As the continent with the greatest area of land situated in the intertropical zone, "Africa is accordingly the uniformly hottest continent of all. The closer one moves towards the tropics, the drier the heat becomes and, conversely the moister it is near the equator... More than half the continent consists of dry regions."[125]

Conscious of the fact that minerals are probably the most strategic amongst the resources available to man on the earth's surface, Ki-Zerbo recounts the richness of Africa in this regard. His discoveries reveal that

> the ancient basement complex composed of crystalline rocks covering one-third of the continent contains extremely rich mineral deposits. The Copper Belt of Shaba (Zaire), which extends over a distance of more than 300 kilometres, is the world's largest source of copper ore, alongside which radium and cobalt are also to be found. In the Transvaal, in South Africa, a 500 Kilometre strip rich in minerals such as platinum, chromium and asbestos runs on into Zimbabwe. The African diamond-bearing zone has no equal anywhere in the world...the same is true of gold, tin, iron ore—which is almost commonplace—and bauxite, in respect of which Guinea alone possesses more than half of the world's reserves. The gigantic volcanic disruptions produced, among other resources, rocks that weathered into highly fertile soils...[126]

It is also a geographic fact that Africa is principally a grassland continent. Grass occupies 50 percent of the surface area while the additional land is divided into 30 percent for desert and 20 percent for forest. Yet the vegetation zones have varied considerably since the

---

[125.] Ibid., 26–27.
[126.] J. Ki-Zerbo, ed., *General History of Africa*, vol. 1, 131.

very beginnings of time, considering the reality of climate change in the Sahara and in other areas of the world in general.[127]

Also peculiar to the African continent are its large animal resources and cultural diversification. All the regions of the continent experience or have experienced the presence of very large wildlife species at one time or another.[128]

In terms of water resources, it is said that Africa has both some of the highest and some of the lowest rainfall in the world. Therefore, in this connection, Africa can hardly be envied. Though there are many fertile regions, it is also evident that shortage of water is also a geographic reality in Africa. This accounts for the unstable nature of human settlements that the continent experiences in many areas since the prehistoric times.[129]

At a very elementary consideration is the fact that Africa is a continent made up of five regions. This is with respect to certain geographic and natural factors which set some differences to give each region its own identity though, generally, as Africans, there is much in common that defines Africa as a unique continent. This division is explained below through the articulation of Joseph Ki-Zerbo.

3.2 The Five Divisions of the African Continent

3.2.1 East Africa

One peculiarity concerning East Africa is that the earliest known humanly fashioned tools dating from a period ranging between 3 and 1 million years ago were found by the edges of former lakes and marshes close to the Rift Valley in Northern Tanzania, Kenya, and Ethiopia. These tools must have been used for cutting. They showed signs that they were really used, and it was also discovered that they were made by hunters and gatherers.[130] Therefore, there was some technology in this area which continued for over a million years until

---

[127.] Cfr. Ibid., 133–134.
[128.] Cfr. Ibid., 135.
[129.] Cfr. Ibid., 137.
[130.] Cfr. J. Ki-Zerbo, ed., *General History of Africa*, vol. 1, 199.

probably 100,000 years ago. Africa, thus, was one of the places where the makers of tools, *Homo erectus*, emerged.[131] Ki-Zerbo's research shows that tool industries such as the Gondar and Graba III industries at Melka Konture, the Sangoan industries that mixed some Acheulian-type tools and new techniques, as well as the Fauresmith-tool type also existed in various areas in East Africa. Most of these industries were located around Lake Victoria and the Western Rift Valley in Southern Uganda, Rwanda, and Western Tanzania. With the lake sites, rivers, and forests, fishing, hunting, and agriculture were also carried out. These were among the numerous economic and cultural activities that took place around these prehistoric periods. Most of these cultural and traditional elements or activities were discovered to be similarly carried out in the other African regions.[132]

3.2.2 Southern Africa

The first Australopithecus fossil, a juvenile, was found in 1924 in a lime-cemented breccia at Taung in the north of the Cape Province of South Africa. The first adult individual was discovered in 1936, again in an old cave deposit in Krugersdorp region in Transvaal. Such discoveries are also found in Korotoro in the Lake Chad Basin and other areas in South Africa. It is also assumed that some of the early *Homo* forms, as existed in East Africa, were also found in Southern Africa between 1.7 and 2 million years ago.[133]

Equally, minerals like stones, wood, bark, horn, and bones used as tools form part of the treasures of Southern Africa and are used in industries. Some of these industries that have been termed *Fauresmith*, after the site of the Orange River region where these shaped hand axes were first found on the surface, appear to date from 115,000 to 80,000 years before the Christian era.[134] At Chavuma, in Zimbabwe, the industry is characterized by picks and a few hand axes and lighter tools, including points, scrapers, and blades made

---

[131.] Cfr. Idem.
[132.] Cfr. Ibid., 206–209.
[133.] Cfr. Ibid., 210.
[134.] Cfr. J. KI-ZERBO, ed., *General History of Africa*, vol. 1 213-217.

of chalcedony, opaline breccia, quartzite, and quartz. The Twin Rivers industry, in Zambia, which has been dated to about 22,000 years before the Christian era, resembles that from Chavuma.[135] In Swaziland, hematite for use as pigment appears to have been first extracted as early as 28,000 years ago. There are also evidences that the people practiced hunting, sheep rearing, toolmaking, and plants cultivation; and these cultural activities, which continue till this present epoch, are, to a greater or lesser extent, common to Africa as a whole. Ki-Zerbo notices that these cultural or traditional activities were carried out with some level of intellectual aptitude as we read the following:

> There must have been ample opportunity for the hunters to indulge their intellectual interests, some of which are manifest in their magnificent rock arts of the Drakensberg Mountains, Zimbabwe and Namibia. Although much of the art may not be more than 2,000-3,000 years old, it provides a well-documented record of these hunters' life-style.[136]

3.2.3 Central Africa

The Democratic Republic of Congo basin, which is a very significant region in Central Africa, extends from the Gulf of Guinea in the west to the Great Lakes region in the east and approximately from latitude 10° south in Angola and Sahara. It occupies mainly the equatorial zone. It is characterized by plants and forests, consisting of some of the densest forests to be found in Africa. There are equally signs of development in this area consisting of toolmaking, industries, and large-scale migration by the Neolithic pastoralists.[137] The tools made, especially in the Acheulian industry, consisted of

---

[135.] Cfr. Idem.
[136.] Ibid., 220.
[137.] Cfr. Ibid., 222.

very large flakes produced by striking blocks of stones against fixed support. These flakes were then used to make hand axes and cleavers which were heavy-duty tools with curved cutting edges. These industries bore many similarities with those in the other parts of Africa. Fundamentally, it was at this stage of toolmaking that technological innovations were introduced.[138]

Another important historical observation is that off the coast of Cameroon, on the island of Fernando Po, polished axes associated with pottery are found which are dated to the seventeenth century of the Christian era, and similar tools are in use today.[139] This area is also noted for large monuments. The Megalithic monument is a typical example. These are monuments built of rough-hewn or dressed blocks, or standing stones set out in groups or separately, according to a definite plan, such as a circle, a square, or following a certain design. They are normally very spectacular, and this culture is also found in other parts of Africa.[140]

In this area also, the observations of the engravings on rocks were a manifestation of the fact that the people were already familiar with ironworks and the use of tools. It is equally noted that for many years, Central African prehistory consisted only of typology and chronology and very little attention was paid to man.[141]

3.2.4 North Africa

Unlike East Africa, North Africa appears to have lagged behind with regard to two prehistoric issues, namely excavation methods, which have often been neglected and absolute chronology, which is imprecise because of the lack of stratigraphic sequences where soil layers have remained undisturbed in their original state of nature. Thus, in the prehistory of North Africa, instead of looking at man and his environment, we shall look at how man accommodates to his environment. Early human industries, as well as pebble tools, are

---

[138.] Cfr. J. Ki-Zerbo, ed., *General History of Africa*, vol. 1, 227.
[139.] Cfr. Ibid., 239.
[140.] Cfr. Ibid., 232.
[141.] Cfr. Ibid., 23.

evident, especially in Morocco, Algeria, and the Sahara; they appear to be between 1,000,000 and 2,000,000 years old. In the light of chronological and stratigraphic findings, hominids do not appear to have been present in the Maghrib (Maghreb).[142]

Peculiar to this area is the Mousterian[143] industry. The Mousterian industry is the name archaeologists have given to an ancient Middle Stone Age method of making stone tools. This Mousterian culture in the Maghrib is said to be similar to that identified in Europe, and it is also said to have originated in the eastern Mediterranean.[144] It is clear that fresh excavation of minerals at the Tamar Hat site in Algeria have made it possible to date these findings very early and to obtain a clear picture of those Ibero-Mauritians, who were hunters of horned sheep and who lived in coastal caves separated from the sea by marshes. There were also blade industries in pre-Saharan Tunisia, in the Gafsa region, and other pre-Capsian[145] industries and traditions. There are real evidences of the rock arts culture and the engraving tradition that has always been a major characteristic of the region of North Africa from antiquity.[146]

Elementary history tells us that civilization started in North Africa, precisely in Egypt. Hence, Ki-Zerbo explains that "the fact is that the first scientific techniques were brought to the world from the African cradle, and continued to be until the millennia during which Egypt was the teacher of Greece and the entire Mediterranean Basin."[147]

[142.] Cfr. Ibid., 241. The Maghrib region is the region of Northwest Africa, west of Egypt. At first, it was defined as being the region including the Atlas Mountains and the coastal plains of Morocco, Algeria, Tunisia, and Libya though other areas were later added to this.

[143.] The Mousterian is associated with our hominid relatives, the Neanderthals in Europe, and both early modern human and Neanderthals in Africa.

[144.] Cfr. J. Ki-Zerbo, ed., *General History of Africa*, vol. 1, 242.

[145.] Capsian is named after the Tunisian town called Gafsa, and it is, thus, related to the Mesolithic culture of the Maghreb, which lasted from about 10,000 to 6,000 BCE. This culture was both typological and technological.

[146.] Cfr. Ibid., 243-250.

[147.] J. Ki-Zerbo, ed., *La natte des autres (pour un développement endogène en Afrique)* (Paris: CODESRIA/Karthala, 1992), 23.

3.2.5 West Africa

The discovery of remains of early forms of men or hominids has not really been evident in West Africa as in the other parts of Africa. This does not mean that these fossils did not exist there. This is because of some archaeological inaccuracies such as the condition of the climate of this area that has high humidity and the acidic nature of the soil which do not really favor archaeological findings and even preservation of relics. Nevertheless, skull fragments of human specimen, named *Tchadanthropus uxoris*, have been found near Largeau, in Chad, and in other areas in West Africa. There are also historical facts that stone or pebble industries existed in this area. Various types of industries for the production of choppers and other tools are also evident in Nigeria, Senegal, Ghana, Ivory Coast, Togo, and other countries in West Africa. These are dated about 39,000 years ago.[148]

Ki-Zerbo, in his research on African history, realizes that there are many cultural and geographic similarities in the continent though there are certain aspects too that retain the identity of each area and, consequently, of each nation. In this regard, talking about the Late Stone Age and the Neolithic, he intimates as follows:

Over most of West Africa, the Late Stone Age is characterized by the appearance of very small stone tools, known as "microliths." In parallel with North Africa and the Sahara, there was a time when finds from Rufisque in Senegal were attributed to the Neolithic of Capsian tradition, or "Guinean microlithic," which is very widespread in the eastern half of West Africa. In the western half, by contrast, it is absent at the most southerly sites, in the area of Liberia, Sierra Leone and south of the Republic of Guinea.[149]

[148.] Cfr. J. KI-ZERBO, *General History of Africa*, vol. 1, 264-269.
[149.] J. KI-ZERBO, ed., *La natte des autres*, 269.

Yam and rice farming were also very prominent in West Africa, especially in Niger, Nigeria, and Ghana. The cattle rearing in Mali is also worth mentioning, as well as the exploitation of the shellfish and other minerals in these regions. All these occurred between 2,000 and 1,500 years Before Christ. With respect to the Iron Age, it is noted that two civilizations introduced West Africa to the iron industries: the Geramantes of North Africa and the Kingdom of Meroe in Sudan. Prominent in the culture of this area, as in the other regions of Africa, is pottering, making of tombs, with a specific model of the king's tomb, as well as the discoveries of relics and objects or figures that represent the earliest effigies of the ancestors of the present-day people, with specific reference to the Yoruba.[150]

Conclusion

Looking generally upon Africa, an important aspect that could be discerned is that issues which unite her as a continent are more than those that divide. It is but normal that differences must abound, considering that each group of people are united as a region, clan, or nation with distinct peculiarities. Though it is of different parts, segments, or nations, as a continent, the history runs along the same direction and with similar characteristics. One very essential point concerning Africa as a continent is that by the middle and later Stone Age, between 150,000 and 40,000 years ago, humans had developed more sophisticated tools, shaping stone points to use as spearheads and the developing of bows and arrows. This equally implies the hardworking nature of the Africans as a people always searching for a means to survive even with the harshness of nature. They also used a wide range of implements made of bone that were used as needles or fishhooks. Around 10,000 years ago, humans took a hugely important step to begin domesticating animals and cultivating crops.

It is within this context of animal rearing and organized farming that trading and human socialization took a more organized and humane dimension. Trading naturally goes with movements,

---

[150.] Cfr. Ibid., 270-273

and such migrations justified the increase in population as history unfolded. Peculiar to the Africans is also the fact that, at this time of evolving socialization, people started expressing themselves through arts. Arts were used for aesthetic, social, cultural, and religious motives, and Ki-Zerbo sounds convincing that Africa is one of the richest continents in rock art. Peter Hunziker affirms his words that African arts "reflects but also stimulates action and these prehistoric carvings and paintings proclaim the relentless struggle of the African man to dominate nature and also to add to his own nature through the divine joy of creation."[151]

It is worthy of note that the Nile is the cradle of one of the most astonishing and enduring civilizations; it is and has always been an immense legacy to Africa and the world. Ancient Egypt was an African civilization, and the history of Africa can never be written appropriately without it being connected to the history of Egypt. The African historian who evades this problem is either oblivious, fainthearted, or a neurotic. The moral fruit of this civilization is intertwined with the cultural, ethical, and theocentric values embedded in the African tradition in general.

[151.] P. HUNZIKER, ed., *The Story of Africa* (London: K Gygax, 2005), 21.

CHAPTER FOUR

Substantiating Ki-Zerbo's Conception of History as Fundamentals of Social, Political, Cultural, and Religious Practices

WHEN HE RETURNED from exile into his country, Burkina Faso, in 1992, Ki-Zerbo was dismayed to realize that all his previous equipment and his library of eleven thousand volumes had been destroyed or dispersed. Yet with the desire to reconstitute the history of his continent as a strong foundation for development, he decided to reestablish CEDA in his country. CEDA is the *Centre d'Etudes pour le Développement Africain* (Center for Studies for the Development of Africa) which he created in 1980. When he was given the award as one of the outstanding contributors to development in Africa in 1997, he used the opportunity to define the aim of CEDA as follows:

> We must return the institutional imagination of African societies to their tradition of creativity across the widest possible range of science and technology, and on this basis rearticulate a theory and praxis that are appropriate to their situations. We must rebuild the identity from which

the African peoples have become alienated by the
vicissitudes of history and their own amnesia.[152]

The implication of the above statement is that Africans have
been originally creative, and their creativity is reflected in their tradition which is sustained in the sociopolitical and cultural values that
the people uphold. Here lies the bedrock of history. We, therefore,
understand at this point why he summarizes his conception of history, as seen above, as the fundamentals of social, political, cultural,
and religious practices. For him, this can really be implemented or
understood only with sound education—education that involves
both the arts and science of history. By education, Ki-Zerbo does
not mean only Western-style school education but also traditional
education that has produced so many intellectuals, scholars, and scientists.[153] With an example of local education, he takes the field of
African medicine. Without neglecting the Western style of education,
Ki-Zerbo recommends the African traditional style of education as
a social means of transmitting history for the good of humankind.
This point is better presented in the following communication:

> African medicine has stressed the importance of
> some principles, such as the psychosomatic effects
> of certain substances, which Western countries
> have tended to neglect. In other words, African
> countries contain reserves of rationality, of log-
> ical principles, which might well open up new
> horizons in various fields of knowledge... Lets
> take from Europe but let's give something back
> in return. To say that we must start from scratch
> would be to accept a kind of mental apartheid.[154]

[152.] J. Ki-Zerbo, *The Right Livelihood Award* (1997).
[153.] Cfr. J. Ki-Zerbo, *Histoire de l'Afrique noire*, 642.
[154.] J. Ki-Zerbo, in *UNESCO Courier*, 9.

What then are the fundamental social, political, cultural, and religious practices that constitute African history and which serve as an embodiment of the African conception of history in the perspective of Joseph Ki-Zerbo?

4.1. History as Fundamentals of Social Practices

Social practices are those activities that a people involve themselves in as they move on with life in the society, especially in their surrounding communities. We already realized that the Africans were mostly farmers, and they did pasture rearing as well as trading and the manufacturing of tools for the cultivation of food crops, as well as for the improvement of their environment. Sociology revolves around the human person in a society. Therefore, the traditional African values each individual person and pays every respect to the fact that man is supposed to live in solidarity with his fellow man and with the divine world. This is reflected in work, property management, and governance.

4.1.1 The African Notion of Work and Property and the Continuation of History

Africans are traditionally conscious of the necessity to work hard in order to live well on earth. Therefore, history testifies that the African people are basically hardworking. Ki-Zerbo, as we saw above, identifies trading, pasturing, industrial work, arts, and farming as some of the main occupations of the African people as traced in history. Normally, the traditional African would introduce his sons and daughters to work, especially the type of work that they excel in and consider as their source of livelihood. Work, as a source of living for the Africans, goes in line with the conception of property, and property, depending on its type, either belongs to the community at large (under the custody of the king) or to the family, and this is transferred from one generation to the next. This is where the notion of work fits into the concept of history and makes this topic relevant to our subject matter. In most cases in Africa, people work on the land, which is evidently not privatised. It is on this historical fact that Ki-Zerbo figuratively considers land or property in general as the owner of man and goes on to regret the ills of privatization and consumerism in ancient and recent times that breed selfishness and other vices. Hence, while subscribing to the Hebrew consideration that "la terre, propriété, et propriétaire" (the land, the property, and the owner), he goes on to make the following remark:

> C'est la terre qui est finalement propriétaire de l'homme! Depuis l'Antiquité grecque et romaine, on a mis un accent trop prononcé sur la propriété et sur la privatisation de la propriété. En revanche, dans le système africain, on a "désintoxiqué" la propriété privée avant la consommation.[155]

Work at a community level was always coordinated and organized by some delegates, persons who were also good workers with a good sense of judgement.[156] History testifies that this aspect of work is mostly associated with physical power and energy, and it is mostly actualized in a community system, and there was always a headman or a spokesman to lead and to coordinate. Ki-Zerbo observes in this connection that in Africa,

> forces have to be constantly stemmed, collected, channelled, harnessed and mobilised by a sort of mental engineering, working for the individual or the group. This attitude is a dynamic one... the role of the spokesman was not to supervise and impose sanctions, but to advise and proffer guidance so as to ensure that the reckless energy

---

[155.] (It is the land that finally owns the man! Since Greek and Roman antiquity, there has been too much emphasis on ownership and the privatization of property. On the other hand, in the African system, private property was "detoxified" before consumption.) J. KI-ZERBO, À Quand L'Afrique?, 40.

[156.] Cfr. J. KI-ZERBO, in UNESCO Courier, 21.

of the people was not prejudicial to the community as a whole.[157]

Historical objects and events are actually the products of work. Ki-Zerbo's conviction is that Africans, both the men and the women, are, in fact, a hardworking set of people. As they wandered through nature, they discovered many things and shaped them with their natural energy in a manner that had to be of valuable service to their day-to-day lives. He recounted the adventures of the Neolithic of the Sahara and the Nile valley, three thousand years before the coming of the Europeans, as an example, recounting that hard work brought the African people into a unity of culture as he states as follows:

> Pottery appears to have been brought to the Khartoumian culture of Sudan and subsequently to the Sahara and Egypt from highlands of East Africa. This was a decisive human innovation that stepped up the pace of early capital accumulation, as did the spread of cattle-raising. Pottery was also instrumental in fostering the art of cooking, which sets man completely apart from all other animals.[158]

Some of these socioeconomic aspects of the people also came along with some violent encounters. Ki-Zerbo infers that these conflicts arose from man's innate aggressiveness and led to the elimination of the weakest.[159]

Work in Africa as Ki-Zerbo intimates, had to be studied too, not strictly in the formal sense but in what could be considered indigenous knowledge system. This is a knowledge system which endorses knowing with practice, practicing not only particular trades or functions but also performing them as a value-based activity for the good

---

[157.] J. KI-ZERBO, ed., *General History of Africa*, vol. 1, 21.
[158.] Ibid., 315.
[159.] Cfr. Idem.

of one's family and for the entire community. It is in terms of this knowing and sharing that communities have survived for centuries. This, therefore, is not only knowledge and practices of culture, custom, agriculture, medicine, biodiversity, ethno-numeracy, customary law, and other undertakings but, above all, is the rationality of these cultural practices and rites that prompted social consistency, creativity, and skilfulness in activities, such as dance and music, technology of fashioning, clothing, and carpentry. Ki-Zerbo discovers that Egypt had a lot of indigenous knowledge, some of which is still applicable across the world in business sects today, for example, the calendar, paper, pen, and irrigation (shadoof). One can be justified to say indigenous knowledge systems are highly applicable to business processes toward sustainable development in Africa and the eradication or the alleviation of poverty in African states.[160]

4.1.2 History and Political Practices in a Culture of Peace

Every society has its own political systems and even before the coming of the colonial masters, the African society also had its own political system that ensured the maintenance of peace and stability. Peace and stability, therefore, constitute a major aspect of the African conception of history. An African can hardly conceive his history without surrounding it within the framework of peace. Such a culture of peace is also to be understood within the ambient of African solidarity because peace is to ensure that people live together as one family. To make this more comprehensive, Ki-Zerbo tells us thus:

> Non si può esprimere meglio la solidarietà fra tutti gli esseri umani che con queste parole: Il giovane iniziato mandingo, alla domanda Chi sei? risponde "Non sono niente senza di te, non

---

[160.] Cf. J. KI-ZERBO, À Quand L'Afrique?, 129-130.

sono niente senza di loro. Quando sono arrivato, ero nelle loro mani; erano lì ad accogliermi."[161]

In his article "Africa—the Culture of Peace" in *Dossier*, April 2013, Chris Maitho quotes Ki-Zerbo saying:

> African culture is based on peace and on peaceful coexistence. Looking at how African leaders, after liberation wars, have been capable of reconciling with those who dominated, mistreated, crushed and despised them, the ability of African people to take the standpoint of peace is easily recognisable. Moreover, all daily habits of the African people are deeply infused with a culture of peace, from ritual salutations to the way of settling community conflicts. Their manner of speaking and their social behaviour suggest a perpetual appeal to peace with both the universe and one's own neighbours.[162]

In explaining the culture of peace that happens to form a fundamental part in the conception of history for the Africans, Ki-Zerbo makes reference to the aspect of race as not being an issue for the Africans in terms of concepts like racism. In fact, he explains that the concept of race for the Africans does not really call for differences but for living together in pluralism. In this regard, he makes reference to a paper presented by Livingstone in 1952 with "the nonexistence of human races." The point raised here, endorsed by Ki-Zerbo, is that—depending on the criteria selected, whether it be skin color, the shape of the skull, or the nose, the nature of the hair, genetic features, etc.—the resulting map of the races differs every time. He

---

[161.] (Solidarity between all human beings cannot be better expressed than with these words: The young Mandingo initiate, to the question who are you? replies, "I am nothing without you, I am nothing without them. When I arrived, I was in their hands; they were there to greet me.") J. Ki-Zerbo, *Punti Fermi Sull'Africa*, 16.

[162.] C. Maitho, "Africa—the Culture of Peace" in *Dossier* (2013), of April 2013.

draws our attention to the fact that in the light of the most recent advances in human genetics, no biologist nowadays admits the existence of races within the human species. He explains to us that this was one of the reasons for the UNESCO declaration that "race is not so much a biological phenomenon as a social myth."[163] To demonstrate this, Ki-Zerbo explains that in spite of the confusion in living with racial consciousness, this also brings unnecessary inhumanity which again is contrary to the African frame of mind. He says,

> What better illustration could there be of this claim than the fact that in South Africa, a Japanese is regarded as an "honorary white" and a Chinese as "coloured," whereas a man who is considered to be white in Brazil is considered black in the United States. The truth is that all the peoples of the world are of mixed blood, and are likely to become increasingly mixed. Even so, the myth of race continues to do untold harm, since Hitler asserted that between the Aryan "Prometheus of Mankind," and the black "half ape by descent," there was the intermediate Mediterranean type; the racial myth is still very much alive. In the objective development of peoples, two factors contribute to the typical profile of a group: the genetic heritage (heredity) and the environment. Against that background, what can we say about race where the African continent is concerned? It emerges from a great many recent studies that the blacks came into being on the continent some 120,000 years ago and that the black pigmentation was, in fact, a protective adaption to harmful radiation, especially ultraviolet rays. The "whites" appeared on the planet much later— about 55,000 years ago. The Arab-Berbers, who

---

[163.] J. Ki-Zerbo, ed., *General History of Africa*, vol. 1, 102.

are "Mediterranean" types, subsequently spread to the south of the Sahara, the Horn of Africa and the eastern seaboard. In the regions where the Arab-Berber world touched the black group, which also comprises the Khoisan, the Nilotic peoples, the Fulani and the "Ethiopians," certain peoples display distinctive signs of mixed breeding. This is true of certain Tuareg groups, the Haratin and Somali, as well as of certain Fulani and Hausa, Tukuloor, Songhay, and so on, in the Sudanic belt. In this, as in other instances, the decisive factors in the process of differentiation are the geographical environment and the isolation of intermingling of peoples through invasions, migration and intermarriage.[164]

The inference of Joseph Ki-Zerbo after this entire lecture is an anthropological certainty that a slow-moving evolution has always been undergone by groups that were, for a long time, fairly isolated. This calls for natural mixture and interculturalism among human beings. Therefore, as anthropologists, sociologists, and psychologists affirm, contrary to people like Hegel, no human group or race is better fortified than any other as far as the gradation of intelligence is concerned. This is one of the major points we are making in this work. The historical primacy of culture over biology has been basic ever since the offspring of the same ancient couple have roamed over planet Earth, having probably set out from the African continent. Ki-Zerbo, after explaining all these, laments when people will eventually come to realize that it is culture, and not the nuts and bolts of biology, that makes them what they are and that this is the basic fact that can develop our humanity.[165]

Based on a culture of peace, Ki-Zerbo explains that the African political system has its own peculiarities. While acknowledging the

---

[164.] Ibid., 102-103.

[165.] Idem.

contribution of sociology and political science to the understanding, as well as to the development of African political system, he also insinuates that the notion of, or rather the Western concepts, of kingdom, nation, state, empire, democracy, political party, and so on cannot be applied to Africa indiscriminately.[166]

Political issues are always very sensitive, and generally, in every society, it can hardly be denied that the biggest obstacle to good governance does not come from the lack of material means but, more often, from the absence of a positive political will. Consequently, we agree with Rauf Mustapha that "it is only when the political problems are understood then can we acquire solutions on how to solve the economic problems."[167] In his book, *Which Way, Africa*, Ki-Zerbo makes much reference to Basil Davidson who happens to have written the preface of the book, also making reference to Jules Ferry. According to him, when Jules Ferry declared, "The question of the colonies is the question of outlets," he recognised implicitly that the colonies were one of the remedies for social conflict. He asks us then to speculate about what the social and economic history of Belgium would have been without the Belgian Congo. With due respect to some of the positive values in the colonial masters, we are conditioned to understand in this book that many of the first leaders of the African states had contracted the colonialist's disease to such an extent that they believed there was nothing positive to be drawn from the precolonial African system.[168]

Alongside the general distortion of the values in precolonial Africa in the minds of the first African leaders, it was also noticed that even those who held progressive social or socialist views, when they came to power, were often led astray by the logic of Realpolitik which sustains the nation state. This is why the majority of African peoples, far from seeing their lives improve as they had hoped, have

---

[166.] Cfr. J. KI-ZERBO, ed., *General History of Africa*, vol. 1, 32.

[167.] R. MUSTAPHA, "The Constitutional Conference, the Military Factor, and the Future of Democracy in Nigeria," a paper presented at the symposium of Nigerian Political Science Students (NIPSS) (Zaria: ABU Chapter, August 17, 1994).

[168.] Cfr. J. KI-ZERBO, *Which Way, Africa?*, 12.

suffered a deterioration in their circumstances caused by what has been dubbed—in an oversimplistic way—neocolonialism. It is not as if everything precolonial was good or everything colonial is bad, yet Ki-Zerbo insists that the mindset of the Africans must be rearranged; it must be firmly educated because the risk is that thinking of the precolonial era, the positive elements which could most appropriately provide the foundations for our countries to play a role in the contemporary world are dismissed as traditional, unfashionable, and out-of-date.[169] Yet by not considering tradition or culture as contingent on history, he intimates that the consequences are many: dependency on foreign countries and deteriorating terms of trade, capital flight from Africa to industrialised countries, clandestine siphoning off capital by Africa's leaders into safe bank accounts, and egoistical individualism, which is destroying social cohesion at a time when the capitalist mode of production, responsible for spawning this individualism, is not yet fully established.[170]

We prefer to approach the African political system as an embodiment of history in the account of Ki-Zerbo from the points of view of traditional government as well as from the perspectives of leadership and sanctions.

4.1.3 The Historical Situation of African Traditional Government

When he attempts an interpretation of the African traditional system of government, Ki-Zerbo again identifies history as his point of departure. In his account on this topic, one must get into the roots of the African political system, studying it from any topic or perspective from within and not by making references to other systems or ready-made ideas or prejudices.[171] He explains that, traditionally, the African society had a well-structured political system with leaders who exercised their power or authority over the members of their

---

[169.] Cfr. J. KI-ZERBO, *Which Way, Africa?*, 12.

[170.] Cfr. Idem.

[171.] Cfr. J. Ki-ZERBO, ed., *General History of Africa*, vol. 1, 8.

respective communities. He realized, however, that in some cases, these authorities were oppressive to the people, yet it was also with such forceful manifestation or execution of authority that colonizers encountered the fiercest resistance.[172] Amy Niang documented him in the following general observation that he made concerning government in the African sense:

> Africans, he says, "believe that power should be divided among its incumbents. They also believe that stability could be preserved in the multiplication of power." He debunks misconceptions about African history and dominant theories that deliberately confine the history of the continent to the slave trade and the colonial experience. He adds that historical knowledge is a condition to collective liberation as the linkage between historical knowledge and self-worth is undeniable. In Africa, the lack of this knowledge has greatly contributed to underachievement and "mental underdevelopment." Ki-Zerbo is a man of vision and a soothsayer but he does not read Africa's future in the sand of its drying soil; he uses the dialectical process of history as an investigative method to uncover the true past of the continent in order to understand the underpinnings of Africa's value systems. He then tells us what a de-structured society can expect to see: the import and application of values that do not fit its peoples, which eventually will lead to the destruction of cultural identity.[173]

[172.] Cfr. Ibid., 18.

[173.] A. NIANG, "Joseph Ki-Zerbo, the Historian and His Struggle" in *Pambazuka News* (2005), n. 256.

In the political governing, some societies were really so very well organized to the extent that they became empires. Among the many examples of empires that Ki-Zerbo explains is the Ethiopian Empire. He explains that "from the thirteenth century onwards, the Ethiopian royal chronicles provide a record of the imperial reigns, continuing into the twentieth century with the Amharic chronicle of the Empire of Menelik II."[174] Some of the documents containing similar facts were also found in the nineteenth century onward, furnished by documents in the archives of those European powers and in those of Addis Ababa and even Khartoum.[175]

Another very important issue concerning government in Africa is that government was never an issue for a particular people though leaders were available and respected. Fundamentally, community dignity was everybody's concern. Each person took care of the other, and the dignity of every human person was highly prized. This respect for individual and community sanity and sanctity was everybody's business, and it was a system of life that was traditional, meaning that it was handed down from one generation to another as a historical rhythm of nature even though there was always a governing body with the power to ensure this vertical and horizontal flow of equanimity. Hence, "power and history were everybody's business and it is this that accounts for the popular and 'democratic' inspiration that so frequently informs the African concept of history."[176] He also observed that autocratic government also existed and it was actually the duty of everybody to flee from such a form of government.

Ki-Zerbo, however, does not limit his conception of history to the ruling class or to great world spectacular events as some historians make of history. In his consideration, political history was for all; it is social history. In the same way, economic history was not concerned with what the people produced and what their needs were or with the ways in which they were commandeered into the service of the privileged classes. Instead, it dealt with the technical discoveries made

---

174. Ibid., 47.
175. Cfr. J. KI-ZERBO, ed., *General History of Africa*, vol. 1, 47.
176. Ibid., 20.

by scientists and the decrees made by ministers to develop national growth policies. Therefore, African specialists may not necessarily need to copy other systems of government for Africa, but rather, they need a keen knowledge of African history and the African system.[177] In an attempt to illuminate this point, he says thus:

> When for example, they claimed that Africa had highly centralized empires and kingdoms similar to those of Europe, they tended to overlook the fact that those structures had been built at a very heavy cost of human lives, whereas African village democracies, founded on maximum individual autonomy, probably represented more worthwhile achievements.[178]

Thus, in an interview with Bahgat Elnadi and Adel Rifaat in the *UNESCO Courier* magazine on the first of September 1993, Ki-Zerbo firmly suggests that any democracy in Africa today must recognise the peculiarity of the traditional African system of government that is founded on the very nature of the African people, as testified by history. Accordingly, he explains that "a democracy based on the constitutional solidarity of the African system could make Africa a credible member of a new planetary partnership."[179] If democracy is not so considered, then it would be an external matter, and this, for him, is the problem with democracy today, especially in Africa. "Democracy," he emphasises, "is a delusion, a placebo, if it is only a matter of outward forms."[180]

[177.] Cfr. J. KI-ZERBO, ed., *General History of Africa*, vol. 1, 24.
[178.] Idem.
[179.] J. KI-ZERBO, in *UNESCO Courier*, 9.
[180.] Ibid., 13.

Viewing the situation of Africa today, therefore, with regard to state government, while appealing for the values of traditional government to be examined and adapted, he intimates as follows:

> What is required is not so much the abolition of African nation states but their transformation into new institutions better suited to address the realities, interests and values of peoples. In this task, a vital part will be played by civil society, which, through its dialectical relationship with authority, and in conjunction with the political class, transforms the state and the nation.[181]

The African system always recognised that government is out for the common good; it goes with good leadership and the leaders have the duty to execute sanctions in cases where rules are transgressed.

4.1.4 Leadership and Sanctions with Regard to History and Government in Africa

The concept of government logically goes with that of leadership. In traditional Africa, government and leadership took the form of the present-day states with a head of state. This idea also contributes not only to the history of Africa as a continent but also to the African conception of history. It is in this consideration that Ki-Zerbo's infers as follows:

> The recent history of pre and post-colonial Africa, from *Osei Tutu* and *Anokye* of the *Asante* to *Shaka* or *Samory*, and right through to some of the present day heads of state, does not detract from this mental picture of the "meaning of history" that Africans have. We should hasten to add, however, that their idea of a leader who is a driving force

---

[181.] J. KI-ZERBO, *Which Way, Africa?*, 7.

behind history is almost never reduced to the car-
icature-like image of any one as the prime mover
in the whole of human progress.[182]

This is because there is always a dynamic group, with the assignment to assist the chief or leader in his administration. This group
is often composed of some dignitaries with moral rectitude and also
some personalities with inferior statutes such as griots, spokesmen,
and servants. Each person has his own role and acts according to
prescribed norms. Each member of the governing body in his own or
her own way is a part of the heroes in history. Women, in some cases
and contrary to certain persistent misconceptions, also form part of
this team, especially in matrilineal societies or in situations where
such is bound to apply.[183]

Leadership and government in the traditional African setup are
equally based on human dignity. Hence, the African, as Ki-Zerbo
intimates, cannot think of his history without attaching to it this
primary value of the dignity of each individual, and every law that
governs the people was based on the natural law that did not depend
on man but on the Supreme Being, found in the deeper being of
each person and defined and implemented by the rulers of the people. Laws were equally constructed along this reality, and Ki-Zerbo
is firmly convinced that this link between natural laws, human laws,
and human dignity is found in all cultures. "L'idée de droit au niveau
des droits naturels et du respect de la dignité humaine, existe dans
toutes les cultures humaines."[184] Yet Ki-Zerbo goes further in the
African context to link up this respect for the human person; human
dignity with community solidarity, calling it a moral law. "En Afrique
précoloniale, les gens considéraient que la solidarité était un devoir
moral, pas seulement juridique."[185]

Ki-Zerbo also explains to us that leadership and rules must go
with sanctions. The primary role of the governing body is to ensure

---

[182.] J. KI-ZERBO, ed., *General History of Africa*, vol. 1, 18.
[183.] Idem.
[184.] J. KI-ZERBO, *À Quand L'Afrique?*, 129.
[185.] Ibid., 130.

peace and tranquillity. This explains why, in this connection, government activities have an intrinsic religious value. Accordingly, it is only in a contextual manner that a dichotomy is made between the political and the religious. Both form part of a dynamic social system of living. Punishments are not only given to ordinary citizens who act contrary to community norms but also even to those in positions of authority, following the ethical content of authority or leadership, without which no power would be capable of doing good. With many historical details given, Ki-Zerbo affirms that "popular wisdom bears witness to this idea in many tales which depict despotic chiefs who are finally punished, thus drawing the moral of history."[186]

The influence of Basil Davidson on Joseph Ki-Zerbo is very evident. It is under the inspiration of his work, *The Black Man's Burden*, that Ki-Zerbo wrote his book *Which Way, Africa?* In this book, he makes concrete use of the traditional African saying that "it is not the king who possesses kingship, but kingship which possesses the king." Here he indicates that in a typical African society, even between ethnic groups not subject to the same law, there were judicial and cultural bridges indicating the existence of a common patrimony or a common will to exorcise past or possible future conflicts. His investigations clarify the point that the African societies were governed through a set of norms that were ethnic, interethnic, and supra-ethnic, thus national in scope.[187] He frantically regrets that this culture was dishonourably put to death as he goes on to proclaim:

> The decision to condemn this culture to death was truly a crime of continental genocide, which continues to bear its bitter and poisonous fruits. "Salvation must come from outside. For nothing of value grows in the dark primitive forest of the uncivilised human mind": this sentiment reflected the blindness of the first Africans to be emancipated, legally but not culturally, who

---

186. J. Ki-Zerbo, ed., *General History of Africa*, vol. 1, 21.
187. Cfr. J. Ki-Zerbo, *Which Way, Africa?*, 14–15.

were content to chant the refrain, "They need Christianity and the example of the English."[188]

4.2 History as Expressed in Cultural/ Religious Practices

Certainly, we are versed with the word *culture* in this work. That, notwithstanding, we still have a duty to present it in Ki-Zerbo's perspective even though it may not be very much diverse from the other conceptions we have seen. Joseph Ki-Zerbo perceives culture as the creative life of a people, which transforms the natural and social environment. It includes both the most prosaic aspects of the people's existence (tools and agrarian methods), the more subtle elements such as ownership, how to smile, how to celebrate love and death. He also insinuates that the transmission of culture to future generations by an educational system remodeled modernization in the authenticity and liaison with universal culture. Thus, as a result, culture is not static.[189] Accordingly, he reminds us of the vastness of this term by inscribing that "parlare delle identità culturali africane significa trattare un tema immenso, difficile da circoscrivere, perché tocca tutti gli aspetti della nostra vita in quanto popoli e in quanto nazioni."[190] It becomes evident, therefore, why culture takes a central place in the field of history, implying the geographic, religious, ethical, sociopolitical, and all other aspects of a people's existence. It is the conviction of Ki-Zerbo that all through the course of history, strong beliefs in simple benevolent principles, such as the importance of family over the individual, the respect of elders, the spirit of sharing and good neighborliness, human communion in joy and sadness, have been the bedrock of existence for the Africans. Unfortunately, he realizes that the degradation of these principles with the so-called modernization has shattered prospects for Pan-Africanism and devel-

---

[188.] Ibid., 15.

[189.] Cfr. J. KI-ZERBO, *Generation Joseph Ki-Zerbo* in URL: < *http://www.fondationki-zerbo.org/IMG/pdf/A_propos_de_culture-Joseph_Ki-Zerbo.pdf,* > (accessed on March 13, 2014).

[190.] J. KI-ZERBO, *Punti Fermi Sull'Africa,* 79.

opment. Nevertheless, he warns us that "liberation for Africa will be Pan-African or will not be."[191]

Today, the debate over Africa, he observes, is entangled in endless and ineffectual squabbling over the legitimacy of pseudo-democracies and misleading conflicts. But he argues that the conception of power, as well as its management in today's Africa, has nothing African in it. In fact, political formations in precolonial Africa are rich with institutions based on a division of power with the greater possible number of people.[192] According to Ki-Zerbo, genuine knowledge of the natural and social setting is needed. Again, to this concept of culture, he fits in the necessity of education. Therefore, he insists that "Africanisation is necessary in order to give back to education its role as an instrument to perpetuate African society."[193] Thus, in order to draw the necessary inspiration from the African culture to guarantee the sustenance of African values in the society, education must be localized; it must be "immanent in the local social setting."[194] He considers the reform of the school system of Africa as a sine qua non for the growth and development of the society. This change for him must also involve the introduction of African languages into the educational system and the necessity to promote persons as the supreme value, solidarity, creativity, and ongoing initiation. Consequently, for the implementation of all these, he proposes a complete change in curriculum and working methods, in African schools, making them community, social, environmental, and value orientated.[195]

Another aspect that Ki-Zerbo highlights is that even though Africans had their own sociocultural or religious systems, they also came in contact with and were affected by the Islamic and Christian religions. The evidence is that the period up to the threshold of the fifteenth century of the Christian era is not as poor in written sources

---

[191.] A. NIANG, "Joseph Ki-Zerbo, the Historian and His Struggle" in *Pambazuka News* (2005), n. 256.

[192.] Cfr. Ibid., no. 256.

[193.] J. KI-ZERBO, *Eduquer ou périr*, UNICEF-UNESCO (Paris, 1990), 101.

[194.] Ibid., 87.

[195.] Cfr. J. KI-ZERBO, *L'éducation permanente en Afrique* (1972), Revue Orientations 43, 13.

as might be thought. There is much documentation on this fact that kept improving as we move on from Herodotus to Ibn Khaldun and Ibn Battuta. There are also some Arabic sources that show the external origin and transcend the undeniable social and cultural similarities and differences of some values. Yet this is often seen as the beginnings of a new and fuller trans-Saharan solidarity, dating back to that of Neolithic times.[196]

4.2.1 Religious and Ethical values

One point that is so firmly engraved in Ki-Zerbo's conviction is that for the Africans, sin has a social dimension and must be purged from all angles, considering that it disturbs the normal ethical flow of events. This is the idea that prompted him to make the following assertion:

> This lofty view of the role of ethics in history is also found in "traditional religion" belief, which regards sin as being anything that disrupts the equilibrium of the forces and is liable to harm the community. This may seem a mystical view of things, but it exerted an objective influence on real-life history.[197]

Ethical principles are part of the community system of life, and he continues to explain that in certain Black African systems, as in most other parts of Africa, moral authorities, which are not essentially distinguished from the normal political authorities, are capable and actually have the community mandate to sanction the conduct of public affairs or of chastising all persons who act without the sense of propriety. Some of these groups operated in the form of secret

---

[196.] Cfr. J. Ki-Zerbo, *General History of Africa*, vol. 1, 41-42.
[197.] Ibid., 21.

societies and people appealed to them in various forms for protection and for the execution of justice.[198]

It is equally the conviction of Ki-Zerbo that religion is the strongest force that binds the African community together. Their faith is bound to their existence. This, for him, explains why Christianity and Islam penetrated their system because they were already used to a life of faith, a life that pays respect and reverence to God. Hence, they could blend Christian and Islam beliefs to their tradition and customs.[199]

Since community living is very paramount in the African society, truth stands out as a towering value that sustains this community lifestyle. Truth in the ethical and epistemological or ontological sense is always separated from jokes and even lies in comic circumstances, considering that truth in itself expresses the reality of life in the community; it expresses the authentic cultural and traditional values which are situated at the very core of history.[200] These are the facts about the community, and it is on authenticity that the people are bound as a community with a certain definition and not merely as a group of people. To this effect, Ki-Zerbo intimates:

> Genuine traditionalists have a scrupulous regard for truth. For them, lying is not merely a moral fault, but a ritual taboo which, if violated would put an end to their foundation. As the saying goes: "Better for the world to be cut off from you than for you to be cut off from yourself through lies." Apart from the esoteric teaching provided in the great schools, traditional instruction is dispensed by the community and the family, and is also directly bound up with everyday living. Tales and legends are rich in practical and moral lessons, while proverbs are missives bequeathed to poster-

---

[198.] Cfr. J. KI-ZERBO in *UNESCO Courier*, 9-11.

[199.] Cfr. Ibid., 13.

[200.] Cfr. J. KI-ZERBO, ed., *General History of Africa*, vol. 1, 64.

ity by the ancestors. Some games based on mathematical laws train the mind while transmitting
ciphered occult knowledge: the *Banangolo* game
in Mali, which is based on a numerical system
connected with 266 *siqiba* of signs corresponding
to attributes of God, is an example.[201]

By way of worshiping, there were times that many areas in the
traditional African societies were attached to several gods and goddesses irrespective of their general claims to monotheism. In North
Africa, for example, as far back as the time of the late predynastic or
Late Gerzean phase of their history, "the culture came to be dominated by the worship of the falcon god, while the South had originally venerated the god of *Seth*, variously identified as a jackal or a
giraffe."[202] Equally, at some point, the goddesses who were to prevail through the Pharaonic period appeared and other deities such as
Horus were worshipped. As a social activity, religious worship or ceremonies were very much organized. Population groups were centered
on the worship of particular divinity and were organized into prov-
inces or norms, each with a distinctive emblem that accompanied the
chief and traditional dignitaries into ceremonial occasions.[203] This, of
course, had to do with the relationship that the people had with the
transcendent.

4.2.2 Man's Relationship with God, Spirits, and the Extraterrestrial World

Ki-Zerbo attests to the importance of solidarity in the African
culture as said above. He equally recognizes that this solidarity
among the people has its roots in their common belief that there is
a supreme God taking care of all in a socially bounded community.
He goes on to intimate that people did not live their lives in sep-

---

[201.] Ibid., 64-65.
[202.] J. KI-ZERBO, ed., *General History of Africa*, vol. 1, 309.
[203.] Cfr. Ibid., 310.

arate compartments, either in relation to their bodily needs, with another separate life for engaging in social relations, and yet another embracing art, philosophy, education, and so on. All these different strands are woven together to form a single whole, even in relation to God and the ancestors or spirits, or with the extraterrestrial world in general. Such an all-inclusive approach to life also raised patterns of body sanctification which fulfilled the twofold function of signalling ethnic identity and satisfying an aesthetic urge.[204] Practical example of such a life that expresses religion and ethnicity is taken from the coins used in the Guinean, Sierra Leonean, and Liberian culture. The iron coins served at the same time as currency, as protectors of houses and land, and as resting place for the spirits of the departed and the ancestors.[205]

4.2.3 Theism and Ancestral Veneration as a Cultural Heritage

Theism is a basic religious culture in Africa that can never be overlooked in the conception of African history. As we mentioned in the first part of our work, quoting from some authors, including Geoffrey Parrinder, history testifies that Africa is, basically speaking, a religious continent. Even before the coming of the missionaries, the people communicated with God and they were generally conscious of the basic principles of morality.[206] Yet that which presently fits into our subject matter is the way this theism constitutes a cultural heritage, in other words, how it is conceived as an element of history.

We agree with Ki-Zerbo, as mentioned earlier, that God is conceived by Africans in relation to the ancestors and other spiritual beings. Martin N. Nkemnkia also clarifies that we cannot approach religious matters, especially when it comes to the issue of history, and specifically creation, with a purely scientific disposition but rather by carefully examining and appreciating the language expressions as in

---

[204.] Cfr. Ibid., 144-145.

[205.] Cfr. Ibid., 145.

[206.] Cfr. G. PARRINDER, *Religion in Africa* (England: Penguin African Books Ltd., 1966), 39.

the myths and other figures of speech involved in the transmission.[207] Consequently, with reference to many other African thinkers, he illuminates better the point of Ki-Zerbo concerning the indispensable role of oral tradition, with specific reference to myth, the symbolic and literary use of language in general, in the study and expression of history for the Africans.[208] In this regard, without a thorough study of the African terminologies and expressions, it may be difficult to understand properly the cultural heritage of the African people which conveys their history. We shall use a few words or concepts to explain better.

The word *ancestor*, in the English sense, is etymologically derived from the Latin word *antecessor*, stemming from the infinitive *antecedere*, which is a synthesis of two words *ante*, meaning "before," and *cedere*, meaning "to go." Nominally speaking, therefore, the word *ancestor* means one who goes before or one who has gone before. Connotatively, an ancestor is "one from whom a person is descended, especially at a distance of time; a forefather."[209] However, the traditional Africans see deeper into this word. The Bangou tribe in the western region of Cameroon, for example, uses the traditional name *mfeussi* for an ancestor. *Mfeu* means "to return or to go back" and *Si* means "God." Thus, *mfuessi* or an ancestor for them is a member of a family who has returned or gone back to God. They are spiritual beings, so their mode and form of existence have changed after death.

Newell S. Booth explains that it is an essential fact in African history as handed down to successive generation that, at death, the breath of a man leaves him; his spirit has left him at this point, and he no longer has strength to dwell in the present but in the extraterrestrial world. Thus, death is the passage into a new stage of life.[210]

[207.] Cfr. M. N. Nkemnkia, "L'Origine dell'universo nella 'Vitalogia' delle culture Africane," in A. Pavan and E. Magno, eds., *Antropogenesi* (Milano: Società Editrice il Mulino, 2010), 180–187.

[208.] Cfr. M. N. Nkemnkia, *African Vitalogy*, 30–34.

[209.] M. Webster, *Webster New Collegiate Dictionary* (New York: G & C. Merriam Co., 1956), 33.

[210.] Cfr. N. S. Booth, ed., *African Religions, A Symposium* (London: NOK Publishers Ltd., 1977), 40.

Actually, the ancestors are still very active among the people; hence, they are often described as the living dead. However, not every dead person becomes an ancestor. Some major prerequisites are required, which includes the following:

> Since ancestors are custodians of societal ethics, for a person to be qualified as an ancestor, he must have lived an exemplary moral life.
> He must get a proper burial according to the traditional rites.
> Even though some conditions (such as a life of virtue, taking good care of persons, especially children) may accept a childless deceased person to be an ancestor, it is generally a condition that for a person to qualify as an ancestor, he must have had at least a child who has to continue his lineage. As John S. Mbiti puts it, "For the Africans, the lack of children means a physical and spiritual extinction, since the ancestral spirits depend for their survival on the remembrance in the minds of their descendants."[211]

The main activity or function of the ancestors is that they act as intermediaries between God and man. To pacify them is to pacify God, and to be at peace with them is to be at peace with God. God still has His supreme role and His indisputable place. Placide Tempels explains this better that in Africa, "no one doubts the fact that life belongs to God and creation is certainly His work. However the preservation and respect for life are regarded to be the business of the ancestors."[212] This is because, "the ancestors are our predecessors…and secondly that in their spiritual state, they know more than we can, being in unhindered touch with the essence of things (God)."[213] It is through the living dead that the spirit world becomes personal to men. They are still part of their human families and peo-

---

[211.] J. S. MBITI, *African Religion and Philosophy*, 175.
[212.] P. TEMPELS, *Bantu Philosophy, Présence Africaine* (Paris, 1969), 78.
[213.] Cfr. J. MIDDLETON, "Ancestral Spirit Mediumship," in *Africa* (1973), vol. XLII, no. 2, 125.

ple have personal memories of them.[214] This is why sacrifices of pacification, thanksgiving, and supplication destined for God are offered to them. Though we shall explain the concept of sacrifice more when handling the concept of naming, it is sufficient at this stage to know that the offering of sacrifices is linked to the concept of evil or illness. Evil, just like illness, for the Africans, is a defect that needs to be handled and since God is the Supreme Being, His power triumphs over every evil. Yet as Jacob Olupona observes, "God is seldom a direct source of illness but He may send diseases and death through the lesser deity and the spirits."[215]

The idea of a life after death, which is used to explain the reality of the existence of the ancestors, forms an integral part of history in almost every culture. Western philosophical thought also uses the concept of the preexistence of the soul to explain this. As Battista Mondin confirms, "From Plato to Kant, the enormous majority of philosophers do not consider death as the extinction of the whole of man but only as, one part, the body. The other part, the soul, continues to subsist in the world of spirits."[216] Descartes, for whom the spiritual nature of the soul is beyond question, retains that there is no plausible argument against the soul's immortality.[217] The tenability of the existence of the ancestors, therefore, can be philosophically substantiated from the point of view of the immortality of the soul.

The perspective of Immanuel Kant about the destiny of the virtuous souls is similar to the African notion of ancestor. According to Kant, practical reason teaches man the way to bring his will into line with the moral law, to live a virtuous life. Man progresses in virtue and in perfection. "This indefinite progress is possible only in the supposition of an indefinite duration of the existence and the

---

[214.] Cfr. J. S. MBITI, *African Religion and Philosophy*, 83.

[215.] J. K. OLUPONA, ed., *African Spirituality, Forms, Meanings and Expressions* (New York: Crossroad Publishing Company, 2000), 158.

[216.] B. MONDIN, *Philosophical Anthropology* (Rome: Urbanania University Press, 2005), 270.

[217.] Cfr. S. TWEYMAN, ed., *René DESCARTES Meditation on First Philosophy in Focus* (New York: Routledge Taylor and Francis Group, 1993), 156.

personality of this same rational being, which is called immortality of the soul."[218]

Even though St. Thomas claims that the souls of the dead by their nature can have no knowledge of what goes on in the material world, he also acknowledges, like the Africans do, that God can dispense them and communicate any form of knowledge and activity to the material order.[219] Along the same line of thought, Pedro Meseguer intimates that "the souls of the dead in themselves know no more than the knowledge they acquired in this world, but God can communicate all classes of knowledge to them."[220] Whatever the case, the fact remains, as Mbiti insists, that "whatever science may do to prove the existence or non-existence of the spirits, one thing is undeniable; namely that for African people, the spirits are a reality to be reckoned with... And it demands more than academic attention."[221]

Joseph C. Chakanza, while confirming the intensity and extensiveness of the traditional practice of veneration of the ancestral spirits in Africa, infers that African history cannot be conceived without an affirmation and elucidation of this reality. Yet he indicates that this tradition or culture in itself has no historical dating. It cannot be pinned down to an era that it started, but it has always existed.[222] The African past is real, and it has its own system of conception and transmission. Belief in spirits or the supernatural is apparently as old as mankind. This is why, generally speaking, as John Mbiti observes, all African traditional religions, including African ancestral religions, have neither founders nor reformers.[223]

In a more radical way, Chinua Achebe argues that "the African's past, with all its imperfections, was not one long night of slavery from which the first Europeans, acting on God's behalf, delivered

---

[218.] I. KANT, *Critique of Practical Reason*, in L. WHITE, trans., (Cambridge: Cambridge University Press, 1956), 140-141.

[219.] Cfr. THOMAS AQUINAS, *Summa Theologica*, 1a. q. 89, a. 8.

[220.] P. MESEGUER, *The Secret of Dreams* (West Minister: Newman Press, 1961), 153.

[221.] J. S. MBITI, *African Religion and Philosophy*, 91.

[222.] Cfr. J. C. CHAKANZA, ed., *African Ancestral Religion* (Zomba: Kachere Series, 2002), 65.

[223.] Cfr. John S. MBITI, *African Religion and Philosophy*, 4.

them."[224] Africa has a history that is conceived and transmitted as African history proper. It is embodied in tradition and culture, and it is founded, situated, and sustained in a living community that is essentially interconnected with the extraterrestrial world of the great God and the ancestral spirits as expressed below:

> Many forms of power have been attributed to ancestors, especially in ancient times but this power generally lies within the scope of the society's needs and the ability to seek and receive help in a crisis. To offer the ancestral spirits both recognition and gratitude, certain types of shrines are erected at which prayers, animal sacrifices, masquerades, or similar ceremonies are performed.[225]

In Chad, the *qir Ka*, for example, has been regarded as a powerful ancestral male figure, and it plays a prominent role among the social and the ethical life of the *Sara* people. Legal rights, identity, and land are part of the power and the ancestral heritage that is conferred to succeeding generations according to the local traditional customs.[226] Therefore, in line with ancestral veneration is the ethical life of the Africans.

Another prominent issue that cannot be left out in viewing the African notion of history is witchcraft and divination which are also connected somehow to the activities of the ancestors. Within the concept of witchcraft and divination, the people attempt to find a solution to the issue of evil. Though they know fully well that evil, just like sickness, is part and parcel of the present imperfect world, they use the diviners, and to some extent what is considered as witchcraft, as a means of handling this reality. Though some exaggerations are recorded in this domain, the Ghanaian thinker, Kwame Gyekye, argues that mediumship, divination, and witchcraft involve modes

---

[224.] C. ACHEBE, *Hope and Independents* (London: Heinemann, 1988), 30.

[225.] W. F. PAGE, ed., *Encyclopedia of African History, Ancient Africa (Prehistory to 500 CE)* (New York: Facts on File Inc., 2001), 191.

[226.] Cfr. Idem.

of cognition that clearly distinguish African from European epistemology. For him, generally speaking, this is a mode of knowing for
the Africans; certain individuals are born with special psychic abili-
ties. Telepathy, clairvoyance, psychokinesis (psychokinetic) and pre-
cognition are in the African context aspects of divination and spirit
mediumship. Divination is a result of the activities of the discar-
nate minds, that is, spirits. Thus, it links the spiritual and physical
worlds.[227]

4.2.4 Transmission of History in a Communal Living

African ethics, in line with its orientation to the divine, which
has already been explained, is fundamentally reflected in the communal lifestyle of the people. Thus, situating his novel on the Nigerian
landscape, the prominent African writer, Elechi Amadi, affirms that
any analysis on African history must recognize that, it is thanks to
the supervision of the community by the ancestors, that the ordinary
African society is known for its tradition, propriety, and decorum.
Excessive or fanatical feelings over anything were frowned upon and
even described as crazy, given that people were expected ordinarily to
control their emotions.[228] Decorum and propriety imply self-respect,
the respect for each human person, mutual respect, especially respect
for the elders, and an ultimate attachment to a communal system of
living.

From birth, an individual is welcomed as a member of a community with great joy, accompanied by singing, dancing, and some
ritual celebrations. The indigenous African way is far from individualistic existence; it is to hold up the community and understand
the individual and the rest of the world, with reference to the community. It is from his or her community that the individual gets
his or her identity. Similarly, it is through the relationship that the
individual has with his or her community that he or she feels alive. It

---

[227.] Cfr. L. M. BROWN, ed., *African Philosophy—New and Traditional Perspectives*
(Oxford: Oxford University Press, 2004), 149.
[228.] Cf. E. AMADI, *The Concubine* (London: Heinemann, 1966), 165–166.

does not really matter if the group concerned is defined geographically like a village or sanguinely in terms of direct or indirect consanguinity; the result is the same. The community, in various respects, is the family. This also explains the concept of extended family in Africa. Consequent upon this communal system of living is the fact of authentic existence which implies that a human person is a human person because of his association with other human beings. John S. Mbiti further explains that

> only in terms of other people does the individual become conscious of his own being, his own duties, his privileges and responsibilities towards himself and towards other people. When he suffers, he does not suffer alone but with the corporate group; when he rejoices, he rejoices not alone but with his kinsmen, his neighbours and his relatives, whether dead or living. The individual can only say, "I am because we are, and since we are, therefore I am."[229]

Incumbent upon this is the pain of ostracism. In a typical African society, to be ostracized from the community is the most severe of all punishments; it is tantamount to death. This primacy of the community is also a major strand in the African understanding of right and wrong. That which is to offend the deities is often linked up in one way or another to an offense against an individual or the community as a whole or to what might threaten the natural order. This explains why the weight of many, if not all actions, is judged with a pragmatic or practical mind frame; in terms of how much such an action is to harm or destabilize the community.

Solidarity implies hospitality. Principally, African hospitality can be looked upon as that extension of generosity, giving spontaneously without attached strings; it is the inclination and the enthusiasm to give, to help, to assist, to love, and to carry one another's

---

[229.] J. S. MBITI, *African Religion and Philosophy*, 106.

burden without necessarily placing profit or rewards as the driving force. With a deep insight of the African culture, Austin Echema considers that the best way to express the idea of solidarity is that in the heart of the traditional Africans is "an unconditional readiness to share."[230] It is explained that African hospitality is one of the few facets of ancient African culture that is still intact and strongly practised today by most Africans in spite of all the excesses of the contemporary external influence.

In view of the above, George Ikechukwu Olikenyi explains that despite the destabilization of traditional life by colonialism, foreign worldviews, technology, and modern living, African hospitality has held rather well to the extent that it is often described as a way of being an African.[231] Therefore, Mercy Oduyoye represents the true African culture as well as true Christianity when she inscribes that hospitality is "inherent in being African, as well as in adhering to a religion that derives from the Bible." It is "given a religious meaning, and linked with the ancestors, Christ and God."[232]

Similarly, Moeahabo Phillip Moila sees African hospitality as that which embodies the entire philosophy of African peoples. It is not a theory but a way of life,[233] a reality that is even difficult to express exactly in the English language. Julius Nyerere expresses it in his emphasis on African solidarity in the concept of *Ujamaa*. This concept of African hospitality or solidarity is normally perceived and presented as a lived reality and not a theory to be preached. Ali A. Mazrui was intelligent enough to have realized that the drifting away from such a traditional African value is one of the major ills of colonialism. For him, "Nyerere's socialist thesis' entire scaffolding rests on

---

[230.] A. ECHEMA, *Corporate Personality in Igbo Society and the Sacrament of Reconciliation* (Frankfurt: Peter Lang, 1995), 35.

[231.] Cfr. G. I. OLIKENYI, *African hospitality: A Model for the Communication of the Gospel in the African Cultural Context* (Nettetal, Steylerverlag, 2001), 102.

[232.] M. A. ODUYOYE, *Introducing African Women's Theology* (Sheffield: Sheffield Academic Press, 2001), 94.

[233.] Cfr. M. P. MOILA, *Challenging Issues in African Christianity* (Pretoria: CB Powell Bible Centre, 2002), 1.

the fundamental question: where do we go from here?"[234] Of course, as a rhetorical question, the answer is obvious. With the study of history, we need to reclaim the destroyed values of African culture, of which solidarity is one of the most vital. This is why, along the same track of Ki-Zerbo, Mazrui prescribes education as a priority value in Africa today, for it does not only expose the real African cultural values as hidden in history but also empowers the Africans and opens their eyes to the actual implications of whatever step that is taken in issues concerning their existence in a world so vast and intricate.[235]

The concept of solidarity is also expressed as *Unhu* among the Shona of Zimbabwe, *Ubuntu* among the Nguni speakers of Southern Africa, *Utu* among the Swahili speakers of East Africa, and *Umundu* among the Kikuyu of Kenya, among others. Archbishop Desmond Tutu explains the *ubuntu, botho* of South Africa, for instance, as the essence of being human. One knows when it is there and when it is absent. It speaks about humaneness, gentleness, and hospitality, putting yourself on behalf of others, being vulnerable. It embraces compassion and toughness. It recognizes that my humanity is bound up in yours, for we can only be human together.[236] In a more practical way, Nelson Mandela explains:

> A traveller through our country would stop at a village, and he (or she) didn't have to ask for food or for water. Once he stops, the people give him (or her) food, entertain him (or her). That is one aspect of Ubuntu (and generally African hospitality) but Ubuntu has various aspects. Ubuntu does not mean that people should not enrich themselves. The question therefore is: Are you

---

[234.] A. A. MAZRUI, ed., *Julius K. NYERERE, Africa's Titan on a Global Stage* (*Perspectives from Arusha to Obama*) (Durham: Carolina Academic Press, 2013), xviii.

[235.] Cfr. A. A. MAZRUI, *The African Condition* (*The Reith Lectures*) (London: Heinemann, 1980), 63.

[236.] Cfr. N. TUTU, *The Words of Desmond Tutu* (London: Hodder and Stoughton, 1989), 69.

going to do so in order to enable the community around you to improve?[237]

The above quotation brings us to the level of property and hard work, illuminating the fact that riches and property are also seen in the light of community living because life was all about caring for one another.

Alongside the theme of solidarity and work is that of suffering. Martin N. Nkemnkia discusses the theme of African solidarity in good times and in troubled times, considering that man's real destiny is not this present world. In explaining the communal facet of suffering that has a religious and a mysterious significance, Nkemnkia explains thus:

> Within the African context of the extended family, no one can suffer privately or alone. The participation is almost immediate. Pain and suffering is almost always given a religious interpretation. It is commonly thought that one suffers because he has broken his relationship with others, the world, the ancestors or with God. There is a cause for every suffering; however, it is cloaked in mystery. In the whole of African culture, there is a religious background which links everything and everyone.[238]

Basically, it is within this context of African solidarity, with the valorization of the human person that Ki-Zerbo explains how economic and political values, and consequently, development, are attained in the real African sense.

Development is normally considered from the socioeconomic and political perspectives of men and the society in which they func-

---

237. A. EIDE, *Disability and Poverty: A Global Challenge* in URL: < http: //books. google.it/books, > (accessed on December 28, 2014).

238. M. N. NKEMNKIA, *African Vitalogy*, 114.

tion. From the social perspective, Julius Nyerere summarizes the essence of the African society when he states that "in our traditional African society we were individuals within the community. We took care of the community and the community took care of us. We neither needed nor wished to exploit our fellow men."[239] Therefore, the excess corruption that by a certain logic dehumanizes the African society as seen in the body of this work is not, strictly speaking, of the African spirit. Thus, to put things straight, Africa must come back to the base, that is, to their African essence, as a solid point of departure.

Economically, it is very evident that Africans have always been hardworking people who earn their living from their own energy or toils. In fact, in the traditional African conception, work is both a necessity and something to be appreciated. There is something spiritual; there is something aesthetical about work. Broadly speaking, work is part of the human existence; it enriches the biological, emotional, physical, aesthetical, and even spiritual aspects of the human person and, consequently, of the entire community. Therefore, apart from being a normal way of earning a living, work is also perceived as a means of coming together for mutual assistance and for the structural growth of the community as a whole. In this case, groups and teams (and it may even be an entire village coming together) are formed for the purpose of working together on the land, building, etc.[240]

Justus Mbae's article, "Work in the African Traditional Culture," explains that in the Western world, the concept of work has come to take on a commercial value. Work is often associated with the marketing of services and anything that has no economic value seems to be excluded from the definition of work. For example, rearing children may not count for work unless, of course, it is also paid for.[241] Contrarily, however, for the Africans, the emphasis is not placed on

---

[239.] J. Nyerere, *Ujamaa: Essays on Socialism* (Nairobi: Oxford University Press, 1968), 6-7.

[240.] Cfr. J. Mbae, "Work in the African Traditional Cultures" in *Research and Documents (Property and Work in the Perspective of Inculturation)* (Nairobi: Opus Matriae-Focolare, 1997), 32-33.

[241.] Cfr. Ibid., 30.

the economic aspect of work, valuable as it may seem. Rather, as said earlier, the traditional African perceives work as both necessary and something to be appreciated in itself. There is something sacred about work, and the end product of work is something beautiful and to behold. This concept is well presented in Chinua Achebe's book, *Things Fall Apart*, where we learn that a title was society's recognition for bravery and hard work was a substantial contribution to the well-being of the community.[242] Therefore, essentially speaking, Africans are not a lazy set of people as they seem to present themselves today in some perspectives. Something must have gone wrong somewhere which can only be redressed if Africans review their essential nature and come back to their undistorted personalities and vision of reality as testified by history.

No one can dispute the fact that African history has many nasty stories from slave trade to colonization and now to neo-colonization. This also calls for a hearty understanding when evaluating affairs concerning Africa in the past, in the present, and even in the future. We can understand this better if we reflect on the following words of William Edward Burghardt DuBois:

> It would be conservative, then, to say that the slave trade cost Negro Africa 1,000,000 souls. And yet people ask today the cause of the stagnation of African culture since 1600! Such a large number of slaves could be supplied only by organized slave-raiding in every corner of Africa. The African continent gradually became revolutionized. Whole regions were depopulated, whole tribes disappeared; villages were built in caves and on hills or in forest fastness; the character of peoples like those of Benin developed their worst excesses of cruelty instead of the already flourishing art of peace. The dark, irresistible

---

[242.] Cfr. Cfr. J. Mʙᴀᴇ, "Work in the African Traditional Culture," in *Research and Documents (Property and Work in the Perspective of Inculturation)*, 32.

grasp of fetish, took firmer hold on men's minds. Further advances toward civilization became impossible.[243]

The above notwithstanding, it takes an optimist or a historical pragmatist like Ki-Zerbo to remind us, with profound conviction, that coming back to the rudiments of the African conception of history would lay a firm foundation for a better Africa. Therefore, from every point of consideration, hitherto, we subscribe to Ki-Zerbo's proposition that history, as cruel and controversial as it may seem as a concept and as a lived reality, is an irrefutable point of departure as well as an irreplaceable reference and a foundational bearing for any way forward in life.

Basically, politics is to coordinate the people in their socioeconomic endeavors toward authentic living. Strictly speaking, Africa followed the regal system of government by chiefs, kings, or "fons" of the tribes, clans, and villages. The power to govern is not conferred by another authority, superior to the one who receives the task to wear the regal dress or to govern. It is the tradition itself that desires that the kingdom or the tribe should be represented by an authority and the chiefs, "fons," or kings have as their primary task service, protection, and preservation of the culture for the benefit of the people, individually and as a collectivity.[244] This implies that even if Africa were to adopt a different form of governance today, it must be based on this basic foundation in order to succeed. Even democracy, which almost the entire world is advocating for today, existed in other forms in the traditional African settings. The following proposal of Owusu Maxwell clearly summarizes the point we are advancing in this section:

African democracy may require the integration of indigenous methods of village cooperation with

---

[243.] W. E. B. DuBois, *Africa*, 46.

[244.] Cfr. M. N. Nkemnkia, "Property and Work in Africa," in *Research and Documents (Property and Work in the Perspective of Inculturation)*, 51-52.

innovative forms of government, combining the power of universal rights with the uniqueness of each district's or nation's own customs and respected traditions.[245]

African culture and religion revolve around solidarity with other individuals in the community as well as with the forces or elements of nature. It was already explained by the concept of vitalogy of Martin Nkafu that Africans live a holistic system of life. Little or no dichotomies are made between other life matters and religious convictions, for example. Therefore, we continue to emphasize that even before the coming of the missionaries, the people communicated with God and they were generally conscious of the basic principles of morality. With the day-to-day divine consciousness in their daily activities, Nkafu goes on to convince us and to add to Ki-Zerbo's utterances concerning the fidelity of the Africans to God and to their ancestors in a living community that a person should be understood globally, from birth to death, as a religious reality, considering that for the Africans, life was intimately linked with religion. Therefore, there is no unbeliever in the African traditional society.[246] It is in the same understanding that John Mbiti explains that the "African is notoriously religious, and each people has its own religious system with a set of beliefs and practices. Religion permeates into all the departments of life so fully, that it is not easy or possible always to isolate it."[247]

Irrespective of the valorization of the African traditional system of solidarity consciousness, the issue of male chauvinism is also a historic affair that bears a negative mark in the African traditional

---

245. O. MAXWELL, "Democracy and Africa: A View from the Village," in *The Journal of Modern African Studies*, v. 30, n. 3 (1991), 384.

246. Cfr. M. N. NKEMNKIA, *African Vitalogy (A Step Forward in African Thinking)* (Nairobi: Pauline's Publications Africa, 1999), 67.

247. J. S. MBITI, *African Religions and Philosophy*, 1.

heritage. Presenting the situation of the traditional African woman, Musimbi Kanyoro makes the undermentioned observation:

> African women are custodian of cultural practices; for generations, African women have guarded cultural prescriptions that are strictly governed by the fear of breaking taboos. Many aspects that diminish women continue to be practised to various degrees, often making women objects of cultural preservation. Harmful traditional practices are passed on as "cultural values" and therefore are not to be discussed, challenged or changed. In the guise of culture, harmful practices and traditions are perpetuated. Practices such as female genital mutilation, early betrothals and marriages, and stigmatization of single women and widows, (polygamy, domestic violence) hinder the liberation of women.[248]

There are also some fundamental criticisms concerning the whole issue of African solidarity. Irrespective of all the advantages presented by a social life style as lived in Africa and the fact that it is an integral part of African culture, some abuses are also registered time and again. Some people take advantage of the mutual assistance they receive from the community to grow in laziness. With the phenomenon of traveling abroad for greener pastures as evident today in African, some people, especially the youths, make no effort to find jobs or to struggle with work that could make them to earn a living back home. They prefer to remain perpetually dependent on their relatives and friends that are struggling to raise money abroad. This attitude, to say the least, is exploitation.

[248.] M. KANYORO, "Engendered Communal Theology: African Women's Contribution to Theology in the 21st Century," in N. NJOROGE and W. D. MUSA, eds., *Talitha Cum! Theology of African Women* (Pietermaritzburg: Cluster Publications, 2001), 159.

Other Africans use the basic quality of respect for elders and for authority to exploit others, especially in cases where religious values are coded with some kind of fundamentalism. Thus, even though Africans believe in the potency of God and the mystery of nature, they can easily give up even in things they can handle and instead attribute it to divine decisions. These, however, are extremes found in almost all cultures. We find the play *Swamp Dwellers* by Wole Soyinka a good piece to represent this vice in the traditional African set up. The characters in *Swamp Dwellers* are confronted with the ordeals of flood, a natural disaster, yet the chief priest, the Kadiye, projects a serpent that needs to be fed through him. By this, he exploits the people and increases their miseries. While the villages suffer from starvation because of food deprivation in the midst of economic depression, the Kadiye remains fat. He is well-fed because he consumes the food destined for the serpent, the god who is believed to be balancing the ecosystem, depending on the offerings made to him. Igwezu, a character in this piece of drama and an ideal son of the Swamps, is posited as tired of depending on the supernatural assistance for a meaningful existence. Despite all the sacrifices made, he remains essentially unsuccessful. He even loses all his possessions, and worse of all, his wife is seduced by his own brother, Awuchike, who, paradoxically, has disengaged himself from all ties of family, religion, and tradition. The reality of loss causes Igwezu to compromise his nobility and challenge the existing exploitative and unfair societal set up with the following questions:

> If I slew the fatted calf, Kadiye, do you think the land may breathe again? If I slew all the cattle in the land and sacrificed every measure of goodness, would it make any difference to our lives, Kadiye? Would it make any difference to our fates?[249]

[249.] W. SOYINKA, *The Swamp Dwellers in Three Short Plays* (London: Oxford University Press, 1983), 39.

The Kadiye, therefore, takes advantage of his position and the submissiveness of the people and their religion to grow rich by deceiving them, knowing that he could never be challenged. Therefore, with due recognition of the strength of these valuable qualities, Africa still needs to grow in a bid to resist exploitative authority. Such ills of exploitation or fatalism are not really presented as dominant or cultural aspects, but they existed in one form or another, and as a matter of fact, they constitute part of the evil in the world. Even though we had already discussed the problem of evil, Emmanuel Eze presents the idea of Kwame Gyekye concerning such weaknesses in the society as stemming from the heart of men. Evil, in the African context, he insists again, is not from God. It comes basically from man's conscience, from his own actions and wrong choices and not from God. It is from such evil in people that such manipulative way of destroying the human society is generated. There may be also some spiritual forces in action, but in any case, evil never goes uncovered and unpunished.[250]

Africa is not the only continent that, to a greater extent, links up religion and tradition as concepts that sustain history. In the Eastern worldview, Confucianism is also presented with similar trends, especially with its concept of *re*. We shall examine this in the following chapter, considering the comparative nature of our research.

4.2.5 Preservation and Transmission of History in Arts

Art is one of the ways in which the traditional African exercised his energy as a hardworking individual and a maker of tools. Art was intended not only to keep oneself busy or for the sake of entertainment and pleasure or to produce tools as instruments to develop the environment but also as a way of preserving history. From a general perspective, Ki-Zerbo identifies that "man, by definition, has always been a toolmaker. At the same time, he has also been a maker of works of arts."[251] Yet historically speaking, Africans have excelled in

---

[250.] Cfr. E. C. Eze, ed., *African Philosophy, an Anthology*, 468-470.
[251.] J. Ki-Zerbo, ed., *General History of Africa*, vol. 1, 284.

prehistoric art more than any other continent as Ki-Zerbo's research identifies in the following citation:

> In spite of the damages caused by the elements and in spite of pillaging by Man, notably during the colonial period, Africa is still the continent with the greatest number of specimens of pre-historic art. These are to be found mainly in the upland regions and mountain massifs, especially in the cliff formation running along the edges of the mountains and overhanging existing or dried-out water courses... There are few African countries where artistic remains have not been discovered, although it is true that they are not all of prehistoric origin.[252]

Art was also used as a form of chronology, a form of keeping dates or to record historical events. Although later developed by archaeologists in recent times, this stratigraphic method of preserving and observing arts consisted of classifying objects on a timescale according to the place they occupy in the sequence of superimposed ground layers. Works of arts may also be tentatively dated from the animal species they represent. Such works of art included engraving on rocks or stones, painting, and jewelry making.[253]

Pottery and sculpture were other artistic means of preserving history. This is historic because it is being carried out today and has formed part of the African heritage. It is revealed that plant glazes are still used in Africa today for varnishing or decorating both pottery and houses, and they were already known at that time. It is an embodiment of history to observe that most of these works of arts represent particular types of animals with various histories and mannerism; some are drawings with mystical symbols and some, even

---

[252] Idem.
[253] Cfr. Ibid., 285–287.

involving an active or emotive ritual in which men who are some-times masked defer to animal totems.[254]

In his attempt to adequately communicate the value of arts in the African conception of history, Ki-Zerbo made reference to the term petrography and explains it as follows:

> The term "petrography" has been coined to describe rock art. In point of fact, this art is a kind of writing to which the key has to be discovered before it can be deciphered. This is why it is important to describe the sign first, before going on to decode it and ascertain what it means... However, it should be borne in mind that a sign is not only a sign of something, but a sign that means something to somebody and, as such, involves a form of symbolism. For that symbolism to be understood, familiarity with all the social and spiritual representations of the human group involved is necessary. In the final analysis, only the entire cultural context can provide the key to the interpretation of an aesthetic message. Only by fitting together the various cultural pieces is it possible to reconstruct the historical patterns into whose fabric they are woven.[255]

While insinuating that arts, poetry, pottery, sculpture, and music are used in expressing African history, Ki-Zerbo also insinuates that the traditional craft and trades are the great channels of oral tradition, therefore, great vectors of history. They perceive the craftsman's work as important because it is in the image of divine creation. Ki-Zerbo goes on to make reference to the *Bambara* tradition which teaches that when *Maa Ngala* (God) created the universe, he left things unfinished so that man could complete them, alter them, and

---

[254.] Cfr. Ibid., 288.
[255.] J. Ki-Zerbo, ed., *General History of Africa*, vol. 1, 290.

finally perfect them. In this case, it is just obvious that every craft or trade is loaded with symbols.[256]

As it is with archaeology, Ki-Zerbo explains that *art* is illuminated by many other disciplines, and it is mostly approached through familiarity with the entire environment, taking into account geology, social status, political structure, myth, and religion. On the other hand, by recording rituals, scarification, hairstyles, costumes, and scenarios, art acts as a museum of cultural, and even physical, anthropology. This is why it is a very valuable criterion for the establishment of history. Therefore, he maintains that history is, accordingly, at the very center of art. He gives an example of the Yoruba land, where the same artists carved in wood and later ivory while others worked in clay and then in bronze. It is this switch from one material to another which helps us comprehend and appreciate the aesthetic forms used in working ivory or bronze. This form of changeover was also common in prehistoric periods, where the artists, switching from basketwork to pottery, often accounted for the shape of decoration of pots. In the same vain, masks arts were also common, and they were a reflection of life in the villages and often recognized as personalities, even by children. Cowries are also some important elements used in works of arts. Ki-Zerbo wants us to understand that arts and artists, by and large, are of a great contribution to making the history to which they are witness, and they also have a very religious significance.[257] He cites a few examples which we are recounting in his own words below:

> This is true of the large Bobo bird, buffalo and ancestor masks, for instance. In some circumstances, masks are consulted and accordingly serve as intermediaries for certain social groups in the context of the established pattern of forces. The cowries mentioned by Ibn Battuta at the court of Mali in 1352 were primarily intended

---

[256.] Cfr. Ibid., 65.
[257.] Cfr. J. KI-ZERBO, ed., *General History of Africa*, vol. 1, 139-141.

for use as coinage, but they also served as adornments and as statutory gifts on social occasions and at religious ceremonies. To embark on the history of certain African societies without a knowledge of the rich language of cowries inevitably produces a defective version of their evolution. Some paintings show men bending down using tools, or women leaning forwards in a characteristic gleaning posture. It is not easy to tell whether the figures are meant to be gathering food from wild plants or actually cultivating cereal crops, as might be suggested by the number of grindstones and grinders that have been found. At Battle Cave, young girls are depicted setting off on a food-gathering expedition, with their digging-sticks over their shoulders.[258]

Like the musician, weaver, and other artists, the smith also works in the same mystical and creative universe. In the Fulani culture, for example, he is known as the first son of the earth. His forge, which is called the *fan*, always contains water in a small pot, fire, the air of the bellows, and a small pile of earth. These elements are known as the four mother elements of the world.[259] As master of the knife, he performs the circumcisions. It is also known that the black-furnace smith, who both extracts and smelts metal, possesses the highest degree of knowledge—knowledge of metals, minerals, as well as knowledge of plant life. He is also capable of dictating a seam of gold by merely examining the plans and pebbles on the surface of the earth in a particular area.

History also reveals that in the traditional African community, natural wealth was not exploited merely for profit-making, but in communion with the universe. Fundamentally, the craftsman's work, like the work of the artist in general, was not a straightforward cre-

---

[258] Ibid., 140-141.
[259] Cfr. Ibid., 66.

ative activity. Their work was not confined to the acts and gestures of production. It was embodied in the whole way of life with prohibitions and obligations; it was a function that created social status.[260]

Teaching and learning went on in the field of arts. Education was lifelong, most often till the age of forty-two, and even after this age, they were still required to listen to more experienced persons. "Young craftsmen, after their initiation, set out to travel from village to village, sometimes with their tools on their backs, so that they could improve their skills by contact with fresh sources of experience."[261] This was history, orally, and concretely transmitted.

4.2.6 Language, Oral Tradition, and the Transmission of History

At this historical epoch, Ki-Zerbo has no problem with the studying of foreign languages in Africa. His cry is that cognizance should be taken of the fact that the African people, in any case, had their own languages. Any authentic study of the history of Africa must, therefore, recognize and research on the importance of language in the unfolding of history. With reference to French, as is taught in his own native country, for example, he says, "French should increasingly be learnt as a modern foreign language, taking the substratum of the African languages into account."[262]

The most salient point is that the Africans see a bond between history and language. Ki-Zerbo also notices this in the Fulani expression that "we meet the past in stories," and in his observation, even the Greeks and the Arabs have the same thought, yet for the Africans, as he insists, owing to the lack of written sources in many instances, history is seen less as a science and more as a form of wisdom and as the art of living substance through speech. As science language has a twofold bearing on history. On the one hand, it is a system, a system and a tool of communication, a historical phenomenon while, on the

---

[260.] Cfr. Ibid., 66-67.
[261.] J. KI-ZERBO, ed., *General History of Africa*, vol. 1, 70.
[262.] J. KI-ZERBO, *Histoire de l'Afrique Noire*, 642.

other hand, history is a product of language both as discourse and as historical evidence.[263]

Naming is also another arm of language that has much to do with the African conception of history. The science that concerns itself with the study of names or name places (toponyms) is known as onomastics. This science would have much work in African because names as used in language always have connotations that detect authentic historical contacts, convergences, and influences. Thus, names of persons, places, and events evoke eloquent historical characters, atmospheres, and even integrity.[264]

Language, as oral tradition of history, Ki-Zerbo insists, must be well scrutinized. Referring to it as oral text in the context of African history, he recounts the following feelings of regrets:

> There are a substantial number of oral texts, but they have been neglected because the history of Africa was for centuries viewed exclusively from outside. And yet they are extremely valued because they come from within Africa. Of course they need to be carefully sifted and subjected to critical analysis before they can be considered as credible evidence.[265]

The old people in this connection are always considered as relevant sources of history. Ki-Zerbo explains this using the words or rather a proverb by one of the old wise people of his country, Hampate Ba, that "when an old man dies in Africa, a library disappears."[266]

The fact is that until the twentieth century, written documents were the basis for any historical reconstruction worthy of that name. Yet in the case of Africa, owing to the relative scarcity of written documents, history has been compelled to overstep its habitual

---

[263.] Cfr. J. Ki-Zerbo, ed., *General History of Africa*, vol. 1, 89.
[264.] Cfr. Ibid., 94.
[265.] J. Ki-Zerbo, in *UNESCO Courier*, 9.
[266.] Idem.

bounds.[267] Oral tradition, Ki-Zerbo insists, is a living museum of the whole stock of sociocultural output stored up by peoples who were purported to have no written records. The old men who are its custodians have become the last vestiges of an ancient landscape which historians are seeking to restore. As the African proverb goes, "The mouth of an old man smells bad, but good and salutary things come out of it."[268]

It is also good to understand that oral tradition as an instrument of history takes different forms and that which is closest to the written source is considered by Joseph Ki-Zerbo as the institutionalized or formalized text. In this case, as he explains, a body of state functionaries were constituted with the responsibility of administering the collective memory. Such a group was well trained, and they kept records of particular happenings and of the meanings of certain events or object with their actual or symbolic implications. Hence, he explains with a concrete reference to some African nations:

> Thus, among the Moose, in Burkina Faso, in Mali, or in the kingdom of Abomey, what is now Benin; there were organised corporations which were responsible for managing collective memory. The members of these corporations were trained in specific places, each of which had its own traditions. In these places, masters taught their pupils a curriculum that took several years to complete... To give you an idea of just how reliable these texts may be, in the land of the Moose, in Burkina Faso, the head of the *griot* had to recite the genealogical list of the *"Mogho-Naaba"* every day! It was out of question that he should forget.[269]

[267.] Cfr. J. KI-ZERBO, ed., *General History of Africa*, vol. 1, 139.

[268.] Ibid., 3.

[269.] J. KI-ZERBO, in *UNESCO Courier*, 9.

In no way is Ki-Zerbo saying that written documents are unimportant. His emphasis is that as far as African history is concerned, the predominance of spoken word over written in many societies has to be acknowledged and that though both the written and the spoken words are complementary, the spoken words even seem to be richer as explained below:

> Oral language remains richer because it can bring into play such features as accents, intonation, silences and tempi, because it can adapt itself to different environments, because it keeps closer to people for whom it is sometimes the only vehicle of expression, and because it conveys cultural features that cannot be found in writings. Thus spoken language and written documents are complementary elements that are essential for reconstructing a people's culture, especially in Africa.[270]

The graphic tradition which is also used to justify the African writing tradition is justified in the Egyptian tradition. Yet writing at this time was done as a form of art. It is very evident that the Egyptian hieroglyph is essentially pictographic; its value as a sign and in terms of effectiveness lies in its materialization of living beings, objects and ideas. Hieroglyphic writing is also prominent in various sophisticated forms in the graphic symbols of many African people.[271]

Conclusion

Though it is very clear that African history has been, down the ages distorted and misrepresented and even considered as nonexistent by some people as we said at the very introduction of our work, our idea here was not merely defensive for the sake of defending Africa.

[270.] J. KI-ZERBO, ed., *General History of Africa*, vol. 1, 94.
[271.] Cfr. Ibid., 95.

Rather, our attempt was to defend a certain truth, a certain reality that could assist Africa to fit in the general picture of globalization, and that could also ensure historical truth, for the sake of truth, as an epistemological object of the mind for authentic living. It is in this regard that we again vouch the very words of our author, Ki-Zerbo, which, to an extent, summarizes the aim of our work as expressed earlier in the introduction. He says,

> Our purpose here is not to write a history designed to settle old scores, but rather to embark on a scientific undertaking, in a bid to shed light on the darkness in which the past of the African continent...is still shrouded...this is a remarkable experiment in international co-operation which is making it possible to restore to the people of Africa their own past, not merely for pleasure or amusement, but in order to enable them to understand the present and rid themselves of their complexes, so that they can move forward and build the future.[272]

Consequent of the above citation, our work is not merely the recounting of history but, rather, a reflection on history as a concept. The historical aptitude of Joseph Ki-Zerbo is affirmed by Romain Rainero who refers to him, as well as other African personalities such as Cheikh Anta Diop, Ahmadou Hampate Ba, and Nazi Boni, as veteran African historians, stating that they are known to have written a *new* history of Africa, being truly objective and not taking sides as if to revenge, as the tendency is with some other African historians.[273] Rainero equally emphasises the misconception that some writers, especially Western historians, have published concerning the African continent, irrespective of her strategic sociopolitical and geographic

---

[272.] J. KI-ZERBO, ed., *General History of Africa*, vol. 1, 1.
[273.] Cfr. R. RAINERO, *Storia dell'Africa: Dall'epoca Coloniale ad Oggi* (Torino: Eri-Edizioni Rai Radiotelevisione Italiana, 1966), 18.

importance to the world at large.[274] He further explains concerning the vastness of Africa as follows:

> L'Africa è il secondo continente al mondo per estensione, ma comprende il 22 per cento delle terre emerse. Il deserto del Sahara, da solo, è grande quanto gli Stati Uniti. In realtà questi ultimi, insieme con Cina, India, Nuova Zelanda, l'Europa dell'Atlantico a Mosca e gran parte del Sudamerica, potrebbero trovare posto entro le linee costiere Africane.[275]

Innocent C. Onyewuenyi also confirms some of the misunderstandings or misrepresentations of the African continent when he recounts that "a look at the world map leaves no doubt that Egypt is in Africa, yet how many of us are educated to think of it as a Middle East power?"[276] He proceeds by stating that the so-called Africa South of the Sahara was devised to cause at least a mental separation of Egypt and North Africa from the rest of Africa, whereas Herodotus, the father of history and a Greek, and many other ancient writers, testified to the blackness of the Egyptians of their time.[277]

Peter Hunziker also explained the existence of industries, especially iron industries, for the making of tools in Africa as well as the Egyptian civilization and socioreligious organization. He insinuates that in West Africa, the knowledge of iron smelting may have come from the Phoenicians who, in 800 BC, founded the colony of Carthage on the North African coast. The skills may have crossed the

---

[274.] Cfr. R. RAINERO, *Storia dell'Africa: dall'epoca Coloniale ad Oggi,* 5.

[275.] (Africa is the second continent in the world by extension but includes 22 percent of the land area. The Sahara Desert alone is as big as the United States. In reality, the latter, together with China, India, New Zealand, Atlantic Europe in Moscow, and most of South America, could find a place within the African coastlines.) J. READER, *Africa, Biografia di un Continente,* Maria NICOLA, trans. (Milano: Oscar Mondadori, 2003), 7-8.

[276.] I. C. ONYEWUENYI, *The African Origin of Greek Philosophy* (Enugu: SNAAP PRESS Ltd., 1994), V.

[277.] Cfr. Ibid., 24.

Sahara Desert with the Berber nomads who dominated much of the North African plains. It has also been suggested that iron smelting may have started in Africa itself, without any outside influences.[278] However, there are challenges involved in integrating the concept of history the future of a nation or a continent.

[278.] Cfr. P. HUNZIKER, ed., *The Story of Africa* (London: K Gygax, 2005), 21-28.

CHAPTER FIVE

Consequences of an Authentic Consideration of the Concept of History

McGRATH'S POSITION, BUILDING on the ancient Greek conviction, is that history is that which the surviving records of past peoples enable historians to recover through research and reflection; it is an attempt to discover and understand what happened—that is, all that men have suffered, thought, and done—the entire life of a people or of humanity.[279] In the same regard, John Parker and Richard Rathbone, as they write about the history of Africa 'affirm that, in writing history, historians are bound to *unpackage* a range of political, social, and ideological entities that, for a long time, have simply been taken for granted... This un-packaging has been directed towards the ways in which societies and individuals have seen themselves in the world.[280] This is a lot of work for the historiographers, especially in places like Africa, where transportation, internet, and records still remain difficult due to poor roads and electricity supply. Yet much is handled by oral tradition as a quasi solution to this challenge.

Henry Odera Oruka has also written much on the topic of oral tradition as an essential element in the African conception of history.

[279.] Cfr. M. HILL, *The New Catholic Encyclopedia* (Washington, DC, CUA Press, 1967), 13–14.

[280.] J. PARKER and R. RATHBONE, *African History, a Very Short Introduction*, 4.

In this regard, he has exploited the thoughts of many wise men and women in the African community, explaining how, by their wise utterances, they communicate to the world or, rather, they present history to others. He refers to this system of communication as sage philosophy.[281] Oruka assumes that a large part of the African precolonial culture and thought systems has remained intact even after the end of colonialism. This, he believes, like Ki-Zerbo, is a body of history. It rests in the sages and is better transmitted by them. These sages form an integral part of the African conception of history as he explains thus:

> Most of the "tribal" cultures and thought remained intact even after colonialism. And there were people whose education and view on life were wholly or mostly rooted in this. So, I decided to select my sample from among the people considered wise by their own communities and who were at the same time free from the effect of Western scholarship... Such people, I believed, were genuine representatives of traditional Africa in a modern setting.[282]

Oral tradition equally moves along with the concept of myth. In the African context, via myths, rational explanations of origins (people and spirits as well as other terrestrial and extraterrestrial events) are studied. John S. Mbiti reminds us that "both history and pre-history are dominated by the myth."[283] Oliver Onwubiko defines a myth as follows:

> A myth is a story which is believed to be true and has its origin in a far distant past history of a people and their culture. Man made them himself as to answer the questions that have troubled his

[281]. Cfr. H. O. ORUKA, *Sage Philosophy: Indigenous Thinkers and Modern Debate on African Philosophy* (Leiden: E. J. Brill, 1990), 33.

[282]. Ibid., 6.

[283]. J. S. MBITI, *African Religion and Philosophy*, 23.

mind since the origin of time. These questions which often border on religion and philosophy, have sometimes found answers in myths which then become "philosophical" explanations for the "primitive man."[284]

It may be true that myths are not established from chronological or verifiable facts of history, but at the same time, they are drawn from and are founded on the facts of life. They are founded on what the founders of myths are very conversant with. They make a deep impression on the people. Considering the life of the Africans as a vital force and as explained by the concept of vitalogy that perceives no aggressive dichotomies in existence, the point that is emphasized here concerning the importance of myths in the concept of history for the Africans is that in the preliterary era, myth, even in its *non-literary* form, provides the most effective means by which religious beliefs were both preserved and transmitted from generations to generations.[285]

Oliver Onwubiko goes further to identify four kinds of myths—natural, religious, ritual, and hero myths—and through these myths, African thinking about history is variedly exposed. Cultural myths deal with stories about the gods and other cultural elements, how they affect events concerning the daily life of the people, with daily gifts such as fire, medicine, music, dance, and other cultural gifts or benefits. Natural myths still revolve around the gods but, this time, attached to the natural phenomenon of life. Its references are the mountains, valleys, water, as well as other natural benefits and natural disasters. Ritual myths explain why religious and other acts are done with a particular pattern. Finally, the hero myth posits some heroic legendary traditional figures invested with a common pattern that satisfies the human desire for idealization.[286]

[284.] O. ONWUBIKO, *African Thought, Religion and Culture*, vol. 1 (Enegu: SNAAP Press, 1991), 39.

[285.] Cfr. O. ONWUBIKO, *African Thought, Religion and Culture*, vol. 1, 38-39.

[286.] Cfr. Ibid., 40.

Added to the above fact that the concept of history as explained by Ki-Zerbo fits into the objective standards is equally the importance that he gives to it. Building a nation, Ki-Zerbo says summarily, cannot be done without recourse to the history of the people in question, the case in point, we know is Africa. As if to affirm this basic position of Ki-Zerbo, Pope St. John Paul II makes a very radical remark that "Africans do not have to copy the foreign models of Western 'know-how.' They should be especially attentive to the values of their own spiritual inheritance, in the view of an intercultural encounter with other world visions."[287] Ki-Zerbo, we should remember, is insisting on history as the foundation for a better society today and for the future. Putting these in other words, by making a striking reference to the African scholar, St. Augustine, Fritz Stenger states, inter alia:

> Nobody can save Africa from oblivion without the collaboration of the Africans themselves. Saint Augustine said that God created you without you, but will not save you without you. If yesterday the history of Africa was shaped in one way or another by foreigners, what Africa will be tomorrow will largely depend on your efforts today. Therefore, work hard towards the construction of a living environment for all, with a special thought of your children who will be your pride tomorrow.[288]

Again, it is a major challenge to decode the myths so as to get into real history, and it is in an attempt to encourage the African people to embark on this challenge that Ki-Zerbo dedicated his studies

---

[287.] JOHN PAUL II, *Ecclesia in Africa*, nn. 42-43.
[288.] F. STENGER, ed., *Africa Is Not a Dark Continent*, 23.

to the field of history as presented by another historian, G. Galchi, as follows:

> Il proposito che ha ispirato il grande affresco dell'Africa nera composto da Joseph Ki-Zerbo è il recupero del passato della convinzione che nessuna società possa progettare il proprio futuro se non basandosi appunto sulla memoria di ciò che è stato un popolo o una nazione. Il ruolo della storia è di propiziare la coesione sociale, saldando fra di loro le varie sezioni di una collettività le diverse generazioni andando o ritroso nel tempo.[289]

In such a challenge to delve into research came the certainty of another outstanding African historian, William Edward Burghardt DuBois, concerning the situation of Egypt with regard to Africa. He insists with unwavering certainty that from every point of consideration, it is an error to count Egypt out of Africa, for its belonging to this continent is not only a geographic reality but is also a historical certainty and an anthropological veracity. As if using the same vocabulary with Joseph Ki-Zerbo, he proclaims thus:

> It is one of the astonishing results of the written history of Africa that almost unanimously, in the nineteenth century; Egypt was not regarded as part of Africa. Its history and culture were separated from that of the other inhabitants of Africa... The Greeks looked upon Egypt as part of Africa not only geographically but cultur-

---

[289]. (The purpose which inspired the great fresco of black Africa composed by Joseph Ki-Zerbo is the recovery of the past in the belief that no society can plan their future if they do not just rely on the memory of what was a people or a nation. The role of history is to propitiate social cohesion, welding between them the various sections of a community or different generations going back in time.) G. CALCHI, ed., *Africa: La Storia Ritrovata* (Roma: Carocci editore, 2007), 22-23.

ally, and every facet of history and anthropology proves that the Egyptians were an African
people... It is especially significant that the science of Egyptology arose and flourished at the
very time that the cotton kingdom reached its
greatest power on the foundation of American
Negro slavery. We may then without further ado,
ignore this verdict of history, widespread as it is,
and treat Egyptian history as an integral part of
African history.[290]

The third volume of the *General History of Africa* series, with
M. M. El Fasi and I. Hrbek as editors, titled *Africa from the Seventh
to the Eleventh Century*, does not only endorse the fact that Africa is
the cradle of civilization but also challenged the Africans of today to
get involved in the study of their own history following their own
categories, insinuating that oral tradition is an absolutely important
element in defining the African conception of history.[291]

Corresponding to the ideas of Joseph Ki-Zerbo, B. A. Ogot
insists that the main role of history is to offer the defence or the solid
grounds for humanity, the durability, the historicity, the complexity,
and the wealth of African societies together with their culture. He
insinuates that

history formed the core in the overall socialization of the individual in society. It was evident
to us that historical consciousness and historical study are as old in Africa as man himself. In
nearly all societies, historical details were carefully preserved in one form or another and were
transmitted from one generation to another...

[290.] W. E. B. DuBois, *The World and Africa*, Kraus-Thomson Organisation, New York 1976, 99.

[291.] Cfr. M. M. EL FASI and I. HRBEK, ed., *General History of Africa, Volume III—Africa from the Seventh to the Eleventh Century* (California: University of California Press, 1988), xix.

> History had a purpose, which had to be thor-
> oughly understood and grasped by all members
> of the society.[292]

African history, like the study of other histories, is of great intrinsic interest; it is also of immense relevance to understanding and providing solution of present-day problems, especially as the society becomes more and more multicultural.[293] John Parker and Richard Rathbone applaud the African historians such as Addullahi Smith, Dike and Ajiyi from Nigeria, A. A. Adu Boahen from Ghana, and Bethwell Ogot from Kenya who, after completing their first degree in the new African universities, continued their professional train-ing by studying PhD in Britain before returning to build up history programs in their home nations. Of course, he did not omit other historians like the Senegalese Alioune Diop, Cheikh Anta Diop, and the poet, Léopold Senghor.[294] It is in this respect that Cyril Lionel Robert James admires Aime Cesaire's *Cahier d'un retour au pays natal* (Return to My Native Land), published in the middle 1930s. What James says of Cesaire's great hymn celebrating the wanderings of the Black historical imagination equally applies to his historical works in which he sees it to be too normal as Ki-Zerbo himself emphasizes that the past of mankind and future of mankind are historically and logically interconnected and that Africa and Africans should express their historical uniqueness in the process of integration into world culture.[295]

A major challenge in the presentation of African conception of history in the perspective of Ki-Zerbo is that it gives very little attention to some of the controversies that emanated within the very construction of this concept. Within the African historians them-

---

[292] B. A. OGOT, *Reintroducing Man into the African World* (Nairobi: Bookwise, 1987), 225.

[293] Cfr. B. A. OGOT, *My Footprints on the Sands of Time: An Autobiography*, Trafford, Victoria 2003, 94.

[294] Cfr. J. PARKER and R. RATHBONE, eds., *African History, a Very Short Introduction*, 126-28.

[295] Cfr. C.L.R. JAMES, *The Black Jacobins* (New York: Vintage Books, 1963), 402.

selves, some laxity exists while some do not take seriously some of the core issues others hold very firm. It is argued, for example, that Anglophone and Francophone nationalist historians advocate for decolonization, but they developed divergent methodologies of recuperating the African past through their writings. Thus, there is a certain linguistic iron curtain, causing their historical and conceptual ideas, valuable as they are, to continue to be divided along linguistic lines without any substantial endeavor to arrive at a reasonable cross-fertilization. It is also manifested that, fundamentally speaking, the postcolonial Anglophone and Francophone historians are keeping up with the tradition of acting in isolation from each other.

There is an observation to this effect that while the department of history in the Francophone universities give pride of place to the teaching of Egyptology as necessary but omit ingredients of the history of Africa that accentuates the African origin of Egyptian civilization, Anglophone history departments, on the contrary, are not engaging themselves with such historical exigencies. This point was manifested in the famous encounter between the former president of France, Nicolas Sarkozy, and the students of Cheikh Anta Diop University in Senegal on July 26, 2007. In this encounter, the speech presented by Nicolas Sarkozy was considered humiliating and Hegelian in every respect. The irony is that when Nicholas Sarkozy unearthed the old myth of the nonexistence of African history, an enthusiastic rejoinder came exclusively from Francophones and French Africanist scholars while their Anglophone counterparts maintained an embarrassing silence as if they are not Africans or as if this insult from Sarkozy did not include them.[296]

Ki-Zerbo, we realize, did not get very deep into such debates, and the reason we can give to this is that his was to trace that which unites both camps in a common destiny, the struggle to recover the African past as contained in the cultural heritage of the African people, in the name of history. This is also our primary preoccupation in this work. In this regard, therefore, the Anglophone and Francophone schools

---

[296.] Cfr. A. B. KONORE (ed.), *Petit précis de remise à nouveau sur l'histoire africaine à l'usage du president Sarkozy* (Paris: La Découverte, 2008), 9-10.

of history shared the same concerns about the defamation of Africans as a strategy for colonial supremacy and the prolongation of colonial rule. Ki-Zerbo goes primarily for the intellectual and physical capacities that intellectuals sought to defy such European ideological standpoint by providing a counter-treatise that was to liberate the Africans from inhuman pre-considerations. Though he recognized the differences between both schools, he recognized, as a historical reality that the very history has conditioned them to operate within the confines of such diversities as their colonially carved spheres.

What was important for him was that as African nationalist historiographers, their research was characterized by the establishment of a counter-discourse to the abhorrent European historiography of domination, particularly during the struggle for political independence in the 1950s and 1960s. This, for him, was a way to correct the biased and racist historiography that served the colonial ideological apparatus of domination.[297] Hence, many other historians were motivated, as Ki-Zerbo was, to embark on the historical adventure. It is also observed that this nationalist historiography was a concerted intellectual effort not only of African intellectuals but also of some non-Africans (European and American) scholars. Thus, the decolonization process was attained through an alliance between African nationalist historians and White liberals.[298] The stinging reality is that right into the nineteenth century, when some African countries had already had independence, and with a good number of African *intellectuals* (intellectuals by the European standard), such sarcastic lectures against Africans and the African continent prevailed.

---

[297] Cfr. H. OCHWADA, "Historians, Nationalism and Pan-Africanism: Myths and Realities," CODESRIA's Thirtieth Anniversary Conference, Dakar-Senegal, 10-12 December (2003), 6.

[298] Cfr. P. T. ZELEZA (ed.), *The Study of Africa, Vol 1, Disciplinary and Interdisciplinary Encounters* (CODESRIA, Dakar 2006), 138-140.

In 1960, Hugh Trevor-Roper, during his inaugural lecture at the University of Oxford, underlined that there was nothing like African history. His very words are published by John D. Faga as follows:

> Perhaps in the future there will be some African history to teach. But at present, there is none; there is only the history of Europeans in Africa. The rest is darkness...and darkness is not the subject of history. There is only the unrewarding gyration of barbarous tribes in picturesque but irrelevant corners of the globe.[299]

Evidently, his lecture was just the normal European conception that theirs was a salvation mission to Africa, the divine mission to civilize and develop the primitive. This Eurocentric historiography of Africa must be understood in terms of ignorance, social prejudice, cultural chauvinism, and an inherent desire to dominate. Yet the fact that Ki-Zerbo and his team are belaboring is that the rejection of the existence of African history or an African conception of history is a betrayal of reality and an effort to bury the past with the use of an unsound logic that generates power and a false history that is embroiled with deceit and blatant egocentrism.

With the discoveries of Cheikh Anta Diop, many have come to appreciate African creativity, especially as expressed in the Egyptian sagacity, while, on the other hand, his historical works have aroused violent responses from many European historical circles. The works of Diop demand a dispassionate evaluation and appraisal. In fact, most of the historical works of Cheikh Anta Diop were to scientifically and historically prove that ancient Egypt was a Negro civilization. Thus, his firm conviction, as the Egyptian historian Gamal Mokhtar also endorses, is that "Egyptian antiquity is to African culture what Greco-Roman antiquity is to Western culture. The building up of

---

[299.] Cfr. J. D. FAGE, *Africa Discovers her Past*, Oxford University Press, London 1971, 7.

a corpus of African humanities should be based on this fact."[300] In defending the affinity of the Egyptians to the other African nations, as opposed to the White race, Diop gives reason and methods, based on melanin dosage test, osteological measurements, blood groups, the Egyptian race according to the classical authors of antiquity, the Egyptians as they saw themselves, the divine paths, witness of the Bible, cultural data, and linguistic affinity.[301] Even Herodotus, the father of history, seems to have supported this claim. The American sociologist and historian William Edward Burghardt DuBois was one of those who greatly inspired Diop; he worked along the same research path with him, making use of his system, facts, and scientific ideas. The facts that he makes, as if to summarize the points of Anta Diop concerning African civilization, are in the following citation:

> Africa is an old and storied continent. It is probable that out of Africa came the first civilization of the world, and certainly, in that continent the tragedy of the history of mankind has played its greatest part. To the Grecian world, to the Roman Empire, as well as to the American and modern European worlds, Africa has been of supreme importance, and it is well worth while to know something of its peculiar situation, history and meaning.[302]

Diop continues to insist with evidences (scientific and archeological) on the similarities between the institutions of precolonial Africa and those of ancient Egypt. He revealed that the great Egyptian civilization, which is the source of inspiration to subsequent world

---

[300.] G. MOKHTAR, ed., *Ancient Civilizations of Africa*, volume two of UNESCO's *General History of Africa* (California: University of California Press, 1981), 49.

[301.] Cfr. Ibid., 28-51.

[302.] W. E. B. DuBois, *Africa, Its Geography, People and Products* (New York: Kto Press, 1977), 3.

civilizations, is Negro-African in origin and in Africa came the discovery of the first Homo sapiens.[303]

With the strength of the mind and of the pen, therefore, Diop, like Ki-Zerbo and the other historians, had thoroughly deconstructed the myth of the Black man being depicted as a stagnant creature, without a history and without any contribution to world civilization. Nevertheless, though Ki-Zerbo had some obstacles in this struggle for the rehabilitation of the dignity of the African personality and culture, just like many Africans following the same course at the time, Anta Diop had a greater price to pay for this.

Diop's message and his thesis for Egyptology was not what a colonizing power, principally France, desired to hear. The French colonial policy of assimilation and paternalism was fabricated on the myth of European or Western superiority. In the like of Hegel, it was their general conception that the colonized peoples were backward and incompetent of standing on their feet or governing themselves without French paternalism.

It was known at the time that any ideology which blatantly challenged French colonial policies was bound to be fought off. Accordingly, French authorities retaliated on Diop. He was refused the right of defending his doctoral thesis on the origin of Egyptian civilization, a decision that was only reconsidered when France was put under pressure to accept independence in the late 1950s. His conviction was that African history cannot be complete without Egyptology, and it was as a challenge to the nonchalance concerning the teaching of African history in European schools and even African schools that follow colonial syllabus as Diop kept insisting that Egyptology should logically be included in the curriculum of all African universities as a way of enabling Africans to trace, appreciate, and reconnect with their historical links and contribution to world civilization. That which is interesting, irrespective of some historians who still struggle to oppose him, is that Diop makes it categorically clear that this thesis about the "Africanness" of Egypt was accepted as

---

[303.] Cfr. C. A. DIOP, *Civilization or Barbarianism*, 40.

a self-evident truth for millennia stretching from classical antiquity to Napoleon Bonaparte's campaign in Egypt in 1799.[304]

5.1. Arts, Names and Symbols

5.1.1. Arts

Peter Hunziker is quite correct when he says that a more settled lifestyle also prompted the African people to express themselves through arts and crafts.[305] He quotes the very words of Joseph Ki-Zerbo that "Africa is one of the richest in rock art. Images painted with vegetable dye adorn caves in the Sahara, Tanzania and South Africa. Such art gives us a unique glimpse into the life of these people, showing them not only at work—hunting and fishing—but also at play, dancing and socializing."[306]

Accordingly, it is inferred that "these prehistoric carvings and paintings proclaim not only the relentless struggle of the African man to dominate nature but also to add to his own nature through the divine joy of creation."[307] This is why art is a vital subject of African history. It is of great cultural and traditional value and, consequently, is embraced by all generations. African arts can basically fit into the Western concept of aesthetics. Since it reflects the tradition of the people, works of art, therefore, are a portrayal of African values, attitudes, and thoughts, considering that they are the products of the past realities of the people that remain evergreen; this is where arts fit adequately to the concept of history. With a work of arts, many stories are told, a long history is recounted, and an ethical value is concretely represented and explained. Art, therefore, is the product of the African experience; consequently, it provides a way of conceiving history for the Africans.

[304.] Cfr. C. A. Diop, *The African Origin of Civilization: Myth or Reality*, in M. Cook, trans., (Westport: L. Hill and Company, 1974), 45.
[305.] Cfr. Cfr. Peter Hunziker, ed., *The Story of Africa*, 21.
[306.] Idem.
[307.] Idem.

Through the study of African art, we can study the questions which have long preoccupied historians of Africa. Frank Willett certainly understands this so well. In his book *African Arts*, he intimates that, generally, art, in the African continent, is an old practice which does not only arouse the religious and aesthetic sentiments of the people but also stimulates deep historical discoveries and explanations to real phenomenon.[308] Arts did not only generate items that were used to sustain the day-to-day life, but extensively, they also depicted all aspects of life as clarified in the following extract:

> During much of Africa's history, art, especially in the regions south of the Sahara, was designed to reflect all aspects of life. Many of these works were highly functional, including such items as beads and jewellery, pottery, household furnishings, cups and spoons, cloths, and even certain types of weapons. Other works gained importance or value because they were created with certain methods of production or in accordance with particular religious beliefs, cultural practices, or inspiration. Products like these frequently are based upon social myths as well as on both family and regional history.[309]

From the above citation, it becomes evident, as Frank Willett explains further, that irrespective of the plain aesthetic value that may be embedded in some works of arts, fundamentally, in the African culture, art is never done for art's sake or for mere external beauty. It must always have a real value. This is an aspect which he also uses to

---

[308.] Cfr. F. WILLETT, *African Art* (Singapore: Thomas and Hudson Inc., 1993), 35–41.
[309.] W. F. PAGE, ed., *Encyclopaedia of African History and Culture*, 21.

underline one of the differences between European and African arts as inscribed below:

> It has commonly been asserted that there is no "art for art's sake" in Africa, and also that all African art is religious. In the western society, where art critics speak of "art for art's sake," they mean that the artist produces an object which is valued for itself, which attempts neither to instruct nor to edify, a product which the artist is concerned exactly with the solution of artistic problems of composition, colour or form. The content of the work of arts is secondary to these considerations.[310]

Evidently, real African artists are like sacred personalities. They are somehow dispensed from the normal social lifestyle of the people as they spend most of the time in contemplation and composition. Yet their works become public as soon as they are accomplished. They work with inspiration, so much that the works of arts that they produce—be they carvings, poetry, or music, far from revealing some historical phenomenon or personalities—are significantly symbolic, communicating, or actually representing some transcendental realities or personalities. Some are used as rituals with great religious tenets. At some points, the works of art are out to evoke our emotions by passing across a certain message. For example, a sculpture of a baby, which requires that one must assist a young wife in achieving motherhood, is done with an exceptionally large head. This is to ensure that with the assistance of the people, the child will be healthy, beautiful, and intelligent.

Fundamentally, therefore, to properly appreciate the African works of art, one needs to be conversant with the mysteries and transcendental attitudes of the culture that produces it. Thus, we dare to insist that the understanding of the particular cultural view-

---

[310.] F. WILLETT, *African Art*, 156.

point, their conception about nature, God, and the spiritual world in general, is a key to understanding African art. This we perceive as probably one of the most vital issues in today's world. Explaining in a more scholarly manner the idea that African art has always had transcendental, ritualistic, and a symbolic or a generally social functional attribute (which implies a definite mystical quality which is feasibly based on history), Chinua Achebe, using the Igbo Nigerian experience, asserts thus:

> The practical purpose of art is to channel a spiritual force into an aesthetically satisfying form that captures the presumed attributes of that force. It stands to reason, therefore, that new forms must stand ready to be called into being as often as new (threatening) forces appear on the scene. It is like "earthing" an electrical charge to ensure communal safety... Art must interpret all human experiences, for anything against which the door is bared can cause trouble.[311]

Consequent upon our reflection so far in this section is the acknowledgment of the essential liaison between arts and history as already presented by Joseph Ki-Zerbo in which art is perceived as a symbol of nonverbal existential life, a vehicle of culture, and, therefore, a tangible channel of history. In the transmission of history for the Africans, art comes after words. Writing, we should remember, has a historic and a natural relation to arts. In this regard, Martin Nkafu explains that "L'arte Africana è un'arte simbolica... L'arte tribale è veicolo di comunicazione e di dialogo non verbale...l'arte possa essere considerata come mezzo naturale di espressione sociale dopo la parola. Essa è un tipo di comunicazione della cultura e del sapere a tutti."[312]

[311.] C. ACHEBE, "The Igbo World and Its Art," in E. C. EZE, ed., *African Philosophy, an Anthology*, 436.

[312.] (African art is concretetly symbolic... Tribal art is a vehicle of communication and nonverbal dialogue... Art can be considered as a natural means of social expression after the word. It is a type of communication of culture and knowledge

5.1.2 Names and Symbols

As revealed to us through Ki-Zerbo, names are not given in an arbitrary manner in the African culture. Everything that is of immense value has a name that is either full of symbol or, in itself, has a strong historical implication. This explains why the concept of history in the African culture can seldom be authentic without studying the connotations of certain names. This could be names of persons, items, ceremonies, or events. The following declaration by Martin Nkafu Nkemnkia is a real endorsement to this line of reasoning concerning the African conception of history:

> Names of persons and places always carry both a meaning and an accompanying story (history). For example, the name *Ndem mbo*, that is, "God the creator," refers to the eternity of God and implies that the person bearing this name (a finite being) participates in the infinity of the Infinite. The names of persons and places characterize the form and the value they represent.[313]

Accordingly, the name *Ndem mbo*, as explained above, gives us a mental representation of the history behind all reality as stemming from the omnipotence and infinity of God. It is equally a reminder to man as a creature that he or she must also continue to procreate. The implication of the name is that the human person too has to embark in the function of procreation in the world, making it a better place to live in. It may not only be ascribed to those who bear the name, but like any other traditional name, it serves as a reminder to humanity, a reminder of a certain historical reality, and also serves as an assignment or a challenge for the present and the future generation.

---

to all.) M. N. NKEMNKIA, *Dove Un Giorno Regnava la Foresta* (Milano: Paoline Editoriale Libri, 2014), 54

[313.] M. N. NKEMNKIA, *African Vitalogy*, 34.

The name *Barah* (modern), for the Nso people of Cameroon, is among one of those names that have a historical significance. A child, therefore, is named *Barah* as a historical remembrance of the colonial masters who came into the land. In the same culture, the name *Verdzekov* (we are in the forest) is used as a reminder of the time when the traditional people chased the Christians into the forest at Shisong (a village in Nso, Cameroon).[314]

[314.] Cfr. T. H. MBUY, *The Faith of Our Ancestors* (unpublished work, Rome 2012), 146.

CHAPTER SIX

Situating the African Americans in the Philosophy of History

6.1. African Americans and the African Traditions

GRANTED THAT BLACK people are present in every continent in the world, the African Americans form a distinct group of people who deserve a special attention which we can subject to the field of philosophy of history. This approach will make more meaning if we are a little vest with the concept of philosophical hermeneutics.

Etymologically, the word *hermeneutics* implies a process of making intelligible what was once foreign and impenetrable. Hans-Georg Gadamer emphasises the role of the past in constituting any present or future understanding. Any understanding whatsoever, he argues, is conditioned by the affections, concepts, and practices of the cultural heritage and circumstances of the participants in conversation.[315] Thus, the concern of "philosophical hermeneutics is not what we do or what we ought to do, but what happens over and above our wanting and doing."[316] It is, therefore, about how we interpret persons and perspectives with all precautions and prejudices taken

---

[315.] Cfr. G. AYLESWORTH, "Dialogue, Text, Narrative: Confronting Gadamer and Ricoeur," in *Continental Philosophy IV, Gadamer and Hermeneutics* (London: Routledge, 1991), 62.

[316.] H. G. GADAMER, *Truth and Method* (London: Sheed and Ward, 1975), xvi.

into consideration. Philosophy of history, as we already established, primarily and remotely concerns itself with such cultural heritage and circumstances that define a people in their present state.

It is universally acknowledged that the invaders of Africa, who came principally from western Asia and Europe, did not come with good intention. Accordingly, John Henrik Clark, in his book titled *African World Revolution*, reminds us that the invasion of Africa that took place for over a thousand years was, to say the least, a waging of war on the African culture. It was his very conviction that "they had no respect for the African religious customs, and they looked with disdain on all African ways of life alien to their understanding. These invaders made every effort to destroy the confidence of the African people."[317] Our inference is that such an attempt to reorientate the mindset of a people had a tremendous effect on the Africans, not only those who form the African Americans in the United States but also those in the motherland, as well as those who consciously migrated into the United States, Europe, and other continents. As Clark explains, religion or spirituality, for the Africans, is s daily affair as he says,

> Religion or spirituality (the more correct term) was part of the totality of our life. It wasn't a Sunday occurrence; it was a total occurrence. It determined much of our life.
>
> How can we have a revolt, a spiritual revolt, without the assumption that we're trying to destroy the Church when in actuality we're trying to strengthen the Church, trying to give it a new mission, a new destiny and a new will?[318]

[317.] J. H. CLARK, *African World Revolution* (New Jersey: African World Press, 1996), p. xii.
[318.] Ibid., p. 9.

The new mission is, in fact, the spiritual revival that is expressed in the Pentecost experience. We can now understand why the outreach and community-oriented spirituality is more common among the African Americans.

Practically, the first impulse of the Blacks after slavery was to distant themselves from White people who generally considered them as inferior. Many all-Black towns were set up and managed as free of White authority although this had to be stopped because with Black independence came the total loss of the labor that Whites totally depended on. The increasing White supremacy over the Blacks also led to a lack of trust in the banks or the courts. This greatly influenced the mindset of the Blacks since they could principally *trust* only in the things that they could hold in their hands and at that very moment. With this mentality, their focus was mainly on satisfying themselves and assisting other Blacks in communal outreach programs. This seems to be the strongest point in the African America philosophy of history, and it is deeply rooted in the communal lifestyle of the traditional Africans.

With due consciousness of their roots being in the motherland, Africa, the African Americas are attracted to the *kwanzaa* celebration that normally begins on December 26 and lasting for seven days. *Kwanzaa* stands for a celebration of community, family, and culture. It is a means to help African Americans reconnect with their African roots, a reminder that their heritage is truly Africa. Dorothy Winbush Rilley explains that *Kwanzaa* was first celebrated on December 26, 1966, in Los Angeles by Dr. Maulena Kerenga, his family, and friends. And the core principles of Kwanzaa reflected the typical African style of living as has already been expressed in this book. These are presented as the *Nguzo Saba* (the Seven Principles) which Kerenga expressed as follows in Swahili, a language of East Africa: (1) *Umoja* (unity), (2) *Kujichagulia* (self-determination), (3) *Ujima* (collective work and responsibility), (4) *Ujamaa* (cooperative economics), (5) *Nia* (purpose), (6) *Kuumba* (creativity), and (7)

Imani (faith).[319] *Kwanzaa* is purely an African culture, and it is feasible in the African American community. This is why they take time yearly to celebrate it as a way of asserting who they really are and the richness and pride of their foundation.

6.2. The African Americans as a People

We cannot, however, undermine the fact that the authentic culture of the African Americans, as Africans, was reshaped by new realities as soon as they entered America, following the realities of the slave trade deportation. The history of slavery and racism is always at the very foundation of the African American thought, and this forms an essential constitutive element in their worldview or their social and psychological dispositions.

Philosophy of history is concerned with the mindset, and one's mindset is conditioned by various cultural or traditional factors. Philosophy of history goes further to challenge these mindsets for the betterment of persons and societies. Therefore, with a mindset that rises above negativity, with a mindset that purifies the dark side of history (as difficult as this may be), unfair as the social or political policies may appear, the Africans, be they abroad or at home, can do more for themselves than what the government or the foreign countries (for those in the motherland) can do for them. Nonetheless, we have been insinuating all along that the slave trade, colonization, neo-colonization, and racism have done much harm to the world, specifically to the Africans (in Africa and in the United States), and something needs to be done to put a complete end to these evils. Those who still dare to claim that these vices have ceased to exist cannot, in any way, dispute the fact that their effects are still corrosive in our society and something needs to be done to heal the wounds.

In the United States of America, we cannot deny that the effects of slavery and the reality of racism need to be redresses, and urgently too, if we need a healthy and a truly united society. Many people are

---

[319.] Cfr. D. W. RILLEY, *The Complete Kwanza, Celebrating our Cultural Harvest* (New York: Harper Collins, 1995), 3

convinced that this is the reason why crimes and disease are more in the African American communities. In this regard, Mehrsa Baradaran intimates that some of the extremes of the African Americans, as expressed in their manner of living, were created through various racist public policies.[320] This, again, is an indication that something needs to be done urgently to address the acidic effect of racism. This is certainly the message that the crises in the United States of America today, caused by the killing of George Floyd, is portraying to the world.

6.3. Racism, Culture, and the Philosophy of History

The brutal killing of George Floyd is certainly very significant in the evolution of world history. This happened at the time when the global COVID-19 pandemic made news in all corners of the world. The transition from the quarantine state of home confinement into the spontaneous rioting along the streets of various cities in the world, especially in the United States of America, was eminent. This is very significant in the philosophy of history of every continent and culture, especially the African Americans. This is because, at this time, human beings in every part of the world became conscious of the fact that racism is like a virus, historically proven to be more dangerous than the coronavirus. This inference is valid because, as if to confirm the reality of racism, especially in the United States of America, everybody could watch the White policeman, Derek Chauvin, placing his knee on the neck of George Floyd while the latter died in excruciating pains, crying, "I can't breathe. I can't breathe." With this grotesque incident, even the greatest racist was pushed to sympathy—sympathy not only for George Floyd but also for the psychological, sociological, and political stagnation that racism has inflicted on the Black race, which has distorted not only the morale or the dignity of the African Americans as a people but also their general outlook of life.

[320.] M. BARADARAN, *The Color of Money: Black Banks and the Racial Wealth* (Gap Har, 2017), p. 281.

Dr. Cheryl Grills, a professor of psychology at Loyola Marymount University, expresses this reality in the following words:

> These are very difficult and trying times for people of African ancestry in this country, and in fact, in the world. We black folks have been essentially dealing with centuries of racial oppression. Our souls, our bodies, our minds are under duress... We are in a broken social system in society, and as Dr. King put it, in 1968 he did an address to the American Psychological Association, and he said, "What has penetrated substantially all strata of negro life, is the revolutionary idea that the philosophy and morals of the dominant white society are not holy or sacred, but in all too many respects, are degenerate and profane." So, essentially what we're dealing with is a situation that is not righteous, it's not just. It has no empathy or compassion for the humanity of black people, and in the midst of yet another assault, a reminder that we are seen as less than human, we're being called on to rise above the situation.[321]

For those who say African Americans are lazy, I say Africans are not lazy. This was explained in the previous chapters of this work. Something went wrong somewhere. Correspondingly, without justifying vices, without neglecting the importance of positive thinking, the importance and necessity to make use of available opportunities and the need to adopt a firm and humble or humiliating disposition to challenge the status quo and excel as some African Americans have done, we still wish to remind those who say African Americans are more into drugs, alcohol consumption, banditry, and general carelessness that there is a relationship between psychology and reality as

---

[321.] C. GRILLS in https://abc7.com/george-floyd-protests-los-angeles-downtown-la-dr-cheryl-grills/6222321 (accessed on June 14, 2020).

Dr. Grills indicated in the citation above. It is in this connection that I submit to and recommend that we genuinely and empathetically reflect on the following words of Reverend Al Sharpton in his eulogy at George Floyd's memorial service on the fourth of June 2020:

> You put us in, but you had your knee on our neck. We could run corporations and not hustle in the street, but you had your knee on our neck. We had creative skills, we could do whatever anybody else could do, but we couldn't get your knee off our neck. What happened to Floyd happens every day in this country, in education, in health services, and in every area of American life, it's time for us to stand up in George's name and say get your knee off our necks... Michael Jordan won all of these championships, and you kept digging for mess because you got to put a knee on our neck. White housewives would run home to see a black woman on TV named Oprah Winfrey and you messed with her because you just can't take your knee off our neck. A man comes out of a single parent home, educates himself and rises up and becomes the President of the United States and you ask him for his birth certificate because you can't take your knee off our neck. The reason why we are marching all over the world is we were like George, we couldn't breathe, not because there was something wrong with our lungs, but that you wouldn't take your knee off our neck. We don't want no favors, just get up off of us and we can be and do whatever we can be.[322]

---

[322] A. SHARPTON in https://www.rev.com/blog/transcripts/reverend-al-sharpton-eulogy-transcript-at-george-floyd-memorial-service (accessed on June 14, 2020).

It is very clear to the world at large that the United States of America is a great country. This is why immigrants from all over the world, especially from the less-developed countries, want to be citizens of the United States of America. However, the fight against racism is a very strong one that requires divine assistance alongside the human efforts. This is because history testifies that America is a country or a continent that was founded on the premise of White supremacy and White superiority. This is a reality that has prolonged the battle against the vice of racism, a struggle that is also supported by the many wonderful anti-racist White Americans.

In the midst of widespread Black Lives Matter protests, a number of cities in the United States of America have decided to take down Confederate monuments. These anti-racist movements have intensified in recent days as hundreds of thousands of protesters have taken to the streets to fight against police brutality and racism following the killing of George Floyd in police custody on May 25. A number of Confederate statues have already been torn down.

Going back to 2017, Will Drabold in his article titles: "The ACLU Joins the Fight to Bring Down Confederate Monuments" cites Jeffrey Robinson as he talked about the confederate monuments. Jeffrey is convinced that "these symbols, which Trump has defended as historical treasures, were built to perpetuate a lie that Southern leaders fought for liberty, not to protect slavery." According to him, this was inauthentic. While supporting the tearing down of confederate monuments, he insinuated that "when we do not deal with the ugly truth about our history, we have no chance of going forward in any kind of a productive way… Getting rid of the Confederate monuments will…make us deal with the truth."[323] To further explain the

[323.] J. ROBINSON in https://www.mic.com/articles/184042/the-aclu-defends-the-free-speech-of-white-supremacists-but-now-wants-confederate-monuments-removed (accessed on June 14, 2020).

reality and necessity to tear down confederation monuments, citing the case of Robert Lee[324] in Charlottesville, Robinson states inter alia:

> Even as the national movement to remove Confederate monuments across the U.S. gains steam, more than 700 monuments still remain on public land. The push to do away with them, led by racial justice group Color of Change, has seen an explosion of support since far-right protesters gathered in Charlottesville to protest the removal of a statue of Confederate leader Robert E. Lee.[325]

As we discuss issues of culture and religion in this work, we find this topic very relevant to our subject matter because a people's culture, that is, a people's mindset subsists in their history. In defense of history and hysterology, we must insist on the importance of preserving monuments, considering that monuments explicitly represent historical realities. In this perspective, we have the right, the duty, and the responsibility to preserve monuments or statues. The controversy comes in because, though they represent historical realities, they convey the emblem of White supremacy. Just a gaze onto the monuments enacts the memory of slavery in all its brutal and inhuman guises. If racism is still evident in this great nation, then the inference is that White supremacy still exists as a culture, at least for some of the people.

A culture that places one race as being superior over another deserves no sympathy from the perspective of philosophy of history.

[324.] Robert E. Lee was the most prominent Confederate military leader during the American Civil War (1861–1865). He stood in support of chattel slavery and defended the enslavement of African Americans. He was born in a very prominent family in Virginia, and he spent his early years surrounded by enslaved African Americans.

[325.] J. ROBINSON, in https://www.mic.com/articles/184042/the-aclu-defends-the-free-speech-of-white-supremacists-but-now-wants-confederate-monuments-removed, mo-(accessed on June, 14, 2020).

Rather, such a culture has to be reexamined and radically eradicated for the good of the society. By supporting the destruction of the Confederate monuments because it represents bad cultural memories, we are not being unnecessarily political, neither are we taking sides with a certain party in a political debate. Rather, situating ourselves in the domain of culture, we being faithful to the precepts of philosophy of history. This is our interest in this publication.

At our introduction, we explained that philosophy of history is very concerned with values—values that are embedded in culture. It explains the need to learn from history, to eradicate the bad features of history, and to encourages the good, all with the intention to make the world a better dwelling place. One primary question to ask is whether it is necessary to preserve a culture that enacts negative values, a culture that endorses hatred, a culture that resuscitates bitter and inhuman memories, a culture that portrays how superior a particular race is as opposed to another race that is considered inferior.

If we were to sympathize with the idea of maintaining these monuments for the mere reason of preserving history, then we must ask the nature of the history that is being preserved and whether it was necessary at all to enact such monuments or to preserve monuments with acrimonious connotations.

Sometimes we contemplate on the ideas of those who wish to preserve confederate statues for reasons of aesthetics. Nevertheless, any argument to maintain such statues from the perspective of aesthetics crumbles under its own very premise. This is because Alexander Gottlieb Boumgarten (1714-1762), who is often considered as the father of aesthetics and advocate aesthetics as a new and distinct discipline in philosophy, highlighted *good*, *truth*, and *beauty* as a trinity concept in the study and application of classical aesthetics. According to him, aesthetics must aid logic. Such Confederate monuments may reflect historical truths, yet they are void of beauty and goodness, considering, as Jacques Maritain indicates, that the beautiful is that which gives joy, a joy which goes above and beyond the object known. Therefore, an object which objectively connotes hate does not delight the soul. Such an object cannot be considered as good and cannot be apprehend as beautiful.[326]

It is in line with the above arguments that Jefferson Robinson propagates for the complete destruction of the confederate monuments, considering that their very presence is to preserve a heritage of hate.[327] He intimates that

> as long as we continue to perpetuate the myth of Confederate innocence—the idea that good men on both sides fought over distant abstractions and then came together again in brotherhood— we continue to lie to ourselves.[328]

These are some of the bitter historical realities that have affected the psychological mind frame of many Africans. The radical castigation of the grotesque Nazi regime in Germany is in direct opposite to what we find in the United States. This, according to our judgment, substantiates the meaning of culture in particular and the philosophy of history in general as Joshua Zeitz briefly explains below:

> In Germany, you won't see neo-Nazis converging on a monument to Reinhard Heydrich or Adolf Hitler, because no such statues exist. The country long ago came to grips with the full weight of its history. But you'll find Nazis and Klansmen in Virginia, circling a statue of Robert E. Lee, a traitor who raised arms against his own country in the defense of white supremacy.[329]

[326.] Cfr. *J. Maritain, Arts and Scholasticism*, E. Joseph W., trans. (Oxford: Oxford University Press, 2005), p, 36.

[327.] J. ROBINSON in https://www.mic.com/articles/184042/the-aclu-defends-the-free-speech-of-white-supremacists-but-now-wants-confederate-monuments-removed (accessed on June 14, 2020).

[328.] Ibid.

[329.] J ZEITZ, *in https://www.politico.com/magazine/story/2017/08/20/why-there-are-no-nazi-statues-in-germany-215510.*

What a paradox!

6.4. Theocentric Faith

Like the traditional Africans, the African Americans are basically theocentric in their faith. Alongside their history, there is a strong faith in God and the ancestors who basically dwell with God. Accordingly, irrespective of the dark side of their history and the challenges posed by the unfair contemporary sociopolitical atmosphere, there is a strong sense of hope and theocentric confidence. Accordingly, Toni Tupponce, a parishioner of Our Lady of Consolation Catholic Church, head of the Black culture commission and the principal of the Tupponce Enterprise II Inc. Program director presents the following reflection on Sunday, June 21, 2020, in Our Lady of Consolation Catholic Church:

Except for God.

Has there ever been a time like this? Have we ever known such heartbreak and dismay? We feel alone—void of the physical comfort of friends or family when we've needed them most—as we find our way through the challenges to our spiritual, emotional, and physical health.

Even in the midst of all this, our brothers and sisters continue to die in the streets because of the color of their skin, and our children have taken up the fight for justice and the right to live fully as human beings in a country built by their enslaved ancestors. Their parents in the sixties and seventies, their grandparents in the forties and fifties, and their great-grandparents fought the same injustice in the twenties and thirties. Their frustration and tears break our hearts. We pray that through their fight we will know justice and they might know peace!

On this Sunday, God's servant, Jeremiah, speaks to us. Yes, there is terror on every side. There are those who hope to destroy and deceive us, but the Lord remains a mighty warrior on our behalf.

Yes, all around us, the world has changed seemingly overnight! It may never be the same. Everything we thought that we could count on has been upturned, shaken down, and spun off its axis, except for God!

We are exhausted by social injustice, systemic racism, and the disenfranchisement of our poor, imprisoned, and homeless brothers and sisters. Who will intervene, except for God?

And when we are alone, unsure, afraid, and searching for hope in others, we realize that there is no safe refuge, no lasting peace, and no healing balm, except for God.

We are reminded that as we fight for justice and live for peace, we are to fear no one, except for God!

CHAPTER SEVEN

Understanding the Eastern Philosophy of History

EASTERN RELIGION IS a religion that originates in the Eastern areas like China, Southeast Asia, India, and Japan. Contrarily, Western religions are the religions that have their origin in the Western areas, like Americas and throughout Europe. In the Eastern thinking, like African thinking, religion is often expressed as a way of life, that is, as a way of thinking that condescends into practical living. Therefore, it is said that religion, for them, is not different from politics or philosophy. Contrasting Western religions, which are mostly termed as Abrahamic religions, Eastern religions, like the African traditional religion, often blend philosophy and religious practice together as expressed earlier in the concept of *vitalogy*. Followers of the Eastern religions are quite numerous, and they can be found all over the world.

Buddhism, Hinduism, Sikhism, and Jainism are among the major religions in the East and are all closely associated with India. They share a common way of thinking, including a heavy emphasis on personal duty and natural law, and these are linked to their philosophy of history considering that their ancestors thought in similar ways. They also have a rich ascetic tradition and inclinations to gods. Hinduism, Buddhism, Jainism, and Sikhism maintain belief in *samsara*, the wheel of life. In the Eastern thinking is conditioned by three main aspects: *samsara*, *karma*, and *nirvana*.

Samsara denotes a series of lives, death, and rebirth for every individual. The place of everyone in this present life was determined by his/her actions in a previous life. Your actions in this present life can either bring you back into the next life as a higher creature (human or inhuman) or a lower creature, and judgment is explained by the law of *karma*. It is objective justice: "God is fair and gives you exactly what you deserve." Other Indian religions such as Buddhism believe that *karma* merely follows a law of cause and effect.

Eastern philosophy is comparatively one of the oldest, as Hinduism, known be the oldest religions in the world, along with Jainism, Sikhism, and Buddhism. Believers of Hinduism are guided by dharma or religious living, which is synonymous with balanced and righteous living. Hinduism is considered as a polytheistic religion, meaning it worships several gods though Brahman is the principal god who can take on multiple forms. Buddhism, on the contrary, is an atheistic religion. It does not worship any gods. Instead, their adherents are called to pursue the Four Noble Truths and the Eightfold Path toward the goal of achieving Enlightenment *Nirvana*. With a righteous living, one become liberated from samsara, that is, the cycle of death and life caused by karma. Samsara is also depicted as a journey, afflicted by illusion and suffering. It is only in confronting samsara, and finally conquering it, can people achieve true happiness.

Sikhism, on the other hand, has stems from the teachings of Guru Nanak Dev, who rebelled against the Hindu caste system and the traditional beliefs and rituals of Hinduism. Sikhist philosophy of history is cyclical. The followers are called to live a life of virtue; after which, they will return to the universal God, who is formless and yet found in every form. This God is both creator and destroyer. They reject pilgrimages, fasting, and ritual celebrations and concentrate on living ethically, helping the poor, and singing hymns to God.

To better understand the Eastern thinking, we shall, at this point, concentrate on Confucianism.

7.1 The Eastern Thinking as Expressed in Confucianism

Confucianism is an interesting blend of moral, political, social, and religious though. Therefore, it fits into the field of philosophy of history. We find it reasonable using this mode of thinking to represent the Eastern thought though we have briefly presented the major religions already. Confucianism is basically referred to as a Chinese religion, founded on the ideas of Confucius (551-479 BCE). The best source available for studying it is *The Analects*, the collection of the sayings of Confucius or Master K'ung. He was a contemporary of the Buddha (although they probably never met). Robert E. Hume explains that like many great religious leaders, Confucius was eventually deified by his followers.[330] The teaching of Confucius is what is referred to as Confucianism, confirmed by William Bento as follows:

> It embraces some of the more admirable elements of traditional Chinese religion, such as a reverence towards heaven and worship of ancestors. Confucius himself however advocated the achievement of sagehood by man through self-cultivation and inner enlightenment... All the more notable is the fact that even when Chinese profess themselves to be Taoists, Buddhist or Christians, seldom do they cease to be Confucianists. Confucianism is more than a creed to be professed or to be rejected; it has become a patter worked into the fabric of Chinese life and society.[331]

Though the African tradition has neither founder nor a main person referred to as a head, it is based equally on ancestral vener-

---

[330.] Cf. R. E. HUME, *The World's Living Religions* (New York: Charles Scribner's Sons, 1959), pp. 117, 118.

[331.] W. BENTON, ed., *The New Encyclopedia Britannica*, op. cit. p. 1092.

ation and the aspiration toward a better world (heaven). This is a major contrast between the African traditional religion and many other world religions. Another fact, as Huston Smith observes, is that "to understand the total dimensions of Confucianism as a religion, it is important to see Confucius (a) shifting the emphasis from Heaven to Earth (b) without dropping Heaven out of the picture entirely."[332] Confucianism, like all Eastern religion, focuses entirely on ethics. It is through ethics that we can fully understand their reasoning pattern and culture, which implies their philosophy of history. Ninian Smart summarily explains that "Confucianism refers to the official cult or to the philosophical tradition of the Chinese from the time of Confucius (and indeed before)... It includes a strong strand of ethical theory and prescriptions."[333] The focus on ethics conditions us to examine closely the notion of *ren* which is at the center of their ethics.

7.1.1. The General Idea of Ren as in Confucianism

Ren is basically defined as human-heartedness of loving benevolence toward other humans and it is a pivotal ethical notion in Confucianism.[334] Since religion is practiced by human beings, it is incumbent upon man to practice *ren* since man, as Confucius teaches, is to obey the will, laws, or the dictates of *cielo* (heaven). To realize the will of *cielo*, which is mandatory for everybody, man must live a spiritual life, and the spiritual life is a life of sociability or harmony, considering that man is the central of the universe. He is the most important of all creatures though all creatures are important. Therefore, Confucianism is also a religion that stresses the philosophy of holism, considering though that man is the alpha and omega. Every human person has the sentiments of the natural laws, which include justice, reverence, and respect for others according to age and the sentiments of discernment.

---

332. H. SMITH, *The Religions of Man* (New York: Harper and Row, 1965), p. 189.
333. N. SMART, *The World's Religions* (Cambridge: Cambridge University Press, 2002), p. 107.
334. Cf. Ibid., p. 109.

Thus, man must denounce his own will act according to the laws of nature, the will of God which effectively is grounded on love. Love bounds everything, and it is a priceless gift that God has given to all. Therefore, the laws of God are not out of man; they are not external. They are inside man's heart; they are imbedded in man. Humility, magnanimity, sincerity, diligence, and graciousness must all go together to ensure the harmonious atmosphere that Confucianism bases its doctrine on. As he translates the sayings of Confucius, James R. Ware recounts his ideas that "if you are humble, you will not be laughed at. If you are magnanimous, you will attract many to your side. If you are sincere, people will trust you. If you are gracious, you will get along well with your subordinates."[335] All these virtues are based on this simple primary benevolent impulse in man called love, which forms the concept of *ren*. We cannot clearly understand the profundity of this concept in Confucianism unless we get to its historical backdrop.

7.1.2. Historical Basis of Ren

The concept of *ren* is rooted in the notion of filial piety. Max Mueller explains filial piety as a concept that was entrenched in China long before the time of Confucius and can be described as devotion and obedience by the younger members of the family to the elders. This was particularly the case of son to father. This loyalty and devotion to the family was the top priority in Chinese life. Such duty to the family, particularly devotion to the elders, was continued throughout one's life. Max Mueller summarily describes filial piety as "the services of love and reverence to parents when alive, and those of grief and sorrow to them when dead—these completely discharge the fundamental duty of living men."[336] Basically, *ren* is founded on benevolent love. Thus "several disciples asked Confucius about *ren* (*jen*) and his brief answer was 'love men.'" And ancient commentary

---

[335.] J. R. WARE, trans., *The Sayings of Confucius* (New York: New American Library, 1955), p. 110.

[336.] M. MUELLER, ed., *Sacred Books of the East*, vol. III (Ahmadabad, Krishna Press, 1910), p. 448.

says "*jen* is to love men joyously and from the innermost of one's heart."[337]

7.1.3. The Profundity of *Ren* in Confucianism

Ren is existential to man; it explains the fact that man cannot be neutral in a world of multiplicity and diversity. Man must be linked to others. The person who exhibits *ren* exemplifies the ideal of what a human being should be and encourages others to strive toward it. This explains why the word is homophonous with the word for human being (*ren*). *Ren* is (Λ) + (=), that is, man two times which is harmony. Λ (*ren*) and Λ (*uomo*) are the same. Therefore, man is love. In this case, man must always be in harmony. Man must not despise his fellow man because it is going to fall back to him. Without love, man ceases to be man in the real sense of the word. Thus, without saying that it was very easy, James Legge rightly confirms that Confucianism considers *ren* as "a perfect virtue that can be practiced and reached by ordinary people."[338] David E. Cooper sanctions the point that *ren* is like "a gravitational force, giving weight and stability to a person's life,"[339] and it "underlies a whole range of virtues: simplicity, magnanimity, modesty, and so on."[340]

An emphasis on the concept of *ren*, therefore, portrays the Confucian conviction that ceremonial and behavioral propriety is something that involves both the inner feeling and outer act. It is instrumental in teaching individuals how to act well and also very crucial in moral education.[341] Therefore, it is not enough to know God but to put his will into practice, and this is done effectively trough love. Harmony means that we accept diversity and respect hierarchically. In this regard, Roy C. Amore and Julia Ching explain that we can draw from the generic meaning of *ren*, representing

---

[337.] W. BENTON, ed., *The New Encyclopedia Britannica*, op. cit., p.1092.
[338.] J. LEGGE, *The Four Books* (New York: Paragon Book Reprint, 1966), p. 91.
[339.] D. E. COOPER, ed., *World Philosophies, a Historical Introduction* (Oxford: Blackwell, 1999), p. 65.
[340.] Ibid., p. 64.
[341.] Cf. N. SMART, *The World's Religions*, op. cit., p. 114.

proper behavior between people, to signify the pivotal importance of *ren* in the five relationships that act as the center of the Confucian ideology. The five relationships that are depicted in Confucianism are the relationships held between ruler and minister, father and son, husband and wife, elder and younger brothers, and friend and friend.[342]

The interrelationship should be between the individuals according to this explanation. However, there is not the concept of individuals at all in Confucianism because individual value is buried in the family. The good society, according to Confucius, is one that is governed by *ren* or *jen*. He insists on the personal example of the ruler who represents and embodies *ren*. "Hence the state is not unlike a schoolhouse and the ruler the schoolmaster whose purpose is to help his charges become better men."[343] By insisting on *ren*, Confucianism, in Herbert Fingarette's observation, regrets the fact that we all too often just go through the motions, too preoccupied to give our full attention to the relationship. If we consistently and wholeheartedly realized our potential to be the very best friend, parent, son, or daughter humanly possible, we would establish a level of caring and of moral excellence that would approach the utopian. This is Confucian transcendence: to take the actions of everyday life seriously as the arena of moral and spiritual fulfillment.[344]

7.2 *Ren* as an Interrelated Concept in Confucian Tradition and Religion

The function of *ren* is so enormous and profound that it cannot be exhausted nor executed as an isolated virtue. Fundamentally, there are five different avenues to manifest the love of God in Confucian religion. They are *ren*, (love), *li* (interpersonal relationship or social

---

[342.] R. C. AMORE and J. CHING. "Confucianism and Daoism" in Willard G. OXTOBY, ed., *A Concise Introduction to World Religions* (Barnes and Nobles, 1997), p. 449.

[343.] W. BENTON, ed., *The New Encyclopedia Britannica*, op. cit., p. 1092.

[344.] H. FINGARETTE, *Confucius—the Secular as Sacred* (New York: Harper and Row, 1972), ch. 1.

life), *si* (justice), *shim* (faith), and *chung* (fidelity). These are all ways of externalizing the natural law, and they are essentially interrelated. Yet *ren* is most central, and all the other virtues are linked to it. "To love all men" shows the basic meaning of *ren*, which stresses individual ways of practicing *ren*; and "to subdue oneself and return to *li*" stresses *ren* on the other side that to restrain oneself and follow the *li*. Therefore, *ren* is fundamentally linked to *li*. *Li* implies ritual, ceremonial, rules of propriety, good behavior. It also forms a central concept in Confucian education.[345] Accordingly, the smooth interrelationship is not just established with love but also with the rules of love. *Li* is the rule of love to guide the correct way of establishing the relationship. Therefore, consideration for others cannot work without *Li*.[346] Consequently, there is an interactive relationship between *li* and *ren*. Firstly, *li* is made with the principles of *ren*. Confucius said, "If a man be without the virtue (*ren*) proper to humanity, what has he to do with the rites of propriety (*li*)?"[347] This explains why the five relationships—relationship between the rule and subjects, father and son, husband and wife, elder brother and younger brother, friends—created by Confucianism (as presented above) stressed *li* in them. However, there is clearly the authority sequence from the top to the bottom. Each pair of relations has an authority legitimated by *li*. Rule of *li*, or rule with the principles of *ren*, means rule of the man with the perfect virtue.[348]

Confucius also used the concept *xiao ren*, *junzi*, and *sheng ren* to tell the difference of the virtue among the people. He said, "The superior man (*junzi*) thinks of virtue; the small men (*xiao ren*) thinks of comfort. Superior man thinks of sanctions of law, the small man thinks of favors which he may receive."[349] Another terminology that he uses in reference to virtue in the light of *ren* is *chun tzu*, which he

---

[345.] Cf. N. SMART, *The World's Religions*, op. cit., p. 109.
[346.] Cf. J. LEGGE, *The Four Books* (New York: Paragon Book Reprint, 1966), p. 91.
[347.] J. LEGGE, *The Four Books*, op. cit., p. 25.
[348.] Cf. Ibid.
[349.] Ibid., p. 42.

considers as an inner moral force in every person which appeals to harmony.[350]

7.3 The Notion of *Ren* with Regard to Other Religions

We can infer from our presentation so far that religion and morality are closely connected. They are both internal and concerned with a higher law. This higher law for Confucius can be summarized as seen above in *ren*. *Ren* embodies a cross section of moral values which can be well fitted in other religions. Though we shall recognize some variations in approaches to the conception of virtue or love as in Confucianism and in other religions, the general claim is that every religion, worthy of the name exalts the virtue of love expressed as *ren* in Confucianism, especially if we were to consider *ren* in its interrelated perspective

7.2.1 Ren as Expressed in Other Oriental Religions

It is the observation of Ninian Smart that "Westerns have often been confused about religion in China. Often, they refer to Buddhism, Taoism (Daoism) and Confucianism as three religions in china and like three parts of a functioning system."[351] This, of course, involves a great level of ignorance because Buddhism and Taoism have a well-defined monastic embodiment and a class of religious specialists, something which is not common in Confucianism. Of course, the other Oriental religions also preach and practice love and harmony as expressed in the Confucian *ren*. Yet whereas much Confucian ethics revolves around family relationship, "Buddhist and Daoist monasticism provided an escape from the family's structure though the monastic vocation."[352]

Also, "there is a corresponding ethical contrast between the morality to be displayed by the benevolent person in the world,

---

[350.] Cf. D. E. COOPER, ed., *World Philosophies, a Historical Introduction*, op. cit., p. 65.

[351.] Cf. N. SMART, *The World's Religions*, op. cit., 106.

[352.] N. SMART, *The World's Religions*, op. cit., p. 111.

summed up in *ren* or human heartedness, and that of Daoist or Buddhist who is concerned with the *wi wei*, that is, not acting or acting in not acting."[353]Accordingly, we can assert that in the social or religious life for the Orientals, harmony (as expressed in the Confucian *ren*) was the watchword. For Buddhism, it was a spiritual harmony, an interior harmony. Taoists stress the harmony of humans and nature while for the Confucians, it is the harmony of humans with other humans.[354]

7.2.3 Ren Versus Christian Personalism and African Thinking

We had already examined the position of the Africans as far as personalism is concerned. Christianity is not the author of personalism in Africa. Africans tradition, as examined above, is basically built on the importance of the human person as a member of a community. The definition of a human person is incomplete without the community dimension. This is how love is expressed and defined. Evidently, the Christian religion is founded on love, a virtue that is explained almost in the same direction with the Confucian *ren*. In fact, in *The Analects* (XII, 2), we equally read Confucius's version of the Golden Rule (Matt. 7:12) as "Do not impose on others what you yourself do not desire." This is linked to the practice of *ren*.[355] To be very brief in the presentation of the virtue of love in Christianity, we shall refer to the encyclical *Studiorum Ducem* of Pope Pius XI promulgated on June 29, 1923, in which he proclaimed, in a firm biblical manner, that love or charity is the "queen and mistress of all virtues."

In the Catholic perspective, *ren* would be considered as virtue considering that the catechism of the Catholic church no. 1803 defines virtue as a "habitual and firm disposition to do the good. It allows the person not only to perform good acts, but to give the best

---

[353.] Ibid.

[354.] Cf. J. LEGGE, *The Four Books*, p. 37.

[355.] Cf. D. E. COOPER, ed., *World Philosophies, An Historical Introduction*, op. cit., p. 64.

of himself. The virtuous person tends toward the good with all his sensory and spiritual powers; he pursues the good and chooses it in concrete actions'. In the same way as in Confucianism, St. Gregory of Nyssa insists that 'The goal of a virtuous life is to become like God."[356]

Yet there is one major difference being that in Christianity, without minimizing the emphasis on the earthly love, there is more stress on the love of God before coming to man. Thus, unlike in Confucianism where the emphasis is more on humanity, love, as a theological virtue, begins from God before being exercised in the human forum. CCC No. 1822 tells us that "charity is the theological virtue by which we love God above all things for his own sake, and our neighbor as ourselves for the love of God."

Another way to situate *ren* in the Christian context is to discuss love in the light of personalism, considering that *ren* is built on interpersonal relationship and harmony between persons in the society. The concept, personalism, is based in the firmly held Christian conviction that man, as ordained by the Creator, should be the center of all activities in the universe. Jacques Maritain and Bernard Haring emerge from a multitude of thinkers who have profoundly explored this topic.

Personalism is not an abstract philosophy, not a product of thinkers in an ivory tower. It involves listening to the experience of men, to their problems and questions, their anxieties and hopes and perhaps have shared these in their own suffering and in compassion with their fellow men. It is based on a sound interpersonal relationship between persons.[357] In the same channel of *ren* and *li*, Bernard Haring reminds us in the Catholic context that justice designates "a mediation of love. Justice, takes care of other's right in our social relationships... Justice without love, without warmth of the heart, is one of the most crying forms of injustice against personalism."[358] In the same way, drawing from the scriptures, the CCC No. 1805 tells

---

[356.] St. Gregory of Nyssa, *De beatitudinibus*, 1:PG 44,1200D.
[357.] B. HARING, *Morality Is for Persons* (London: Vision Press Ltd., 1972), p. 6.
[358.] B. HARING, *Shalom: Peace* (New York: Image Books, 1989), p. 266.

us that "four virtues play a pivotal role and accordingly are called cardinal. They are prudence, justice, fortitude, and temperance."

The similarities between Christian love as expressed in personalism and the *ren* of Confucianism, notwithstanding, certain distinctions are to be drawn. It is very clear that Confucianism stresses more on ceremonial aspects of *ren*, especially when connected to *li*. Ceremonial and behavioral propriety are things that involve both inner feeling and outer act they are instrumental in teaching individuals how to act well and are crucial, therefore, in moral education in Confucianism.[359] Yet Christianity, specifically Catholicism, is far from being a religion of externality even though they do have rituals.

Another difference is that Christianity, even though respects hierarchy, does not link it to love in some sort mathematical manner as in Confucianism. The virtue of love or charity is also not for the sake of it but is actually willed by God. Christian personalism is emphatic on the point that God has endowed man (in whatever level, age, or social strata) with an intrinsic dignity since man bears the likeness of divine. Each person at his or her own level has value only to the extent that he is created in God's image and likeness and strives to respond to God's love in ways proposed by the gospels. This is precisely why our Lord says that "whatsoever one does to the least of one brother one does it unto him" (Matt. 25:40).

Our study of *ren* is undoubtedly a Confucian expectation of how human nature should be. The fact is that Confucians view each person not only as an autonomous individual but also as a social being whose identity is derived from his interaction within the broader human community. To a greater or lesser extent, this idea is basic to all religions.

However, critics have been able to come out with some flaws in the Confucian thought concerning the concept of *ren*. One of Confucius's statements about acquiring *ren* gives the impression that it is an easy task. He said, "Whenever I want *ren*, it is as close as the palm of my hand."[360] Yet in some instances in his teaching, he also

---

[359.] Cf. N. SMART, *The World's Religions*, op. cit., p. p. 114
[360.] W. BENTON, ed., *The New Encyclopedia Britannica*, op. cit., p. 1093.

accepted the immense difficulties in acquiring this virtue and that the attainment and practice of the virtue was an arduous or even elusive task to the extent that his best student, Yan Hui, was the only person he had known who had exhibited *ren* for any significant length of time. The paradox was reinforced by Confucius's repeated refusal to claim that he had ever attained *ren* himself. Also, subsequent Confucian thinkers such as Mencius (371–289 BC) came up and offered their own interpretations of *ren*.[361] Apparently, it is because of such contradictory and flashy but utopian expectations in an ethical approach to reality that led to the following doubtful remark presented by David E. Cooper concerning Confucius and his doctrine vis-à-vis other great masters:

> Unlike Socrates or Jesus and the Buddha, Confucius has not retained his awesome reputation... More recent judges sometimes sympathize with readers who find his teachings "commonplace and unexciting..." and people of leftist inclinations have presumably been swayed by the mangling he received at the hands of Mao Tse Tong his ideological henchman. More serious however, are the several elements in the currently received, popular impression of Confucius which are unappealing to contemporary taste.[362]

Irrespective of our criticisms (as found in all religions), Confucianism is a people's faith. Faith depends on the perception of those who subscribe to it. As David L. Sills endorses, faith is "one or more beliefs that a person or a people accepts as true, good and desirable regardless of social consensus or objective evidence which are perceived as irrelevant."[363] The fact is that the history of Asia cannot

---

[361.] Cf. Ibid., pp. 1093-1094.

[362.] D. E. COOPER, ed., *World Philosophies, An Historical Introduction*, op. cit., pp. 62-63.

[363.] D. L. SILLS, ed., *International Encyclopedia of the Social Science*, vol. 1 (London: Collier-Macmillan, 1972), p. 455.

be written without Confucianism, and this is what this topic fits into our subject matter. More so, the concept of *ren* can be very much likened to the whole idea of the African personalism which has been explained at various levels in this work.

Conclusion

We have highlighted many different cultures or philosophies of history though the African perspective was given greater attention. Considering that a people's culture is rooted in their history and is equally determined by various geographic, environmental, and even psychological peculiarities, it is cumbersome to compare two cultures in the full and austere sense of the word. Thus, ours in the following chapter will be a quasi-comparative study with the Thomistic-Christian perspective of history. Our intention is to perceive how both cultures can coexist in a world that is facing both the excitements and the challenges of intercultural reality. Consequently, without claiming that the African culture is ideal, our intention is not to use the ideas of Jacques Maritain or St. Thomas as a litmus paper or a yardstick to evaluate or to judge the African culture. We are simply discussing two approaches to reality.

The first problematic in this following chapter would dwell on the very personality of Jacques Maritain as to whether the circumstances that stimulated his vision of history could be similar to those of the African historian, Joseph Ki-Zerbo. Furthermore, while studying the ideas of Jacques Maritain, we shall be asking ourselves what similarities and differences could be perceived when put vis-à-vis the African conception of history that we already discussed in the accent of Ki-Zerbo.

Finally, we shall examine the realities and the effects of an intercultural and postmodern world and decipher what perspective we can propose and present as a way forward for a global culture.

CHAPTER EIGHT

An Overview of Thomistic: Christian Thinking
Typified by Jacques Maritain in Conjunction
with Joseph Ki-Zerbo as an African Thinker

8.1 Jacques Maritain, a Renowned Thomist: What Preliminary Relationship and Contrast to Ki-Zerbo?

ONE STRIKING SIMILARITY to be considered between Maritain and Ki-Zerbo at this initial level is that both studied in the famous Sorbonne University in Paris. Maritain from 1900–1902 while Ki-Zerbo came in from 1949-1953. They both attained the aggre-gation degree. Yet while Ki-Zerbo did history and political science, Maritain studied philosophy. Both became professors at various lev-els and at respective higher institutions of learning. This implies that their insights into the concept of history which they both developed at their respective levels was done with deep intellectual capacity and with due consciousness of the conceptions of their days.

The above veracity, notwithstanding, that which actually stimu-lates us to study these personalities together as presented in the intro-duction of this work is their inclination to a theory of history that is based on tangible human experiences with a directionality and a more authentic and salvific theocentric focus. In their respective cir-cumstances and accents, they both regret the fact that history, as a necessary subject for human development, is not taken as seriously as

it should, having been distorted by philosophers like Hegel and min-
imized by the postmodernists. Ki-Zerbo, for example, to a certain
extent, sees globalization as an arm of postmodernism that destroys
culture and introduces the nihilism of Nietzsche, and consequently
totalitarianism, Machiavellianism, and other doctrines that destroy
true liberty as well as the true values of culture and history that can
work not only for the improvement of the African society but also for
the well-being of persons in the entire world.[364]

In the same reasoning platform, Piero Viotto explains to us that
Maritain criticizes Hegel and his followers for adopting a system of
history that leads mankind to Machiavellianism with their way of
explaining the immanence of God in nature and in world affairs
whereas, quoting from Saint Paul, Maritain expects us to perceive
history as a dialogue between God and humanity.[365] Like Ki-Zerbo,
he is struggling for the reawakening of a system of history that
includes concrete religious living in a culture that is truly human.
The general cry is that "after Hegel, contemporary philosophy has a
reason to rediscover the faith in the power of religion."[366] Therefore,
both thinkers abhor a system of thought that devalues the human
person's strive for authentic and hopeful existence. This is the major
consequence of post-Hegelian thoughts that drove mankind into the
nihilism of Nietzsche, the existential ethics of Jean Paul Sartre, all in
the name of a continental philosophy which, at the end of the twentieth century, developed into a postmodernism that aims at destroying and disregarding of all meta-narratives.[367] Yet Charles Taliaferro
explains to us that there is hope in the return to Thomism and the
natural law theory as he recommends the ideas of Jacques Maritain
as a way forward,[368] ideas that are implied in the African thinking as

---

[364] Cfr. J. KI-ZERBO, *Punti Fermi Sull'Africa*, 263-265.

[365] Cfr. P. VIOTTO, *Jacques Maritain: Dizionario delle Opere* (Roma: Città Nuova Editrice, 2003), 323.

[366] Ibid., 115.

[367] Cfr. C. TALIAFERRO, ed., *The Cambridge Companion to Christian Philosophical Theology* (Cambridge: Cambridge University Press, 2010), 77-78.

[368] Cfr. Ibid., 78.

expressed by Ki-Zerbo. This explains why we feel comfortable discussing the ideas of both together.

Irrespective of the points presented above, one striking difference is that Joseph Ki-Zerbo developed his thoughts within the confines of a continent, the African continent, the African culture. While in Paris, he met some other African students, such as the Senegalese historian, Cheikh Anta Diop, and the former president of Senegal, Abdoulaye Wade, with whom they embarked to develop on the almost-ignored African conception of history. Yet Ki-Zerbo had no ideal historian as it were to hang on. His ideas were based on the general African system of thought from those who lived the experiences, especially his father, as well as on the reality of the African culture. Though Jacques Maritain also centered his thoughts on the Christian thinking, that is, on the Christian culture of history, after facing some existential challenges with Bergsonism and other aspects of life, as would be explained later, he finally found his base on Thomism. Here lies a major difference between Ki-Zerbo and himself. While Ki-Zerbo was somewhat an independent thinker, Maritain developed his thoughts on the Thomistic views. What then is Thomism, and why do we qualify Maritain as an ardent Thomist?

8.1.1 Toward an Understanding of Thomism

Thomism is basically defined as the school of thought that follows the teachings of St. Thomas Aquinas. These teachings, which could be considered philosophical and theological, are principally found in all his works, especially his famous work, *Summa Theologica*. One of the distinguished ideas of Thomism also prominent in the thoughts of Jacques Maritain, whom we have already qualified as a Thomist, is philosophical realism.[369] Some of the Thomistic positions that are relevant to our subject matter, the concept of history, are based on the human person and on moral objectivism. Moral objec-

---

[369.] A Thomistic belief that was posited against skeptics and which holds that things really do exist composed of two parts: prime matter and substantial form. In the human beings, the prime matter of humans is our body, and the substantial form is our soul.

tivism means that the nature of the universe and essences of objects do not depend on the free will of God, but on His intellect and, ultimately, on His essence, which is unchanging. The natural law, the Thomists intimate, is immutable because it springs from the mind of God. Consequently, immoral acts are immoral not simply because God forbids them, but because they are inherently immoral.[370]

Thomism is often expressed as a Christian philosophy, and it is a very broad school of thought with so many other thinkers, alongside Jacques Maritain himself, including Mortimer J. Adler, Vernon Bourke, Frederick Copleston, Jean Daujat, Maurice De Wulf, Dominic of Flanders, Edward Feser, Reginald Garrigou-Lagrange, Peter Geach, Étienne Gilson, Herbert McCabe, Antonio Millán-Puelles, Giuseppe Pecci, Luigi Taparelli, Joseph de Torre, John F. Wippel, and many others. Such a Christian philosophy, in the form of Thomism, was given a strong incentive in the encyclical letter of Pope Leo XIII, *Aeterni Patris*, in August 4, 1879.[371] According to Victor B. Brezik, this document accelerated a Thomistic renaissance in the nineteenth century in the form of an authentic movement that involved studies and publications on Thomistic themes. Consequently, Victor Brezik inscribes thus:

> Like a mighty crescendo which turned Thomism into a leading philosophy of the day, one needs only mention undertakings like the Leonine Commission for the publication of a critical edition of the writings of St. Thomas Aquinas, centres of Thomistic studies such as The Higher Institute of Philosophy at Louvain, the Dominican School of Saulchoir in France, the groups of French and Belgian Jesuits inspired by St. Thomas, the Pontifical Institute of Mediaeval Studies, and names of scholars like Mercier,

---

[370] Cfr. T. M. ZIGLIARA, *Summa Philosophica*, vol. 3 (Paris, 1889), 23-25.
[371] Cfr. V. B. BREZIK, ed., *One Hundred Years of Thomism*, (Houston, Texas: University of St. Thomas Press, 1981), 2.

Grabmann, Gilson, Maritain and a host of others,
as well as the pervasion of Thomism in numerous
Catholic institutions of learning throughout the
world, to realize the immense growth of interest
in and adherence to the doctrine of St. Thomas
that eventually resulted from the firm recommendation made in *Aeterni Patris.*[372]

While accepting, therefore, that Thomism is basically an
expression of Christianity, we are inferring by extension that while
Maritain expresses Thomism, that is, the Thomistic culture as
Christian values, Ki-Zerbo expresses the African culture as African
values. Another significant observation is that almost every religious
community or almost every geographically or historically renowned
group of people has a particular hero that stands as a pillar of faith or
religion. Christianity worships Christ as Lord and God, Buddhism
projects Buddha as the pillar of their faith, Islam talks of Muhammad,
Confucianism refers to Confucius, and we can continue the list.
Contrarily, Africans recognize the Supreme Being as such and no
other concrete personality apart from the respective ancestors who
have their own roles to play in respective families or communities
and not in the general religion as it is with other people.

In view of the argument that Thomism is a very broad school
of thought, it may also be relevant to know not only how firm or
committed Maritain was to Thomism but also the peculiar character
of his Thomism.

[372] Idem.

8.1.2 The Peculiarities of the Thomism of Jacques Maritain

Maritain did not only endorse the thoughts of St. Thomas but he also equally confirmed himself as an ardent Thomist and invited us all to abide by Thomism as revealed in the following declaration:

> St. Thomas had a genius...the most powerful energies of life, of renewal, of "revolution," and what was worth saving in pagan thought and the "discordant clamours" of philosophers. Therefore, we need to have him "teach us Christian philosophy in the social and cultural order" under our "new historical sky" and other skies still in the future, because St. Thomas is always a "contemporary author."[373]

Deal W. Hudson and Matthew J. Mancini refer to Maritain's connection to St. Thomas which started when he developed full interest in the works of St. Thomas in 1910 as an affiliation to wisdom. According to them, this Maritain's romance with wisdom through friendship with Aquinas lasted until the end of his life in 1973 as evident from the spirit that pervaded his writings from 1910 onward.[374]

Deal Hudson and Matthew Mancini again remind us that irrespective of the relationship or the affinity of Maritain to St. Thomas that qualifies the former as a Thomist *per se*, Maritain remains an independent thinker. He is not a mere parody of Aquinas but an interpreter with his own accent. It is in this connection that they made the following declaration:

> One of the greatest dangers one can face in studying Maritain's thought is to think that one is studying a faithful disciple of the principles of

---

[373.] J. MARITAIN, *Some Reflections on Culture and Liberty* (Chicago: Chicago University Press, 1933), 1.

[374.] Cfr. D. W. HUDSON and M. J. MANCINI, *Understanding Maritain, Philosopher and Friend* (Macon, Georgia: Mercer University Press, 1987), 92.

> St. Thomas…indeed Maritain at times, changes
> the thought of Saint Thomas to suit his needs,
> in the same way that Saint Thomas "improved"
> upon Aristotle to make him, at times, say what
> was "upright." Hence to study Maritain as a sim-
> ple twentieth century interpreter of Aquinas is to
> misunderstand both Maritain and Aquinas.[375]

It is in respect of the above conception that we can situate the peculiarity of Maritain's Thomism, both from St. Thomas himself and from the many other Thomistic philosophers. One of the distinctive elements in Maritain's Thomism is his treatment of the concept of intuition, which even goes in divergence to that of his tutor, Henri Bergson, as we shall soon see. In one of his articles, we realized that Edward Feser does not only distinguish the various ages or periods of Thomism but also goes further to differentiate the various positions the respective Thomistic thinkers adopt in the Thomism school. He identified the Neo-Scholastic Thomism, the Laval or River Forest Thomism, the transcendental Thomism, the Lublin Thomism, and the Existential Thomism.[376]

As Feser intimates, the Neo-Scholastic Thomism was the dominant tendency before Vatican II, and its focus was the interpretative tradition of the great commentators on Aquinas, and Reginald Garrigou-Lagrange (1877-1964) is, perhaps, its greatest representative. Its core philosophical commitments are summarized in the famous "Twenty-Four Thomistic Theses" approved by Pope Pius X.[377]

Laval or River Forest Thomism emphasizes the Aristotelian foundations of Aquinas's philosophy and the idea that a sound metaphysics must be preceded by a comprehensive understanding of natural science. Charles De Koninck (1906-1965), James A. Weisheipl

---

[375.] Ibid., 113.

[376.] Cfr. E. Feser, "The Thomistic tradition," part I, in URL: < edwardfeser. blogspot.it/2009/10/thomistic-tradition-part-i.html? m-1_> (accessed on April 14, 2015).

[377.] Cfr. Idem.

(1923-1984), William A. Wallace, and Benedict Ashley are among its main exponents. It is sometimes called Laval Thomism, after the University of Laval in Quebec where De Koninck was a professor. The other label, River Forest Thomism, is derived from a suburb of Chicago, the location of the Albertus Magnus Lyceum for Natural Science. It is also sometimes called Aristotelian Thomism.[378]

Transcendental Thomism, on its part, is associated with Joseph Marechal (1878-1944), Karl Rahner (1904-84), and Bernard Lonergan (1904-84), and it does not generally oppose modern philosophy but seeks to reconcile Thomism with a Cartesian subjectivist approach to knowledge in general and Kantian epistemology in particular while Lublin Thomism, which stems from the University of Lublin in Poland, also sometimes called phenomenological Thomism, like transcendental Thomism, also seeks to combine Thomism with certain elements of modern philosophy though, in a way, that is less radically revisionist. Precisely, it implores the use of the phenomenological method of philosophical analysis associated with Edmund Husserl and the personalism of writers like Max Scheler in articulating the Thomist conception of the human person. Though he later rose above Thomism, the best-known proponent of Lublin Thomisn is Karol Wojtyla (1920-2005), who went on to become Pope John Paul II.[379]

It is in existential Thomism that the uniqueness of Maritain's Thomism shines out though Etienne Gilson (1884-1978) is mostly recognised as its key exponent. Existential Thomism emphasizes the importance of historical exegesis, and it also tends to de-emphasize Aquinas's continuity with the Aristotelian tradition, stressing instead the originality of Aquinas's doctrine of being or existence. Though existential Thomism was sometimes presented as a counterpoint to modern existentialism, the main reason for the label is the emphasis that this approach puts on Aquinas's doctrine of existence.

[378.] Cfr. Idem.
[379.] Cfr. E. FESER, "The Thomistic tradition," part 1.

Contemporary proponents include Joseph Owens and John F. X. Knasas.[380]

The distinctive mark of Jacques Maritain is that he introduced into Thomistic metaphysics the notion that philosophical reflection begins with an intuition of being. According to him, the intuition of being takes place in that very world of preconscious activity, the depths of the soul, which he calls "this limbo of the preconscious." Added to his new direction to the topic of intuition is the point that his ethics and social philosophy sought to harmonize Thomism with personalism and pluralistic democracy.[381]

In October 1913, Maritain published his first book, *La philosophie Bergsonienne*. In this book, he manifested his deviation from his prime philosophical mentor, Bergson, and opted with new vigor for the ideas of Aquinas, most specifically his philosophical system of thought that linked up both intuition and the idea of knowledge by way of connaturality. Consequently, he professed the worth of essence in understanding, insinuating that intuition also revolves around the perception of essence. This is also the main channel through which Bergson's philosophical ideas, rooted in Maritain, became transformed by Thomism, demonstrating a strange effect of the instinct of the intellect towards self-preservation. With this understanding, the thesis of Bergson was involuntarily reordered into the rudiments of scholastic theses, adapting or transforming it to the knowledge system of the celebrated Thomas Aquinas.[382] That, notwithstanding, Maritain had a deviation from Etienne Gilson on this point because Gilson did not accept that essence in understanding, as applied in Thomism, can be known through intuition but through judgment.

The above paragraph again draws our attention to the fact that, like Joseph Ki-Zerbo, whose perspectives we already explored above and many other intellectuals, certain existential factors must have inspired Maritain to embark both in philosophic thinking as a whole and in the Thomistic system of thought, especially as he also places

---

380. Cfr. Idem.

381. Cfr. Idem.

382. Cfr. J. MARITAIN, *Bergsonian Philosophy and Thomism* (New York: Greenwood Press, 1968), 72.

history as a base for philosophical reflections. What resemblance, thus, can we draw from this perspective?

8.2 The Inspiration of Jacques Maritain Compared to That of Joseph Ki-Zerbo

Jacques Maritain's enthusiasm to study the philosophy of history was greatly influenced or motivated by the various conceptions of history prevalent in his days. This again exposes a similarity between Ki-Zerbo and himself, considering that Ki-Zerbo was also conversant with the various ideas of history, especially with the misconceptions and the satiric literature published by philosophers and scholars such as Hegel that his continent of origin, Africa, was a continent with no history, not to talk of having a conception of history.[383] This generated a passion in him to get into historical research, making him to opt for the study of history and political science.

Corresponding to the situation of Ki-Zerbo as presented in the above paragraph, Maritain was not satisfied with some of the trends in the philosophy of history prominent in his days. He considered that they did not meet up with the ideal standards of viewing history as he perceived from the Thomistic platform. Another fact is that as a convert into Christianity, Maritain was influenced by the Christian thinker, Thomas Aquinas. Similarly, Ki-Zerbo, as an African, was also influenced by his father who was an oral historian. While Maritain read the works of Aquinas, Ki-Zerbo listened fervently to his father, yet in both cases, wisdom transpired, and history was created and developed in respective perspectives. Concerning his oral motivation from his father, Ki-Zerbo tells us:

> J'avais opté pour l'histoire d'abord parce que mon père a vécu longtemps. C'était un homme d'histoire. Il avait porté une partie de notre histoire locale, puisqu'il était le premier Chrétien de la Haute-Volta, et il aimait raconter. J'ai donc été

[383.] Cfr. J. KI-ZERBO, ed., *General History of Africa*, vol. 1, 12.

préparé au métier d'historien par cette éducation. J'estime aussi que l'histoire est 'maitresse de vie'. C'est une discipline formatrice de l'esprit, parce qu'elle vous apprend à raisonner dans la logique et au-delà de la science par la conscience. Peu à peu, une double attitude s'est forgée chez moi, l'une consistant à dire: "je veux revenir à mes racines," un mouvement qui est capital pour la constitution d'une personnalité mûre et authentique. Et l'autre constatant les liens multiples reliant ce continent à toutes les régions du monde dans le tissu de l'histoire.[384]

That, notwithstanding, Maritain's approach seems to be broader as he delves into the wider field of the philosophy of history, whereas Ki-Zerbo's preoccupation was mainly on the history and the theory of history of his continent, Africa. This explains why Jacques Maritain, like his mentor, St. Thomas, followed a more academic approach to counter existential issues concerning humanity in general as rooted in people's conceptions of the human person in history. It is also in this connection that some scholars situate his friendship with St. Thomas as we read as follows:

> Jacques Maritain's friendship with wisdom and with Aquinas must be understood within the context of his reaction to the relativism, skepticism and moral nihilism that were consequences

---

[384.] (I opted for history, first because my father lived a long time. He was a man of history. He had worn part of our local history since he was the first Christian of Upper Volta, and he liked to tell stories. So I was prepared for the job of historian by this education. I also believe that history is life master. It is a formative discipline of the mind because it teaches you to reason in logic and beyond science through consciousness. Little by little, a double attitude was forged in me, one of saying, "I want to go back to my roots," a movement that is crucial for the constitution of a mature and authentic personality. And the other is the multiple links connecting this continent to all regions of the world in the fabric of history.) J. KI-ZERBO, *À Quand L'Afrique?*, 11-12.

of the anti-metaphysical and reductionalistic
spirit of his early teachings of philosophy.[385]

Taking cognizance of the above challenges to the Thomist, it
seems obvious that Jacques Maritain had a particular abhorrence for
Hegel's conception of history which caused him to declare that "for
many years, the very notion of the Philosophy of History was held
in bad repute because of Hegel who was its putative father [before
Hegel, however, there was Vico and before Vico, St. Augustine]."[386]
From this remark, Maritain also affirms that many different forms
or approaches to history do exist. He was, therefore, motivated or
inspired by these different approaches to provide his own conception, or philosophy of history, which, of course, was Thomistic in
quality.

Another outstanding difference between the influence or inspiration of Ki-Zerbo and Maritain is that while Ki-Zerbo identified
his target to study history and political science and embarked on
this target directly, Jacques Maritain's academic and spiritual expe-
ditions were a whole mental and emotional journey, a journey that
he made together with his wife, Raïssa. Shortly before he discovered
and became committed to the Thomistic-Christian way of thinking,
Maritain and his wife were drowning into a kind of religious and
philosophical nihilism that was drawing them toward suicide.

Henri Bergson's philosophy of life made a solid mark on
Maritain and was of a very strong influence on him for a while.
They were inclined by Charles Peguy to move from their Sorbonne
University to the Collège de France to hear Henri Bergson's lectures.
They were absolutely impressed and seemed to have discovered a
treasure in Bergsonism, especially the point that one could truly or
absolutely *know what is*. Bergson's emphasis in this case was not on
the intelligence or reason but on a faculty that he called intuition,
which he defined as the kind of *intellectual sympathy* by which one

---

[385.] D. W. Hudson and M. J. Mancini, *Understanding Maritain, Philosopher and Friend*, 93.
[386.] J. Maritain, *On the Philosophy of History*, 1.

places oneself within an object in order to coincide with what is unique in it and consequently inexpressible.[387] To complete this definition, he added that "there is one reality, at least, which we all seize from within, by intuition and not by simple analysis. It is our own personality in its flowing through time—our self which endures."[388]

However, Maritain's satisfaction or consolation with the philosophy of Bergson was not long-lasting. He later realized that Bergson's philosophy was founded on a major understanding of a basic error recurrent in modern philosophy, the "perversion of an intellect which had been separated from its principles and given up to matter."[389] His criticism of Bergson, therefore, was that instead of rediscovering the true nature of the intellect, he "abandoned intelligence and abandoned being, replacing the first by an extra-intellectual intuition and the second by movement."[390]

Maritain carefully places his more modern and flexible sense of intuition in the framework of the thought of St. Thomas. In this regard, he states thus:

> In an "absolutely restricted sense" intuition means, not a knowledge through a likeness, but a direct knowledge of the thing known which is in the subject by itself and as an intelligible in act. This kind of intuition is found in God's knowledge of Himself, the knowledge an angel has of itself and the beatific vision. "The intellect is informed 'immediately' by the essence or the substance of the thing known, *without the means of a subjective similitude of the thing.*"[391]

---

[387] Cfr. H. BERGSON, *An Introduction to Metaphysics*, Thomas Ernest HULME, trans. (New York: Putman's and Sons, 1912), 7.

[388] Ibid., 9.

[389] J. MARITAIN, *Bergsonian Philosophy and Thomism*, 102.

[390] Idem.

[391] Ibid., 150.

It can be understood from this perspective that although Maritain's personal and philosophical indebtedness to Bergson was certainly significant, it was his discovery and understanding of the philosophy of St. Thomas that actually took him out of his spiritual and metaphysical quagmire.[392] Yet it must be emphasised that what actually attracted Maritain to Bergson was Bergson's "criticism of the materialistic world of the scientist and the alternative theory of reality and epistemology he proposed. Despite Maritain's eventual criticism of Bergson's idea years later, initially, they liberated his mind and laid a good foundation for metaphysics and humanism."[393]

Léon Bloy is another personality that can seldom be omitted when discussing the struggles and motivations of Maritain. After being married in 1904, Raïssa and Jacques, in their spiritual and academic muddle, got to know Léon Bloy, and they discovered in him a living example of a person who found God and abandoned himself in utter devotion of God. Due to his influence, Raïssa and Jacques were baptized in the Roman Catholic faith (with Bloy as godfather) on June 11, 1906.[394]

Considering also that we already presented the context within which Ki-Zerbo wrote his reflections on history, to do justice to Maritain and to our work, we shall now examine some of the prominent conceptions of history that Maritain had to contest with to the extent that he wrote an entire thesis on the philosophy of history. In this case, we are also asserting that in spite of the African conception of history and the conception of Jacques Maritain which we shall soon see, other conceptions of history also prevail.

[392.] Cfr. J. TRAPANI, *Poetry, Beauty and Contemplation: The Complete Aesthetics of Jacques Maritain* (Washington, DC: Catholic University of America Press, 2011), 32.

[393.] Cfr. J. TRAPANI, *Poetry, Beauty and Contemplation: The Complete Aesthetics of Jacques Maritain*, 28.

[394.] Cfr. Ibid., 18.

8.3 Various Conceptions of History as Challenges and Motivations to Jacques Maritain

The fact that each generation, as well as social group or culture, perceives life in its own way has given rise to many different conceptions of history. Living in an era with various conceptions or philosophies of history, Maritain was also influenced or inspired to develop his own perspectives, built on the foundation of Aristotelian Thomism. Though there are so many different types of philosophies of history, we shall concentrate here only on four types which seem more relevant to us presently (mostly from the West).

8.3.1 The Cyclical or Fatalist View of History

This view was mainly held by the ancient Greeks. They considered that just as the four seasons (spring, summer, autumn, and winter) repeat themselves year after year, so also does history follow a cyclical sequence. Consequently, they consider history merely as a repetition of preordained events, which could not be affected by human power. Consequent upon this conception is the idea that history has no goal or meaning. History simply repeats itself. Exponents of this school of thought were Herodotus (484-425 BC), who is referred to as the father of history and Thucydides (460-400 BC).[395] We share in the observation of Di Theodore Adorno that this cyclical theory of history leads to stoicism, and it is an inauthentic philosophy of history.[396]

8.3.2. The Providential View of History

Contrary to the cyclical Greek view of defining history in reference to a circular motion, the providential view of history perceives history as having a beginning and advancing in a straight line toward

---

[395.] Cfr. F. COPLESTON, *A History of Philosophy*, vol. VI (New York: Image Books, 1994), 150-164.
[396.] Cfr. D. T. ADORNO, *History and Freedom* (Cambridge: Polity Press, 2006), 272.

a definite goal. History, the exponents of this view insinuate, started with creation, then to the fall of man and the whole of salvation history, leading to the Last Judgment. That which drives history, they claim, is a providential God. This view of history is also called the Christian view of history, and St. Augustine (354-430) is one of the greatest protagonists of this school of thought. St. Augustine is said to have depicted history as a history of struggle between the City of God (*Civitas Dei*), where God-loving people live, and the City of the World (*Civitas Ierrena*), where the people who have yielded to the temptation of Satan live. In his consideration, the real City of God would finally emerge victorious and would institute perpetual peace in accordance with a plan predestined by God. The City of God is a real society with its roots in eternity and its development in time and history.[397] Thus, he depicts human history, from the fall to consummation, into six distinct periods, viz, from Adam to Noah, from Noah to Abraham, from Abraham to David, from David to the Babylonian captivity, from the Babylonian captivity to the birth of Christ, and from the first coming to the second coming. Yet he still left us suspended as to how long the sixth period would last.[398]

This view of history also gives the impression that human beings are instruments moved by God, a kind of predeterminism. Yet St. Augustine also defended human free will in explaining the concept of evil to the extent that some people see a contradiction between his doctrine of predestination and that of free will.[399] The fact, as St. Augustine himself intimates after defining his conception of sin, is that God compels no one to sin though He foresees those who will sin by their own will.[400] Whatever the case, that which is particularly striking in this view of history is its acceptance that there is meaning in history; history has an aim, and it pursues a certain goal.

Many writers consider this as St. Augustine's reinterpretation of Plato's explanation of the two realms—the perfect celestial kingdom

---

[397.] Cfr. AUGUSTINE, *The City of God*, book 14, section 28.
[398.] Cfr. Ibid.
[399.] Cfr. B. GERALD, *God's Decree and Man's Destiny* (London: Variorum Reprints, 1987), xii.
[400.] Cfr. AUGUSTINE, *De Libero Arbitrio*, 3, 4, 11.

and the corrupt terrestrial copy—and as one of his greatest achievements. As Christopher Dawson explains, Christian culture has always
projected a conflict between these two worlds. While the two cities
do not meet spiritually, they intermingle physically.[401] Eternity and
time readily mixed after the incarnation, and because of this, history,
at its deepest level, is informed by eternity; this explains why the
Christian view of history is not merely a belief in the direction of
history by divine Providence, as Dawson explains, but more so, "it is
a belief in the intervention by God in the life of mankind by direct
action at certain definite points in time and place."[402]

8.3.3 The Spiritual (Progressive) Version of History

This view asserts that human beings and not God's Providence
give a driving force to history. History progresses in a straight line
and, necessarily, according to the progress of the human spirit. This
view of history is also called progressive view of history. Giambattista
Vico (1668-1744), one of the exponents of this view, recognizes
God's Providence in history, but he further insinuates that the material world is formed or composed by human beings; therefore, history should not be explicated by God's will alone. Consequently,
while God is pushing at the background, human beings are at the
fore. Voltaire (1694-1778) even took the radical extreme of this view
by excluding God's active power in history. He asserted that it was
not God, but rather the people with higher education, who had
mastered science, namely, enlightened people, that conduct history.
Accordingly, in the philosophy of history, the leading question was
no longer the will of God and divine Providence, but the will of man
and human reason. The philosophy of history was later used to mean
a systematic interpretation of universal history in accordance with a
principle by which historical events and successions are unified and
directed toward an ultimate meaning.[403]

[401.] Cfr. C. DAWSON, *Dynamics of World History*, John J. MULLOY, ed., (Wilmington:
Del.: ISI Books, 2002), 315.

[402.] Ibid., 247.

[403.] Cfr. K. LOWITH, *Meaning in History*, 1.

Hegel presents history as the self-realization of the spirit, or the self-realization of the idea. According to him, reason rules the world, and world history progresses rationally. He thought that reason manipulates human beings. He calls this the *trick of reason*, a phrase that he uses to bridge the gap between the role of the absolute spirit manipulating human beings and the prominence of reason in history. Thus, his view is called spiritual idealistic view of history, or idealistic view of history. In his prediction, the end of history, that is, the rational state, where the idea of freedom would be realized, was to be fulfilled in Prussia. This did not take place, and social problems such as exploitation and human alienation instead became more severe, leading to a revolt against Hegel's philosophy of history and the appearance of historical materialism which again became another view of history.

8.3.4 Historical Materialism

This was championed by Karl Marx who asserted that material forces are the forces that drive history, a conception that is also known as the revolutionary view of history. In contrast to Hegel, who propounded a spiritual view of history and proclaimed that it is idea that drives history, Marx, on the contrary, asserted that it is material force that propels history. Thus, history occurs, thanks to the development of the productive forces, rather than the development of the spirit. As these forces move forward, they meet the old fixed structures of production, and this leads to class struggle between the ruling class—that is, the class that sought to maintain the old relations of production and the class that was the bearer of the productive forces—and sought new relations of production (ruled class).

For that reason, history emanates as class struggle that can reach its peak in revolution, especially in capitalist societies. Consequently, Communist society, which Marx presents as a kingdom of freedom without classes, is realized. The idea of God is kept aside as being distracting to the human materialistic strivings in history. Karl Marx postulated man's economic need as the basic motivating force in history. Though influenced by Hegel, his was a dialectic materialism in which all historical struggles, whether political, religious, philosophical, or ideological, are actual expressions of social class struggles; these struggles are conditioned "by the degree of the development of their economic position."[404]

Irrespective of the convictions of the historical materialists that gave birth to Communism, it is truly testified that the Communist societies that have come into being through revolution, like the Soviet Union, have no freedom; instead, they are dictatorial. Curbing freedom and even their productivity is extremely stagnant. These facts prove that the materialist conception of history is enormously erroneous. Ki-Zerbo made it clear, as seen above, that history is a lived reality; therefore, his criticism of philosophers like Hegel was not only that they had degraded the African continent but also that their approach to history was unrealistically rational. Similarly, Maritain's approach to history is based on the idea that the course of events is rooted in human activity. He repudiated any form of determinism. This served as a basis of his ardent criticism of Hegel, Marx, and Toynbee[405] even though he has some admiration for the Toynbee.

Arnold Toynbee (1889-1975) is a more contemporary historian of British origin. He is known for his view of the past as a succession of civilizations rather than political entities, and his was a panoramic outlook of history. He links up spirituality and historical progress. Thus, he always links up history with civilization. In a concrete way, alluding to ancient civilization, he intimates that in the Nile valley man had to clear jungles and drain swamps before he could plant; he had to subdue and order the wantonness and formlessness of nature before he could create civilization. The vital point, therefore, in Toynbee's analysis of civilizations is that man's great achievements stem from creative acts of the human spirit, and conversely, spiritual and psychological defects ultimately cause a civilization's decline. In his account, therefore, the essential problem confronting the modern West is not material but spiritual. If a civilization is to grow, it must

---

[404.] K. MARX, *The Eighteenth Brumaire of Louis R. Napoleon* (New York: International Press, 1986), 14.
[405.] Cfr. J. MARITAIN, *On the Philosophy of History*, 33.

move from challenge through response to further challenge.[406] This is where Toynbee, like Ki-Zerbo and Maritain, deviates from and opposes the Hegelian and other views which interpret history as a branch of science, governed by mechanical or necessary causality and rational schemata. He sees no strict metaphysical structure in the unfolding of history.

Maritain effectively cites with Toynbee on the above consideration, but he proceeds to argue further against him. According to him, Toynbee misses the mark because "he discards the possibility of having his rational inquiry assisted and complemented by any theological light and a prophetic data."[407] Accordingly, unlike Ki-Zerbo and Maritain, Toynbee seems to limit his theory of history to the terrestrial sphere. Though he claims that civilization is oriented toward religion and it is accelerated by it, he equally intimates that the climax of history, that is the raison d'être of religion is the unity of the "higher religion", that is, Mahayana Buddhism, Christianity, Islam, and Hinduism. This idea, according to Maritain, is "a rather silly prophecy from an author who has never looked for genuine prophetic data where they can be found."[408] Maritain appreciates the fact that the world may be coming more and more united. He endorses Toynbee's vision that mankind must become one family or destroy itself but rejects his conviction that the mission of religion is not defined with respect to God and revealed truth, but rather with respect to mankind and civilization itself. This implies a limitation of religion to an earthly kingdom and an attempt to ignore God's grace while overstating the necessity of nature. Man himself cannot be the supreme aim of religion, else God would be considered as irreligious, as Maritain quotes from Augustine Comte.[409]

[406.] Cfr. A. Toynbee, *A Study of History*, vol. 3 (Oxford: Oxford University Press, 1947), 128.

[407.] J. Maritain, *On the Philosophy of History*, 173.

[408.] Ibid., 175.

[409.] Cfr. Ibid., 173-176.

Conclusion

It is clear from this chapter that by proposing a comparative study in this work, we are out to examine those aspects that could be common in the thoughts of Maritain and Ki-Zerbo, hoping that as we move on in a world that seems to be growing smaller, following the reality of globalization, much could be learned from every school of thought for the well-being of the human person who is the principal subject of history.

We have realized that like Ki-Zerbo, Maritain considers history as a very important discipline that could assist us to improve on the well-being of the human person and the human society. Both thinkers were greatly influenced to pursue history as an academic project. Ki-Zerbo was greatly influenced by his father who was a direct oral source of history, as well as by the fact that throughout his studies at the Sorbonne University, Africa was given little or no attention. Contrarily, there was a lot of literature and philosophical opinions spreading in Europe at the time that downgraded Africa. In a similar manner, Maritain, challenged by the various philosophies of history in his days, was greatly influenced by the works of St. Thomas. Contrary to Ki-Zerbo, however, who concentrated on the history of a people, the African people, Maritain's motivation was like a reaction to various tenets of the philosophy of history that were, according to him, not in line with authentic humanism.

We still need to adequately elaborate the ideas of Jacques Maritain to a relevant proportion to the extent that it would justify our quasi-comparative approach.

Maritain has already been qualified and defended as an ardent Thomist who has a keen interest in history. In the following chapter, we shall be concentrating on some of the sociocultural and political perspectives that make up his definition and presentation of history, placing them vis-à-vis the ideas of Ki-Zerbo.

CHAPTER NINE

Considering the Concept of History and Its Importance in the Light of Jacques Maritain in Confrontation with the Views of Joseph Ki-Zerbo

HAVING SEEN OTHER approaches to history, including the African approach, we are now delving specifically into the thoughts of Jacques Maritain, putting them side by side those of Ki-Zerbo.

Having been challenged by various conceptions of history and with his interest in Thomism, what version of history does Maritain propose to us and how much importance does he attribute to the concept of history in general? One aspect that characterizes Maritain's conception of history or of life in general is his vouch for a philosophy that is uncompromisingly rooted in the paramount value of the human person. This is often referred to as personalism or humanism. Accordingly, history, practically speaking, does not only operate on the ambient of space and time but also has the human person as the principal agent and object.

In this chapter, therefore, after discussing Maritain's version of history and its importance, we shall also examine his conception of space and time as the ambient of history, as well as his social philosophy, since authentic history, according to him, is constructed on genuine humanism.

9.1. History as a Concept

It is of absolute importance to understand that Jacques Maritain himself asserts that "the philosophy of History has the same subject matter as history."[410] Similarly, in the words of William Sweet, "the philosophy of history is inseparable from the activity or discipline of history,"[411] which has been defined extensively in the first part of this work. Therefore, though writing with different motivations and from different perspectives, Ki-Zerbo and Maritain are working on the same platform, and this is what makes a comparative study of their ideas reasonable.

Maritain, like Ki-Zerbo, subscribes to the idea that history operates with all aspects of the human existence in space and time in which there is a double movement—in the direction of good and in the direction of evil. The good is not separated from evil; rather, according to him, they grow together simultaneously. Maritain also adapts St. Augustin's notion of free will to discuss on this, intimating that while nature in itself deals with contingency, in history, where there is a double movement in the direction of good and in the direction of evil, the free will of the human being is also of primary importance. Without downplaying the free will of man, Maritain insinuates that the world, that is, the evil people, cannot escape divine wrath. He does so by alluding to Jesus's parable about the man who sowed good seeds in his farm and the enemy came later to plant bad seeds. Both must be left to grow together, and at the end, God himself, the harvester, would be the one to separate and to destroy (Matt. 13:37-39).[412] In this case, he emphasizes the great role of God, both as the *telos* and the primary mover of history—a conviction that is also well rooted in the African version of life. These ideas certainly were not explained in this intellectual and theological manner, yet they are implied as we can discern in the African notion of history seen above. It is a conception of history which, as Ki-Zerbo also explains, is based

---

[410.] J. Maritain, *On the Philosophy of History*, 4.

[411.] W. Sweet, *The Philosophy of History, A Re-Examination* (Hampshire: Ashgate Publishing Limited, 2004), 5.

[412.] Cfr. J. Maritain, *On the Philosophy of History*, 133.

on the human person, in all his anthropological, socio-political, and religious dimensions.[413]

Maritain, in the above bearing, considers that while historical progress implies the growth of the human conscience, the natural end or goal of history is to attain a mastery over nature, to conquer autonomy, and to manifest all our potentialities in human nature. Yet the absolute or ultimate end of history is beyond history. For him, any philosophy of history that minimizes this fundamental consideration of human free will and the divine existence in the role of history is inauthentic. He equally indicates that for Christian eschatology, there will be a discontinuity between history, which is time and the final state of mankind, which will take place in a world transfigured.[414] Maritain presents this Christian conviction to avoid certain extremes as he explains as follows:

> There is an *anthropocentric* illusion, according to which man himself and man alone, that is to say, either by the power of science and human reason, or the self-movement of human history, is in charge of bringing about the Kingdom of God here below. There is the *satanocentric* illusion, according to which the world is completely abandoned to the Devil, with no kind of veritable progress and of realization of the Gospel, imperfect as it may be, to be hoped for in our social-temporal and political order—a view that is not without some impact in the Protestant world, and also in the Greek Orthodox world. And there is the *theocentric* illusion, which would make the world hic mundus, our historical world, and the social-temporal and political City, into the Kingdom of God.[415]

---

413. Cfr. J. Ki-Zerbo, *Punti Fermi Sull'Africa*, 13-15.
414. Cfr. J. Maritain, *On the Philosophy of History*, 138.
415. Ibid., 151.

The Africans, to say the least, reason in the same direction as the Thomists, avoiding the above extremes. Arguing that God is not the author of evil, they intimate that "evil comes from man's conscience... Man is not a beast to fail to see the distinction between good and evil."[416] Yet the Africans see no emergency reason to analyze their lives in the scholastic manner as Maritain is doing, following the intellectual tradition of his culture. The holistic version of life explains that for the Africans, the life that is lived concretely today and tomorrow speaks for itself even more than analysis and interpretations. It is not as if intellectualization or, rather, analysis and interpretations are not necessary. They are done mainly to accompany or recount history and not to influence people to live the life which they are already living by their enthusiastic fidelity to tradition. An evil man is treated accordingly by the traditional norms and by the ancestors.

The fact remains that as it is with Thomistic philosophy that evil is a mystery to live with and not a problem to be solved, so too is it in the African thinking. Plato, many years before, after recognizing the existential reality of evil, affirmed that "evil can never be done away with, but exists of necessity" and that "they have no place among the gods, but haunt our mortal nature and this region forever."[417] For the Africans, generally speaking, as Martin Nkafu Nkemnkia intimates, evil, as expressed in pain and suffering, is almost always given a religious interpretation; and in the understanding of vitalogy, it is interwoven in the relationship between men, the ancestors, and God though God is always considered as good. There is a cause for every suffering and this concept is often cloaked in mystery.[418]

Maritain's idea is that the good and the evil move on as history progresses, considering that the human person, though rational, has animal aspects. Yet for history to be constituted, it is the role of the rational man, with the application of the senses, as St. Thomas recommends, to gather the objective contents of intelligible data and

---

416. K. GYEKYE, *African Philosophy, an Anthology*, 470.
417. M. BURNYEAT, *The Theaetetus of Plato*, in M. J. LEVETT, trans. (Cambridge: Hackett Publishing Co. Inc., 1990), 176-177.
418. Cfr. M. N. NKEMNKIA, *African Vitalogy*, 112-116.

connections drawn from facts, facts that need to be verified and rationally analyzed.[419]

Maritain also intimates that history deals only with the singular and the concrete, that is, with the events that are contingent. History deals with individual persons and individual events in time. Historical events take place in existential, concrete, individual reality opened to interfering lines of causation.[420] The implication of this point is that the individual or the human person is the subject of history, just as individual events are. Events as such are contingent upon other things. In this esteem, Maritain does not consider history as science in the strict sense of the word since science deals with the universal and the necessary whereas history cannot afford us any explanation by universal raisons d'être. Consequently, he perceives certain dynamism in history, conceding to the idea that history is subject to interpretation since there is no raw fact. He equally detects that historical facts concretely form the basis of societal living. It is for this reason that he presents his view of history in the following declaration:

> No doubt there are no "raw" facts; an historical fact presupposes and involves as many critical and discriminating judgments, and analytical recasting, as any other "fact" does; moreover, history does not look for an impossible "coincidence" with the past; it requires choice and sorting, it interprets the past and translates it into human language, it re-composes or re-constitutes sequences of events resulting from one another, and it cannot do so without the instrumentality of a great deal of abstraction. Yet history uses all these in order to link the singular with the singular; its object as such is individual or singular. The explanation given by an historian, as histo-

---

[419.] Cfr. J. MARITAIN, *On the Philosophy of History*, 10-12.
[420.] Cfr. Ibid., 2.

rian, is an explanation of the individual by the individual—by individual circumstances, motivations, or events. The historical elucidation, being individual, participates in the potential infinity of matter; it is never finished; it never has (insofar as it is elucidation) the certainty of science. It never provides us with a raison d'être drawn from what things are in their very essence (even if it be known only through signs, as in the sciences of phenomena).[421]

In discussing the general definition or consideration of history in the introduction and in the first part of this work, we explained that history deals with facts and that it is an expression of the truth surrounding a people's perception of reality that needs interpretation and even adaptation. This is what Jacques Maritain is likewise highlighting in the above citation, giving another point of homogeneity between his ideas and those of Ki-Zerbo, who, as we saw earlier, spelt out the importance of history in the same light. In addition to this, we have also observed that Ki-Zerbo, like Maritain, also considers the importance of the individual human person and the interpretation of events in history as necessarily contingent. This explains why he castigates the extreme in which chronology is projected as a cult in the study of history.

9.2 The Importance of History

Like Ki-Zerbo, Maritain stresses the importance of history in the understanding and development of culture. He, thus, appeals, especially to the intellectuals, those who take upon themselves the assignment to investigate and write down a people's history for posterity. In this connection, Nicholas Lobkowicz, an admirer of Jacques Maritain, in a paper presented at Notre Dame in 1991, affirmed that almost everything that has gone wrong in the recent history of our

---

[421.] J. MARITAIN, *On the Philosophy of History*, 3.

culture originated in the minds of people who claimed to be investigating on history but come up with unfounded points, people who are university graduates and intellectuals.[422]

Maritain insists on a right understanding and approach to history, insinuating that the world at large can only be transformed by such a correct understanding, application, or adaptation of historical realities. However, Maritain's notion of transformation is more comprehensive. He uses this term to mean a spiritual transformation of the world, not a temporal effort to improve the world itself, which he calls idealistic nonsense. Accordingly, he insists that modern civilization needs to consciously pursue such a transformation, and this requires a total and substantial recasting and transvaluation of cultural principles. In this context, Maritain talks of "a profound transformation of the temporal order."[423]

In recognition of the above Thomistic position resounded by Maritain, Nicholas Lobkowicz also explains that culture, with due respect to the fact that it is rooted in history, should not remain static; it should be dynamic to positive changes. This is equally the position of Joseph Ki-Zerbo. Lobkowicz equally observes that this Maritain's perspective of history is to promote a re-evangelization of our culture and to create a Christian impact upon our culture today by doing almost everything that helps man to be more human, considering that the Catholic faith has much more to say about this subject.[424]

Relating to the above paragraph, a slight difference is observed between the approach of Maritain and that of Ki-Zerbo. Maritain focuses more on the need to *inculturate* (adapting ones culture to the Christian style of worship) the Christian perspective into all cultures, into the general way of living in the world, since Christianity is built on humanism. On the other hand, though Ki-Zerbo does not refuse that the African faith can learn from another culture, be it Christianity or other cultures that manifest personalistic values, he, nonetheless,

---

[422.] Cfr. N. LOBKOWICZ, "Christianity and Culture," in *Review of Politics* (1991), vol. 53/2 of spring 1991, 386-388.

[423.] J. MARITAIN, *The Peasant of the Garonne* (New York: Macmillan, 1969), 231.

[424.] Cfr. N. LOBKOWICZ, "Christianity and Culture," in *Review of Politics*, 386-388.

invites us to understand that the African culture fundamentally is humanistic and needs to be revisited firstly for the progress of the African continent and for the advantage of multiculturalism.

Any project on Africa, Ki-Zerbo insinuates, must be built on the fundamental values that Africa has, as embedded in her culture. Therefore, unlike Maritain who talks on Christian values as a new humanism to be entertained by all, Ki-Zerbo takes the nationalistic cultural foundation based on Africa as his point of departure. For him, each human person has a domestic culture which must be acknowledged as the foundation and fountain of life, without which man would be at the service of history rather than history being at the service of man. In his account, therefore, identity must come first before any other role that a person assumes in life, as he declares as follows:

> Il s'agit du problème de l'identité et du rôle à jouer dans le monde. Sans identité, nous sommes un objet de l'histoire, un instrument utilisé par les autres: un ustensile. Et l'identité, c'est le rôle assumé: c'est comme dans une pièce de théâtre où chacun est nanti d'un rôle à jouer.[425]

For this reason, he depicts history as a practical discipline that must be accompanied by action. It is this action and cultural perspective that illuminates the semblance between the two thinkers, irrespective of their different foundations—one, on the African foundation and, the other, on the Christian foundation. Talking on the necessity to get to our roots in history in order to live a better today and aspire for a better future, Maritain, in explaining the necessity

---

[425.] (This is the problem of identity and the role to play in the world. Without identity, we are an object of history, an instrument used by others, a tool. And identity is the assumed role ; it's like in a play where everyone has a role to play.) J. KI-ZERBO, À Quand L'Afrique ?, 8.

of history within the context of the philosophy of history, declares as follows:

> The philosophy of history has an impact on our action. In my opinion, many mistakes we are now making in the social and political life proceed from the fact that, while we have (let us hope) many true principles, we do not always know how to apply them intelligently. Applying them intelligently depends on a genuine philosophy of history. If we are lacking in this, we run into a great risk of applying good principles wrongly... for instance, we run the risk of slavishly imitating the past, or of thinking on the contrary, that everything in the past is finished and has to be done away with.[426]

We can now understand why both Ki-Zerbo and Maritain castigate the Hegelian thinking and every attempt to limit history only to the rational, that is, to exaggerate the role of reason in history. In Maritain's own words, "Hegel regarded himself as a kind of philosopher-God, recreating not only human history but the whole of the universe."[427] Like Ki-Zerbo who insinuates that history should be at the service of man and not the reverse, Maritain also explains that the Hegelian and Marxian temptation has made a number of our contemporaries subservient worshippers of history, so much that, to a great extent, "history has become for them the Saviour and Redeemer."[428] According to Maritain, they have embraced but a materialistic version of the world and of life. He explains further that philosophies which do not recognize the spiritual and eternal elements in man are erroneous. Conversely, whoever recognizes this spiritual and eternal element in man recognizes also the aspiration,

---

[426.] J. MARITAIN, *On the Philosophy of History*, 17-18.

[427.] Ibid., 1.

[428.] Ibid., 58.

immanent in the person, to transcend, by reason of that which is most sublime in it, the life and conditions of temporal societies. This explains why he opted for the Thomistic philosophy of history that is based on the concrete human person in all guises.[429]

As if to summarize the value or importance and purpose of history as an ideal springboard for an authentic existence, as intimated by Ki-Zerbo and Maritain, William Whitehead, as early as 1941, is known to have made the following proclamation:

> It *is* eminently desirable that we should so relate the law of Divine Providence to the story of man's experience, that we may use the result as a spiritual guide to the experiences that are to come, for that is the chief value of history, the value that comes from a spiritual counsellor and friend.[430]

The above citation that links up history, divine Providence, and the story of man's experience conditions us to bring in Kwame Nkrumah's concept of "consciencism" in the perception and representation of history, as well as in amplifying the importance of history. Nkrumah calls upon the intellectuals and those researching in this important enterprise of history, be they Africans or the Westerners, to be more alert and more conscious of facts and realities—that is, the actual experiences of the people in question rather than selfish politics. Considering that the history of a people must be based on the reality of life as lived by them, Nkrumah indicates that African history must be African history, a history of the African people, seen from reality and from their own perspectives and experience. Accordingly, he insists that African history has its own independent originality and Africa cannot be validly treated merely as the space in which Europe swelled up, and its history should not be interpreted

---

[429.] Cf. J. MARITAIN, *On the Philosophy of History*, 21-27.
[430.] W. WHITEHEAD, "The Development of History," in *Journal of Education*, vol. XIV, 170.

in terms of the interests of European merchandise and capital missionaries and administrators. Hence, he makes the following appeal:

> In the new African renaissance, we place great emphasis on the presentation of history. Our history needs to be written as the history of our society, not as the story of European adventures. African society must be treated as enjoying its own integrity; its history must be a mirror of that society, and the European contact must find its place in this history only as an African experience, even if as a crucial one. That is to say the European contact needs to be assessed and judged from the point of view of the principles animating African society, and from the point of view of the harmony and progress of this society.[431]

The implication is that history must have the face of a society, conscious that a society it made of persons. Maritain, as a typical Thomist, perceives history as based on the human person. Similar to this perception, Joseph Ki-Zerbo, after insisting on the importance of the human person in the study of history, situates genuine development, that is, a development that centers on the primary value of the human person, at the very core and as the actual target of any earnest approach to history. Equally, Jacques Maritain explains that as a prerequisite to the study of history, the historian must have "a sound philosophy of man, an integral culture, accurate appreciation for the human being's various activities and their comparative importance, a correct scale of moral, political, religious, technical and artistic values."[432] The fact that Ki-Zerbo, along the same mindset with Maritain, also presents history as "the fundamentals of civilizations, institutions, structures, techniques, and social, political, cultural and religious practices" sets a good humanistic, sociocultural and political

---

[431.] K. NKRUMAH, *Consciencism* (London: Heinemann, 1964), 63.
[432.] J. MARITAIN, *On the Philosophy of History*, 7.

platform for us to proceed more concretely with our comparative survey.

As already discussed in the previous part of our work, history can neither be conceived nor studied out of the ambient of space and time. This explains why the concept of space and time is so paramount in every culture and is often treated as a twin concept in which one often implies the other as in the African conception seen not only in the thought of Ki-Zerbo but also in the conceptions of John Mbiti and Martin Nkafu Nkemnkia whose ideas were used to buttress those of Joseph Ki-Zerbo. What says Maritain in this regard?

9.3 The Concept of Space and Time: The Platform of History

It is in line with the paramount importance of the concept of space and time in life in general and in philosophy in particular that Maritain, after devoting time to study biology in Heidelberg University, also proceeded to study the works of Max Planck, Albert Einstein (who declared space and time as relative), Louis de Broglie, Schrodinger, Werner Heisenberg, among others, who wrote on issues concerning time and space. Alongside his studies on the works of the above personalities, he attached special importance to quantum mechanics and relativity theory because they call into question the validity of certain commonsense conceptions of space and time.[433]

Our first point of interest is to study the views of Maritain, alongside those of Ki-Zerbo, about space and time within the platform of history. We already saw that Ki-Zerbo's usage of the concepts in question is linked to the conception of myth, and it also carries the idea of eternity as a subject of history. Equally, space and time for the Africans have been presented as a twin concept that embodies a history that has directionality and meaning. Ki-Zerbo appropriately intimates that for the African people, the theme of space and time often involves a significant direction in which its origins tend to be

---

[433.] Cfr. J. P. DOUGHERTY, *Jacques Maritain, an Intellectual Profile* (Washington, DC, Catholic University Press, 1984), 65.

sustained, leading to a future, an eternity. In this case, it can be briefly stated that for the Africans in general, when death comes after earthly life, one goes back to meet God, the Creator of all mankind.[434]

The Thomist follows a similar reasoning pattern as the above, depicting time as a sphere of human interaction and activities that leads to eternity and the salvation of man. Such a position is faithfully endorsed by Maritain as confirmed by the following words of Samuel L. Macey:

> Aquinas accepted a mode of existence in between time and eternity. The Christian existentialist, Jacques Maritain also followed this direction, linking time to man's salvation. The theological question as regards "time" must be posed in the context of the coming (or offer) of salvation, when man is summoned to decision, to accept salvation, in fact, in his freedom.[435]

The difference here between Ki-Zerbo and Maritain is the Christian emphasis which involves the mediation of Christ; this is totally absent in the traditional African perspective, as well as the idea of divine Providence, evil, and human free will which, though present in the African conception, do not constitute an essential focal point in Ki-Zerbo's treatment of history.

Maritain seemingly subscribes to the work of St. Augustine, *The City of God*, where the latter presents the course of history as a rivalry between two communities: the City of God and the world. However, he maintains, again with the accent of St. Augustine, that divine Providence answers that the former would triumph over the latter. In his treatment of history, therefore, one can perceive an underlying directionality. It is for this reason that scholars believe that in St. Augustine, we have the first sustained attempt to find meaning and

---

[434.] Cfr. W. F. PAGE, ed., *Encyclopaedia of African History*, 69.

[435.] S. L. MACEY, ed., *Encyclopaedia of Time*, vol. 810 (Garland: Garland Reference Library, 1994), 327.

purpose in history. St. Augustine, as Maritain affirms and endorses, perceives history as a unified, linear, purposeful process that speaks to and makes sense of the sequence or development of events in time. For this reason, Jacques Maritain refers to his work as the first great example of a philosophy of history. [436]

Maritain is very convinced that the subject matter of history is the succession of time. Time, in its singular consideration, consists of a mass of particular events. Each event is singular and unrepeatable because it is unique to a particular period, person, and circumstance. He insinuates that the formal object of the philosophy of history is the intelligible meaning derived from the unfolding of history. Therefore, time, in itself, has an inner structure, and because of this, each successive period of history has an intelligible structure. It is within this conception that he endorses the Christian-Augustinian approach as he declares as follows:

> Christianity has taught us that history has a direction; that is, it works in a determined direction. History is not an eternal return; it does not move in a circle. Time is linear, not cyclical. This truth was a crucial acquisition of human thought. St. Augustine's philosophy of history was a work of wisdom, both of theology and of philosophy. [437]

At this point, there is an apparent contradiction between the approaches of Ki-Zerbo and that of St. Augustine (endorsed by Maritain), with regard to time as linear and not cyclical. Ki-Zerbo, if we remember, had insinuated that for the Africans, time is both cyclical and linear, contrary to the present treatment of time only as linear and not cyclical. Yet we may not proclaim this as a contradiction because the cyclical system of history that is rejected above by the Thomists is not a rejection of the reality of life getting on seasonally. It is a rejection in relation to eternal recurrence as practiced in

---

[436.] Cfr. J. MARITAIN, *On the Philosophy of History*, 2.
[437.] Idem.

the Hinduism and other Eastern religions. In this connection, both the Thomists and the Africans are on the same track of reasoning. Hence, like Maritain and the Thomists in general, Ki-Zerbo does not subscribe to the cyclical perception of time in terms of eternal recurrence as in reincarnation. Rather, his use of the term *cyclical* was strictly in reference to seasonal changes, especially with the agrarian communities. The converging point, therefore, is that history revolves around the concepts of people, places, and events in time. This explains why humanism or personalism is also an important concept in the Thomistic philosophy of history.

9.4 Personalism: Jacques Maritain Versus Joseph Ki-Zerbo

Joseph Evans, Maritain's dedicated editor, detected that immediately after his conversion to Christianity, Maritain began to reflect more intently on moral and political philosophy and that he made it very clear that Christian politics, based on the dignity of the human person, is the ideal. His effort at this time, therefore, was to establish, in light of a philosophy of history and of culture, the nature of the new humanism which is still being awaited.[438] Maritain's humanism is, by and large, an appeal for an endorsement of Christian personalism in all aspects of human existence, that is, in political, cultural, and social interactions.

The sensitivity of the concept of personalism warrants us to get a bit deeper into its presentation because as we shall soon notice from Maritain's observation, there are many guises of this term though his is specifically Christian personalism, a personalism that is founded on the term person, with his individual natural dignity but which finds expression and meaning in the social context of life.

[438.] Cfr. J. MARITAIN, *Integral Humanism: Temporal and Spiritual Problems of a New Christendom* (Paris: Notre Dame University Press, 1973), v.

9.4.1 Personalism: Founded on the
Term Person as an Individual

Boethius (fifth/sixth century AD) gave a classical definition of person as "an individual substance of a rational nature" (*rationalis naturae individua substantia*). Battista Mondin, after considering the controversies surrounding the concept *man*, considers the study of man as the most complicated. While lecturing that man is the greatest enigma, he also insists that he is a human person from the moment of conception; he is a singularity, unique, and unrepeatable, a substance equal to his dignity and nobility.[439]

In formulating his definition of person, Boethius uses some concepts derived from Aristotle's *Categories*. Indeed, the concept of individual substance corresponds to what Aristotle in the *Categories* calls primary substance (*ousia prôtê*). This refers to that which is neither the predicate of a substrate nor inherent in a substrate because it is itself a substrate (*substrata*). *Substrate* translates the Greek *hypokeimenon*, which literally means "that which lies underneath," which underlies becoming, change, inasmuch as it is its subject, that is, the thing that becomes, the thing that changes and which, in changing, persists. Therefore, the firmness of Boethius's conception of the person which combines a theological origin with recourse to truly philosophical notions—such as nature, individual, substance, rationality, and the recovery of the idea of substance in various expressions of the recent analytic philosophy—seems to go beyond the analysis of language alone.[440]

According to St. Thomas, who laid the foundation for Jacques Maritain and for Thomism as a whole, the name of *person* does not belong to the rational part of the soul or to the whole soul alone. It belongs to the entire human substance, what he also calls subsis-

---

[439.] Cfr. B. Mondin, *Uomini nel Mondo (Personal, Cultura e Valori nella Societa Globalizzata)* (Bologna: Editioni Studio Domenicano, 2005), 45–50.

[440.] Cfr. E. Berti, "The Classical Notion of Person in Today's Philosophical Debate," in E. Malinavaud and M. A. Glendon, eds., *Conceptualization of the Person in Social Science* (Vatican City: Pontifical Academy of Social Science, 2002), 63-65.

tence.[441] This means that the soul as a whole as well as the whole body, and its act of existing constitutes one entire substance. He avoids separations such as the rational soul alone or the body alone. To him, therefore, a human being is always a human person and characteristics such as rational attributes, autonomous willing, consciousness, physical feelings of pleasure or pains are merely consequential and secondary or accidental actions which follow upon certain powers of the soul which themselves follow upon the *essential nature* of the human being.[442]

Battista Mondin, thus, explains St. Thomas's view on the distinction between an individual and a person that it is a logical and not a real distinction.[443] For him, they should not be taken as two realities, separate and distinct. They are the same reality with the logical difference being that the concept of person includes the intellect, liberty, and other perfections that, strictly speaking, may not be implied to the concept of individual. Yet the concept of person does not exclude the individual. It is from this perspective that Jacques Maritain surmises that "the individual is the person." Maritain identifies the individual with the material conception of the human subject and the person with the spiritual dimension. In true Thomistic fashion, human beings are not seen as mere matter or as abstract souls but as embodied souls: "Soul and matter are the two substantial co-principles of the same being, of one and the same reality, called man."[444] This is certainly why, in line with personalism, Gianfranco Basti explains that *il modo di esistere, della persona è il più degno di tutti perchè essa è ciò che esiste per se stessa e non solo in se stessa come le altre sostanza* (the mode of being of the person is the most worthy of all because it is that which exists for itself and not only in itself as the other substances).[445]

---

441. Cfr. Thomas Aquinas, *Summa Theologiae*, Ia. Q. 29, a.1, ans., ad. 2, 3, 5.

442. Cfr. Ibid., IIIa. Q19, a.1, ad.4.2127.

443. Cfr. B. Mondin, *Uomini nel Mondo*, 45-50.

444. J. Maritain, *The Person and the Common Good*, in J. J. Fitzgerald, trans. (London: Geoffrey Bles, 1948) 26.

445. G. Basti, *Filosofia Dell'Uomo* (Bologna: PDUL Edizioni Studio Domenicano, 1995), 338.

Basically, Maritain, like the other philosophers of the Thomistic school, adapted the version of Christian personalism because of the various schools of personalism that proliferated the world in the nineteenth century. According to him, some of these are not really personalistic doctrine but personalistic aspirations, considering that they center on a kind of individualistic and shallow designation of the human person. Actually, he considers such an approach as an error and also goes forth to reject the totalitarian or exclusively communal conception of society which took place by way of reaction against individualism. Accordingly, he considers it a duty to spontaneously react against both totalitarian and individualistic errors that have been incorporated as such into the society. It is in this regard that he makes the following observation and clarification:

> "Personalism"...is a reaction against two opposed errors (individualism and totalitarianism), and is inevitably a very mixed phenomenon. There is no personalistic doctrine, but there are personalistic aspirations, that at times, have nothing in common except the word person... There are personalisms that are Nietzschean in tendency and personalisms that are Proudhonian in tendency, personalisms that tend towards dictatorship and personalisms that tend towards anarchy. One of the major concerns of Thomist personalism is to avoid both these excesses.[446]

Evidently, Jacques Maritain, following the Thomistic tradition and in divergence with Ki-Zerbo, wrote extensively about the human person. His social concern for personalism is evident in his philosophy of history, his works on culture, ethics, and politics. Nevertheless, Ki-Zerbo's works also bear testimony to the African conception of humanism, summarized in self and community respect and also rooted in the fact that each human person has a divine character. He

---

[446.] J. MARITAIN, *La persona e il bene comune* (Brescia: Morcelliana Press, 1963), 8.

does not emphasize on the human person with the same intensity as Maritain. His writings, as it were, are more rooted in the reality of history (with a focus on Africa) and are spiced with his personal experiences, reflections, and suggestions. Yet it is laudable that like Maritain, Ki-Zerbo, in his works, also reflects the fervent importance that the Africans do attribute to the human person, and in this perspective, we can draw a similarity between Maritain and himself. As already mentioned in this work, the Africans do place absolute importance on each human person and shun every form of individualistic tendency that promotes egoism and exploitation. It is for this reason that Ki-Zerbo shuns the extremes of capitalism, liberalism, and other economic, political, and social theories that exploit and show a total disregard to the dignity of the human person.[447]

9.4.2 Personalism in Its Social Dimension

The concept of a person in the sense of Thomistic personalism cannot be complete without the social or community dimension. Naturally, a person requires membership in a society by virtue, both of its dignity and its needs. Maritain explains that, principally, it is through society that a person accomplishes his full human dignity. By relating to, learning from, and loving one another, we accomplish our full humanity. This point is very fundamental in the thought of Jacques Maritain, and it is on it that he constructs his thesis on the common good.

So inbuilt in Maritain's mind is the conviction that individuals exist for the sake of the common good and the common good exists for the sake of persons. Yet he explains further that persons and the common good are not in conflict; the relationship is one "of reciprocal subordination and mutual implication."[448] In the manner of Aristotle and Aquinas, Maritain explains that human beings are social animals and that social life is indispensable, not only for the fulfillment of material needs but also for growth and education, an

---

[447.] Cfr. J. KI-ZERBO, *À Quand L'Afrique?*, 11-12.
[448.] J. MARITAIN, *The Person and the Common Good*, 46.

education that goes with the cultivation of virtues. In this regard, he defines that common good as "the good *human* life of the multitude, of a multitude of persons; it is their communion in good living."[449] Battista Mondin is among the many Thomists who appreciate Maritain's ideas. After referring to other philosophers with a relational focus like Martin Buber, he explains, in the light of Maritain, that "a person realizes his full personality in coexisting, pro-life, proximity, solidarity and participation."[450]

Equally, the African conception of community living is an expression of the Thomistic personalism, if not a little more. This again provides a striking semblance between the thought of Maritain and that of Ki-Zerbo. With concrete reference to the words of Ki-Zerbo, Federico Lenzeriani affirms that in the African conception of the human person, what we can term African personalism flows from the fact that everyone has his or her dignity which is only actualized in a group. The most significant of those values were respect and protection for the individual within the family and the greater social community, deference for elders as holders of knowledge and wisdom, commitment and responsibility to other persons, the family, and the community. There is solidarity with other human beings and tolerance for differences, reciprocity in labor issues, and consultation for government.[451]

Personalism is certainly the most practical focus of any reflection on history considering that philosophy of history is a practical discipline that deals not only with facts but with values. Facts and virtue must be put together if one were to decipher an authentic way forward for humanity. This is a constitutive part of our research. We cannot get to facts and values without getting into the debt of a

---

[449.] J. MARITAIN, *The Rights of Man and Natural Law*, D. ANSON, trans. (San Francisco: Ignatius Press, 1986), 89-90.

[450.] B. MONDIN, *Uomini nel Mondo (Personal, Cultura e Valori nella Societa Globalizzata)*, 58-59.

[451.] Cfr. F. LENZERINI, *The Culturalization of Human Rights Law* (Oxford: Oxford University Press, 2004), 39.

society's system of living. Thus, we affirm the following expression of Ernest Ruch and Kemafor C. Anyanwu:

> In order to understand a system or a world view, one must be part of it; one must live it from within, not merely as an object which satisfies one's intellectual curiosity, but as a mode of thinking and being with which one's whole personality sympathizes.[452]

Regarding the above citation, we are appreciating the efforts of Ki-Zerbo for enlightening us with firsthand knowledge of the authentic African system of life that serves history. Similarly, Maritain writes with an inside knowledge of the Thomistic philosophy. He also has a deep acquaintance with his domestic society, the Western society to which he belongs.

It is also a privilege to me having lived with the African and Western world, experiencing the respective concrete realities that our authors are talking about.

Having lived in the Western world, where, in most cases, one does not know one's next-door-neighbor, where a person finds it strange to be greeted on the street (not to talk of to be visited) by another person he or she does not know, where smiles are mostly superficial, if not for business purposes, where a corpse lying on the street or the sound of wailing or jubilation in a nearby house means nothing to the passersby, and where the stranger is given little or no chance to fit spontaneously into a given system of life, one cannot help boosting Maritain to continue resounding the values of Christian humanism.

On the other hand, having lived the traditional African system where one can get into the home of a neighbor unannounced and is served with a good meal, where the sound of joy or sorrow in a

---

452. E. A. Ruch and K. C. Anyanwu, *African Philosophy, an Introduction to the Main Philosophical Trends in Contemporary Africa* (Rome: Catholic Book Agency, 1984), 1.

particular compound is enough invitation for all to be part of the event in question, and where strangers are well received even before their initial or final destinations are asked,[453] one cannot help joining one's voice to that of Ki-Zerbo in recommending that such a history be taught, adapted, and, if need be, integrated into the sustenance of what Maritain calls Christian humanism.

9.4.3 Maritain's Cultural Approach to History: What Similarity with Ki-Zerbo

Joseph Ki-Zerbo uses the term *culture* as the identity of a people regarding their basic or most fundamental characteristics or worldview. His specification was on African cultural identity. Though Maritain also uses the term *culture* as identifying a way of life; that is, as part and parcel of a people's approach to reality as visible in history, he does not preoccupy himself much with any particular continent or with a geographic group of people. Rather, he examines the cultural trends prominent in the world today, regretting that most have been polluted and have become barely remnants of genuineness and, as a consequence, can only be looked upon as nothing but shadows of what may authentically be termed *culture* as designed by God.

Shifting from all mediocre standards of culture sponsored by all sorts of philosophical trends in the modern and postmodern era, Maritain thinks that it is time to get a new dynamic understanding of culture that would bring us back to the original culture that is rooted in the history of creation. To this effect, he calls for a new vision of culture that has to do with a new humanism which would begin in time or in the present history but would only gain its fullness in the kingdom of God. For that reason, Maritain always discusses culture in the context of humanism which, consequently, blends with to the concept of personalism. In his reasoning, what is normally termed *civilization* is, in fact, culture, and it should essentially conduct man to be more truly human and to manifest his original greatness by enabling him to partake of everything in nature and in history that

---

[453.] Cfr. J. Ki-ZERBO, *À Quand L'Afrique?*, 50-51.

is capable of enriching him as a human person.[454] Thus, he gives the following definition to civilization or culture:

> By culture or civilization is meant the common good, terrestrial or temporal, of the human being... Culture is the unfolding of life properly human, comprising not only the material development necessary and sufficient to permit us to lead a right life here (i.e., the material common good), but also, and above all, the moral development, the development of speculative activities and of practical activities (artistic and ethical) which deserve to be properly called human development (i.e., the spiritual common good).[455]

Evidently, Maritain draws his inspiration from the Thomistic-Aristotelian consideration of culture in the society as practical science, which is in the realm of human action and which is also linked to the freedom of the will. Maritain is fully convinced that this Thomistic outlook on culture is the model and it needs the widest exposure; every society, every community, every philosophy, and every world-view needs to be informed by it. Reflecting on the reality in the world today, it is his conviction that every philosophy must be *corrected* and even *transformed* by Thomism. In this regard, he commissions Thomism also to leave the field of school debates and go out into the fields to propagate its ideals of a culture that breeds humanism and personalism.[456]

At this point, we notice a succinct contrast with personalism in the African context. While Jacques Maritain appeals for Thomistic personalism to grow from the formal classrooms and the books into the streets and the fields, Ki-Zerbo explains that African personalism

---

[454] Cfr. J. MARITAIN, *The Twilight of Civilization* (New York: Sheed & Ward, 1943), viii.

[455] J. MARITAIN, *Some Reflections on Culture and Liberty* (Chicago: Chicago University Press, 1933), 2.

[456] Cfr. J. MARITAIN, *St. Thomas Aquinas* (New York: Macmillan, 1958), 19.

has always existed in the streets and in the fields; it might never even have existed in the books and in the classrooms. In fact, every African and every person who has been to or lived in Africa would conform that the ideals of personalism, as explained in this work, is in the field and more of it needs to be taken to the books for the enrichment of the world.

Thomistic philosophy, as Maritain intimates, is progressive, and assimilative by its very nature, it is a missionary philosophy and it is relevant for all times. Thus, St. Thomas "is in all the fullness of the term, the apostle of modern times," and he "wrote not for the thirteenth century but for our time... He is the most 'present' of all thinkers."[457] Consequently, Maritain appeals that we must be open to the teachings of St. Thomas, his Christian philosophy in the social and cultural order, under our "new historical sky" that leads us to a brighter future, because St. Thomas is always a "contemporary author."[458]

Robert Brennan, as if to authenticate the views of St. Thomas as presented and endorsed by Maritain, cites many sections in his article "The Thomistic Concept of Culture" in which St. Thomas spoke of "the perfection of man's nature in its specifically human and social aspects." In his articulation, that which distinguishes St. Thomas's philosophy of culture and makes it so precious and relevant in the contemporary society, is his emphasis on the transcendental context of the human person in history, contrary to the present-day anti-humanistic, fatalistic, and materialistic ideologies which are unable to see any hope outside the present order of existence.[459]

Maritain, in this connection, perceives his new humanism as a true religion that is from God since it avoids every tendency to narrow it to a specific context, society, or environment. For him, this religion should not only be a choice and a recommendation for humanity; effectively, it should be an imperative for all, considering that it does not only rank above all other cultures and philosophies,

---

[457.] Ibid., 76.

[458.] Cfr. J. MARITAIN, *Some Reflections on Culture and Liberty*, 1.

[459.] Cfr. R. BRENNAN, "The Thomistic Concept of Culture," in *The Thomist*, vol. 5, (1943), 112-23.

but it also unites all and seeks to refine human history which is progressive. Accordingly, he inscribes thus:

> True religion…is not of man or of the world or a civilization or a culture…it is of God. It transcends every civilization and every culture. It is the supreme beneficent and animating principle of all civilizations and cultures, while in itself independent of them all, free, universal, strictly universal, and catholic.[460]

The inference so far is that Maritain's emphasis is on a culture that seeks to transform the world, that aims at a spiritual transformation that transcends the temporal efforts toward material progress which he calls idealistic nonsense. He believes that the mission of Christian philosophy is not only to attain a proper understanding of transformation but to pursue it with consciousness and conviction, considering that modern civilization needs a total and substantial recasting, as well as a transvaluation of cultural principles. This for him is an agenda that should persist throughout our temporary existence.[461]

In his philosophy of history, Maritain subscribes to the view of St. Augustine that the world (and its history) has a certain ambiguity considering that it is in the domain *at once* of man, of God, and of the devil. It belongs to God by right of creation, to the devil by right of conquest, and to Christ by right of victory over the conqueror. He, therefore, considers it the duty of the Christian in the world to challenge the devil in his domain and to extract it from him. The success, Maritain assures, will only be in part as long as time endures.[462] Since the world, strictly speaking, is not theirs, the duty of the Christian "is always only a question of *helping* the world to resolve its problems,

---

[460.] J. MARITAIN, "Religion and Culture," in C. DAWSON and T. F. BURNS, eds., *Essays in Order*, (New York: Sheed & Ward, 1940), 9-12.
[461.] Cfr. J. MARITAIN, *Integral Humanism*, 207.
[462.] Cfr. J. MARITAIN, *The Peasant of the Garonne*, 47.

not resolving them for it."[463] Nevertheless, he calls on the Christian not to isolate and separate his temporal mission from his spiritual vocation. His temporal mission requires him, with his culture of humanism, to enter as deeply as possible into the agonies, the conflicts, and the earthly social and political problems of his age.[464]

Summarily, Maritain considers that this aspiration designed for the Christians toward the humanization of the world can be realized only if saints (men and women striving for holiness at every moment of their daily lives), live with the consciousness of the cross in their hearts—the cross that symbolizes redemptive suffering. With the good things of the world made by God to be enjoyed and the assignment to identify with suffering by practicing redemptive love, Maritain creatively identifies the struggle between self-indulgence and self-denial as the greatest struggle of our age. In this connection, therefore, while the society needs philosophers and thinkers to discover the true and genuine ends of human life, it also needs saints even more to direct mankind to its true historical finality.[465]

The major similarity between the African notion of culture as presented and the Thomistic notion that Maritain has explicated in great detail is that the true theory of history that has to be redemptive can only be adequately understood and applied if we were to reconsider the paramount value of culture, a culture that grows and is adapted to the true values of life. While Ki-Zerbo notices this in the traditional African culture, which is essentially person-centered, Maritain perceives it in Christian personalism or humanism, which, for him, is that genuine Christian culture articulated in Thomism.

In the light of Maritain, Ki-Zerbo applauds the value of personalism or humanism as implied in the African concept of *Ubuntu* which we saw earlier in this work. While making reference to the value of peace and brotherliness as expressed in Thomism and in the Bible, he affirms that "*Ubuntu* puo essere lo strumento piu performativo di questo compito cruciale, ma deve costituire l'obiettivo e il

---

[463.] J. MARITAIN, *Some Reflections on Culture and Liberty*, 35-37.
[464.] Cfr. Idem.
[465.] Cfr. J. MARITAIN, *Integral Humanism*, 73.

senso della pace."[466] Within the background of the African culture that emphasizes the value of the human person as Maritain does, we are also confirming that Kenneth Kaunda, an African traditionalist and former president of Zambia, already confirmed the existence of real humanism among his people and, consequently, among the African people as Martin Nkafu explains below:

> Kaunda considered himself a humanist even though he had never read humanistic works. He defined himself as a humanist on the bases of his beliefs in his people and their capacity and, above all, that one day they will reach perfection, and by perfection did not mean the absence of sin.[467]

Like Maritain, Ki-Zerbo criticizes the excesses of capitalism, insinuating that it leads to a kind of *Darwinism*, and he equally regrets that "Auparavant, le capitalisme fonctionnait selon le slogan bien connu: 'le client est roi' Aujourd'hui, il n'y a presque plus cette référence; le système fonctionne, presque uniquement, pour le compte des échanges."[468]

When Maritain preaches the necessity of spreading humanism in the new civilization or culture, he is equally advocating for a refined form of globalization or mondialization, not the idea of one group or people imposing its culture on others. In the same reasoning, Ki-Zerbo observes with dismay the difference today between the "globalizers" and the globalized in which the former makes the decisions, imposing their culture on the "globalized," who appear as powerless onlookers or passive receptors, treated as sheer pages in a drama being staged. According to him, Africa is losing in this process. He, therefore, insinuates, in the light of Maritain, that glo-

---

[466.] (*Ubuntu* can be the most performative tool of this crucial task, but it must be the goal and the sense of peace.) J. KI-ZERBO, *Punti Fermi sull'Africa*, 146.

[467.] M. N. NKEMNKIA, *African Vitalogy*, 62.

[468.] (Previously, capitalism was operating according to the well-known slogan: "The customer is king." Today, there is almost no reference; the system works, almost exclusively, for trade.) J. KI-ZERBO, *À Quand Afrique?*, 22.

balization would only be authentic if it is done not with any form of imposition or superiority-inferiority attitude but within the ambient of true values that lead to the progress of the human person.[469]

From our discussions so far, one may infer that the Thomistic ideas advocated by Maritain as a new culture or evangelization, to a greater extent, is not a novelty in the African traditional setup. The only outstanding uniqueness is the introduction of the person of Christ, the Second Person of the Blessed Trinity. Indeed, it is because of this flagrant resemblance between the African mode of thinking and acting and the humanism of Maritain that William Kluback explains the admiration that the African thinker and poet, Léopold Sédar Senghor, had for Jacques Maritain as we read thus:

> Nothing brought Senghor closer to Maritain than the rejection of materialism. The poet found in the philosopher's thought an attempt to discover the interrelationship between man and God, between nature and grace. A separation made by the intellect and its natural skepticism was not acceptable to the poet who from his African tradition had always known how intimate and conscious was the divine presence in nature... Maritain was dedicated to reason and to grace, to the divine and the human, to creation and the creator. Senghor was introduced to a philosophy which found a place for every human activity...[470]

9.4.4 The State and Governance

Like Ki-Zerbo, Maritain's conception of a state and of governance revolves around the importance of the human person, his right to belong to the society and to participate fully in the common good.

[469.] Cfr. J. KI-ZERBO, *Punti Fermi sull'Africa*, 245-267.
[470.] W. KLUBACK, *Léopold Sédar Senghor, from Politics to Poetry*, 107-108.

His emphasis is that each person does not only bear in himself the semblance of God the Creator but is, in himself, the very image of God. This, for him, is the mystery of our nature as he proclaims the following:

> It is to this mystery of our nature that religious thought points when it says that the human person is the image of God; the worth of the person, his liberty, his rights, arise from the order of naturally sacred things which bear upon them the imprint of the Father of Being and which have in him the goal of their movement. A person possesses absolute dignity because he is in direct relationship with the Absolute, in which alone, he can find his complete fulfilment.[471]

Consequently, he posits justice, equality, freedom, or liberty and human right as core values or as necessary components of authentic humanism, insisting that it is within this framework that law is situated so that societal life in any given society is well regulated for the good of all. To ensure these core values in the society, Maritain intimates, should be the aspiration of any state or government; in fact, it should be the primary reason for which the state exists as he states:

> On the one hand, the primary reason for which men united in political society need the state, is the order of justice. On the other hand, social justice is the crucial need of modern societies. As a result, the primary duty of the modern state is the enforcement of social justice.[472]

[471.] J. MARITAIN, *The Rights of Man and Natural Law*, Doris ANSON, trans. (San Francisco: Ignatius Press, 1986), 89-90.

[472.] J. MARITAIN, *Man and the State* (Chicago: University of Chicago Press, 1951), 20.

As examples to the above social necessities, Maritain mentions the "right to just wages, work, relief, unemployment insurances, sick benefits and social security."[473]

We had already discussed the spiritual perspective of Maritain's conception of the human person. He realizes with deep regret that in various Western political philosophies, from anarchism to democracy to socialism to communism, the perception of man has always been limited to the material point of view rather than the spiritual; that much is being said about political theorists and economic theories, about production and distribution of wealth, and about the exercise of power, but little or nothing is being discussed about love and about God. He identifies the two extremes of anarchism: libertarianism that abides to the absolute freedom of the individual as its ultimate end and communism that seeks absolute equality for all in the group as its absolute end; yet he regrets that neither of them seems to care much about what we do with our freedom or our equality once we theoretically have them.[474]

Conscious of the various forms of government as experienced in the world, Maritain seems to have vouched for a kind of controlled socialism as expressed in pure capitalism that is based essentially on the voices, the choices, and, above all, the temporal and transcendental values of the people. He was, therefore, a strong exponent of what he calls a democratic faith. Democracy, in his version, represents "the highest terrestrial achievement of which the rational animal is capable here below."[475] Such a democracy, for him, must be based on law and values, and for it to triumph, the people must be adequately educated in a way that they are well sustained and nurtured by the democratic faith. This faith that he also considers a secular faith certainly does not come out robotically in a people. They must be educated or taught from their youth. This is where he situates the importance of education in any democratic society.[476]

[473.] J. MARITAIN, *The Rights of Man and Natural Law*, 113-114.
[474.] Cfr. J. W. COOPER, *The Theology of Freedom: The Legacy of Jacques Maritain and Reinhold Niebuhr* (Mercer: Mercer University Press, 1985), 15-17.
[475.] J. MARITAIN, *Man and the State*, 59.
[476.] Cfr. Idem.

However, Maritain also explains that the endorsement of the democratic faith does not mean the endorsement of a particular form of government. For him, any form of government could be fine, inasmuch as it gives room for an efficient lifestyle, a lifestyle that respects Christian humanism as in the democratic faith. Therefore, "whatever the political regime may be, monarchical, aristocratic, or democratic, democratic philosophy appears as the only political philosophy."[477]

Maritain also accepts that there have been many a number of states that have proudly described themselves as democratic, but in more cases than not, these have been democracies of the individual and not of the person, which is to say that they have borne the heavy stamp of bourgeois liberalism. He calls them false democracies and insists that it is through a sound philosophy of the person that the genuine democracy founded on the vital principles of humanism and, at the same time, a new Christian civilization can be rediscovered. Such a genuine democracy, he insists, must have a Theo-centric inspiration.[478]

As we studiously follow up the perspectives of Jacques Maritain, alongside those of Ki-Zerbo, that which captures our attention at this stage is the importance placed on education by our two authors. On a very similar note, both exceedingly recommend education as a sine qua non condition for genuine development. They seem to have noticed that in the contemporary society, many philosophical or political voices abound, which seem to have derailed man from true personalism or humanism. Hence, only with a radical educational system can such an awareness and reclamation be gotten so that mankind can realize the necessity of brotherly or sisterly love as the simple primary benevolent impulse in man, embedded into him from creation.

More specifically, the political government that is Theo-centric or that is based on a democratic faith with individual and community happiness seems to be the recommendation of Jacques Maritain.

[477.] J. MARITAIN, *Man and the State*, 129.
[478.] Cfr. J. MARITAIN, *Scholasticism and Politics*, M. J. ADLER, trans. (Indianapolis: Liberty Funds Inc., 2011), 84-86.

Similarly, it has been justified in this work that human and community interests are at the very core of the African traditional system. However, Ki-Zerbo reminds us that the African traditional government was a kind of a feudal system, with chiefs ruling their people who were subjects to them. Yet these chiefs and their cabinets knew fully well that upon their authority was vested the duty to restore peace and to ensure that community values were respected, and in most circumstances, this awareness requested them to use the democratic system.[479] This was probably the same idea that stimulated Maritain to make the following recommendation concerning any model political leader:

> Practically, it is normal that the word authority should imply power, and that the word power should imply authority. In so far as it has power, authority descends into the physical order; in so far as it has authority, power is raised to the moral and legal order. To separate power and authority is to separate force and justice. Nevertheless, what is of absolutely primary importance is authority. To "gain" authority is important for him who wants to act on the community. To possess or acquire authority, the right to be followed by the minds and by the wills of other men (and consequently the right to exercise power), is more important still.[480]

In fact, like Maritain, Ki-Zerbo also sees much sense in democracy, if it respects the ideals that it stands for, but regrets that Africa was not well prepared for democracy, that it was wrongly initiated in Africa.[481] In the same manner like Maritain, he indicates that the human person is a special creature of God; therefore, to be a human

[479.] Cfr. J. Ki-Zerbo, À Quand L'Afrique?, 96-97.
[480.] J. Maritain, Scholasticism and Politics, 93.
[481.] Cfr. J. Ki-Zerbo, À Quand L'Afrique?, 77-79.

being is a vocation. Consequently, every form of government or law should aim at ensuring the well-being of the community which implies the well-being of the human person who is to be recognized as exceptionally precious.[482] According to Maritain, every political system must be under the rule of law. He distinguishes four types of law: the eternal law, the natural law, the common law, and the positive law; and he goes on to discuss the interrelatedness of these four types of laws, identifying the eternal and the natural law as the bases.

Maritain, in a Thomistic style, defines the eternal law (divine law) as the law that is directly revealed to us by God and goes on to consider the natural law as self-evident law, law that is universal and invariable, dealing with "'the rights and duties' which follow (necessarily) from the first principle, prompting us that good is to be done and evil avoided."[483] He intimates that this law is not founded on human nature, but rather, it is rooted in divine reason and in a transcendent order, that is, in the eternal law. It is *written into* human nature by God. Therefore, the natural law acquires its obligatory character only because of its relation to the eternal law.[484] The common law, or *droit des gens*, is, for him, an extension of the natural law to the situations of life in society, and thus, it is preoccupied with human beings as social beings (e.g., as citizens or as members of families). Finally, he perceives the positive law as the organization of rules and regulations in the way that they ensure general order within a society. Thus, it must vary from one state to another and must be constructed on human practical reason. Yet natural law stands as the foundation; thus, when a positive law acts against the natural law, it is, strictly speaking, not a law. Evidently, it is in virtue of their relation to natural law that they "have the force of law and impose themselves on conscience."[485]

[482.] Cfr. Ibid., 210-214.
[483.] J. MARITAIN, *Man and the State*, 97-98.
[484.] Cfr. Idem.
[485.] Cfr. J. MARITAIN, *Les droits de l'homme* (Paris: Maison Française, 1942), 90-91.

9.4.5 Arts and the Transmission of History

In the previous part of this work, we realized that for the Africans, art, in all forms, including music and poetry, is produced not only for mere aesthetics or entertainment but also mostly as a medium of driving through a message, that is, as an instrument of history. Every work of art has a message to convey, and here lies the liaison between arts and history. Though Ki-Zerbo goes much deeper into the concept of arts or aesthetic, Jacques Maritain, in his thinking, is on the same rails with him and the general African convictions in this regard. After recounting many great events in history that are immortalized in arts, he explains the intelligence of the artists, saying that the artists have a particular virtue to link man with nature in the course of history. This is the idea that he passes across when he inscribes as follows:

> Ces lieux de la terre sont tout imprégnés de l'intelligence et de l'effort humains. C'est à travers l'histoire que s'accomplit l'union de l'homme et de la nature; et dès lors la nature rayonne de signes et signifiance qui font s'épanouir sa beauté.[486]

Therefore, in the work of arts, the creative self, Maritain writes, "dies to itself in order to live in (its) work."[487] The difference made by Maritain is that he gets more involved in art as an aesthetic discipline or, rather, he gets into the scholarly aspects of art. His wife, Raïssa Maritain, was equally an artist and she also wrote widely on this subject. In a scholastic manner, Maritain makes the following

---

[486.] (The things or places of the earth are all imbued with human intelligence and effort. It is through history that the union of man and nature is accomplished; and from then on, nature shines with signs and meanings that make her beauty blossom.) J. MARITAIN, *L'institution Créatrice dans l'Art et dans la Poésie* (Paris: Desclée de Brouwer, 1966), 6.

[487.] J. MARITAIN, *Creative Intuition in Art and Poetry* (New York: Pantheon Books, 1953), 144.

clarification concerning arts and poetry, a clarification that is often taken for granted by many. He writes the following:

> Art and poetry cannot do without one another. Yet the two words are far from being synonymous. By Art, I mean the creative or producing, work-making activity of the human mind. By Poetry I mean, not the particular art which consists in writing verses, but a process both more general and more primary: that intercommunication between the inner being of things and the inner being of the human Self which is a kind of divination (as was realized in ancient times; the Latin *Vates* was both a poet and a diviner). Poetry, in this sense, is the secret life of each and all of the arts.[488]

It is, therefore, a distinctive feature in Maritain's philosophy, following the thoughts of Aristotle and Aquinas, to discuss art as a virtue of the practical intellect that aims at *making*; art presupposes knowledge, so conjoined to reality and the self that it can be likened to the appetitive harmony of the virtuous person with the good of virtue. As a characteristic of the practical intellect, therefore, art is not a speculative or a theoretical activity; it aims not just at knowing, but at doing. Finally, Maritain writes that the *making* at which art aims is something that is demanded by the end of the activity itself, not the particular interest of the artist.[489] Thus, he considers that what distinguishes the fine arts from the work of artisans is that the fine arts are primarily concerned with beauty; that is, that which upon being seen, pleases.[490] It pleases because it reveals something deeper, something more profound in value, something analogous to deeper reality; it reveals history.

[488.] J. MARITAIN, *Man and the State*, 97-98.
[489.] Cfr. J. MARITAIN, *Arts and Scholasticism*, 13-23.
[490.] J. MARITAIN, *Creative Intuition*, 160.

In the world of academics, any study of arts or aesthetics is hardly complete without reference to the German thinker, Alexander Gottlieb Boumgarten (1714-1762), who is often considered as the father of aesthetics, irrespective of some criticisms that are often imputed onto him. It is generally considered that Boumgarten, in the mid-eighteenth century, did not only coin the name aesthetics but was also the first to advocate aesthetics as a new and distinct discipline in philosophy, being the first to lecture on it in 1742.[491] Boumgarten highlighted *good, truth*, and *beauty* as a trinity concept in the study and application of classical aesthetics, insinuating that "in order to improve reasoning, aesthetics must aid logic."[492] Accordingly, Alexander Boumgarten affirms, by way of definition, that "aesthetics (the theory of the liberal arts, the logic of the lower capacities of cognition *gnoseologia inferior*, the art of thinking beautifully, the art of the *analogon rationis*) is the science of sensible cognition (*Aesthetica*, §1)."[493]

Fundamentally, Jacques Maritain's theory of art or aesthetics is tailored along the lines of classical aesthetics. Yet his deep Thomistic-theological insight makes his handling of this discipline unique as his ideas of some concepts in aesthetics run counter to some of the principal trends in aesthetics and art since the eighteenth century. Maritain insists, however, that his view of the place of beauty in art was more consistent with the nature of artistic activity. He accepts that a work of art is an end in itself but adds that the general end of art is beauty. Thus, since art is a virtue that aims at making, to be an artist requires aiming at making beautiful things.[494] That which is beautiful, however, must be appealing to ethics and must satisfy the

---

[491.] Cfr. K. HAMMERMEISTER, *The German Aesthetic Tradition* (Cambridge: Cambridge University Press, 2002), 6.

[492.] Ibid., 7.

[493.] Idem.

[494.] Cfr. J. MARITAIN, *Art and Scholasticism*, 33.

human person in all his transcendental qualification as he explains thus:

> The beautiful is that which gives joy, not every joy, but the joy of knowing; not the joy proper to the act of knowing, but a joy which goes above and beyond that act because of the object known. If a thing exalts and delights the soul by the very fact that it has been given to its intuition, it is good to apprehend, it is beautiful.[495]

It is within the context of the above presentation that beauty and art, in the perception of Maritain, have a connection to the spiritual and spiritual experience.[496] Consequently, art as a creative activity is ultimately dependent upon and ordained to the Creator. Artistic activity is analogous to the divine free and creative activity and this bears the highest natural resemblance to God's activity; therefore, it has a relation to the divine and to the transcendental of goodness, truth, and unity. Hence, the inspiration of the artist is animated by a certain freedom, not freedom as a license to do whatever one chooses, but freedom in all its forms as an ultimate subject to truth and honesty in the work of the artist.[497] This is why Maritain remarks that the artist gives testimony to the freedom of the spirit, considering that art brings to man a vision of reality beyond reality, an experience of the secret and even sacred meaning of things, an obscure insight into the universe, without which men could neither live morally.[498] Whenever the meaning of a thing is deciphered or diagnosed in any way, history comes into play.

Logically, this section of our discussion leads us to the conclusion that Maritain's idea of art, like that of the Africans, does not only reflect beauty for the sake of beauty; it does not only point to a deeper significance that touches on history but, above all, has a

---

[495.] Ibid., 36.
[496.] Cfr. J. MARITAIN, *Creative Intuition*, p. 178.
[497.] Cfr. J. MARITAIN, *Art and Scholasticism*, 4.
[498.] Cfr. J. MARITAIN, *The Responsibility of Artist* (New York: Gordian Press, 1960), 85.

sacred character that reveals the unity between nature and the divine, between man and God.

Such a sacred character of art cannot be conceived and interpreted without a necessary recourse to history as a concept and as an instrument of culture and vice versa. This explains why Maritain frowns at artists such as Rimbaud, Baudelaire, Valéry, and Mallarmé, for whom "the biblical world was never alive. It had no place in them. Its blood never flowed through their being, and the text never became part of their spirit. These men belonged to the secular world, dominated by the power of reason."[499]

It was revealed in the first part of our work that the African thinker, Léopold Sédar Senghor, shines out as an epitome of African poetry. Irrespective of his Western education, his poems are evidently spiced by the typical African gray matter. His admiration for Maritain, as quoted in the publication of William Kluback, would make an astonishing synthesis between the African and the Thomistic approach to arts, as we read the following:

> Senghor found deep kinship with Maritain, similar to the companionship he found with Claudel, Teilhard, and Mounier. Senghor sought a philosophy and a theory of the arts that preserved the sanctity of the divine and the uniqueness of man. Nothing was so precious to him than poetic creativity, but even the creativity could seek only to approach the divine, never to be the divine. More often, men forget this distinction and seek to find in themselves the divine and they envy God... Senghor believed that in Maritain's thought and, in particular, in his book *Integral Humanism*, he has found the humanism that he longed for. But apart from this title which Senghor found appeal-

---

[499.] W. KLUBACK, *Léopold Sédar Senghor, From Politics to Poetry*, 106.

ing, it was Maritain's writings on art and poetry,
which revealed the essence of humanism.[500]

Conclusion

We have realized in this section that Maritain's approach to history bears much semblance to the approach of Ki-Zerbo. Both of
them perceive history as a practical discipline dealing with concrete
sociocultural and political events operating within the confines of
space and time, with evil as a natural accompaniment, which appears
to be a mystery to live with. However, unlike Ki-Zerbo who concentrated in presenting the real history of Africa and the way the
Africans conceive, preserve, and transmit their history, Maritain
wrote from the perspective of the philosophy of history which, of
course, as already seen in this work, equally has its foundation essentially on the normal conception of history.

The implication this far is that Christian humanism which,
as we must have observed, is also implied in the traditional African
identity, is far from being a reality in the world today because of a
certain deficiency in many people, concerning the very concept and
reality of history. Thus, the opinion of Maritain, as well as that of
Ki-Zerbo, which we also share, is that this generation is pregnant
with certain nonchalance to history, with a certain lack of interest or
certain unresponsiveness to the objective sociocultural and religious
values that history, as a concept, has to offer for the stability of a people. It is a generation that has come to be qualified as a postmodern
generation, and our observation this far is that there appears to be a
tension between the focus that Maritain as well as Ki-Zerbo give to
history and culture and the current trends in postmodernism concerning these concepts. It is this tension that sets the stage for our
next and final chapter.

[500.] Ibid., 97-98.

CHAPTER TEN

The African and Chritstian-Thomistic Conceptions of History: Challenges and Prospectives in a Postmodern Era

THIS CLOSING CHAPTER of our work reiterates the cry or the appeal of Maritain and that of Ki-Zerbo, situating it in another historical epoch which scholars call postmodern, that is, the present epoch in which we live. The rudimentary questions we ask ourselves are, why is the present-day society described as postmodern and what are some of its distinctive elements? How concretely does postmodernism pose a challenge to history or the humanistic call of Maritain and Ki-Zerbo, and what suggestions do we add to what they have given in this work, with the intention of making human history more valuable to be lived and to transmit? These questions constitute the final problematic of this work.

10.1 Toward an Understanding of the Society of Today as Postmodern

Postmodernism is a complicated term or set of ideas. It only emerged as an area of academic study in the mid-1980s. Postmodernism is hard to define because it is a concept that appears in a wide variety of disciplines or areas of study, including art, architecture, music, film, literature, sociology, communications, fashion, and technology. It is hard to locate it temporally or historically because it is not clear exactly when postmodernism begins. Thus, it is always better and easier to begin thinking about it by thinking about modernism, the movement from which postmodernism seems to have grown or emerged. In this connection, Jean Francois Lyotard, one of the key exponents of postmodernism, intimates that "Il postmoderno fa parte del moderno" (postmodernism forms part of modernism).[501]

Etymologically, postmodernism is derived from the combination of *pos'* (after) and *modo* (just now). With attributes which can be traced through the history of modern thought but which take present shape after the Second World War, postmodernism describes our current knowledge with regard to authority, culture, progress, universalization, rationalization, systematization, and consistent criteria for the evolution of knowledge claims. As such, postmodernity involves a radical questioning of the grounds upon which knowledge claims are made and is thereby linked to a sense of liberation from limiting earlier practices. Therefore, following the implication of the terminology of deconstruction (a concept which we already saw in the first part of this work), propounded by one of the most distinguished exponents of postmodernism, Jacques Derrida, there is no absolute truth. As expressed by Paul Karl Feyerabend, "the only absolute truth is that there are no absolute truths."[502] Postmodernism, therefore, defies history, and it gives birth to new approaches to cultural studies, feminist studies, women studies, gay and lesbian studies, and post-colonial theories. Postmodernity is always connected to post-structuralism.[503]

According to Jean-François Lyotard, postmodernism has an outright criticism about metanarratives, presenting metanarratives as general beliefs or systems, including world religions, political ideol-

---

[501.] J. F. LYOTARD, *Il Postmoderno Spiegato ai Bambini* (Milano: Giangiacomo Feltrinelli Editore, 1987), 21.

[502.] P. K. FEYERABEND, *Nonsense on Stilts, How to Tell Science from Bunk* (Chicago: University of Chicago Press, 2010), 253.

[503.] Cfr. V. E. TAYLOR and C. E. WINQUIST, *Encyclopedia of Postmodenism* (London: Routledge Taylor and Francis Group, 2001), 304.

ogies such as socialism or liberalism and even science and reason. In his accent, the present does not need metanarratives because, in an era of global media in which we continuously learn new things about the beliefs and lifestyles of other peoples, we cannot adequately consider one lifestyle or one belief system as the *true one*. This argument consequently contributes to the declining significance of culture and religion and, consequently, of history.[504]

The absence of objective truths and values and the rejection of metanarratives, therefore, stand as one of the foremost characteristics of postmodernism. This also exposes the rebellious attitude of postmodernism to the concept of history. While it is observed that the moderate group of postmodern thinkers encourages historians to take the irrational in the past more seriously, to pay more attention to ideas, beliefs, and culture as influences in their own right, and to emancipate themselves from any approach that stifles and subjects the historian himself or the human persons in general into a straitjacket of socio-science and socioeconomic determinism, the radical group, as we shall soon see, has a total disregard for any kind of objectivity or credibility that may be attributed to history. Even though the entire postmodern philosophy is shrouded in a definition crisis even among its exponents, Stephen Best and Douglas Kellner, while positing postmodernism as a challenging theory, attempted to make a distinction between the moderate and the radical postmodernists as follows:

> Moderate Postmodern theorists like Lyotard (sometimes), Foucault, Laclau, Mouffe, Harvey, Rorty, and others combine modern discourses and interpret the postmodern primarily as a modality of the modern rather than as its radical other. They do not usually carry out extreme attacks on modern theory or make extravagant claims for a major historical rupture, but instead, simply use certain versions of postmodern the-

---

[504.] Cfr. J. LYOTARD, *La Condition Postmoderne* Paris: Les Editions de Minuit, 1979), 7.

ories for specific tasks... Yet in some ways, the more extreme versions of postmodern theory and practice are more interesting than the qualified, in the sense that they more radically challenge existing theories, practices and realities. One of the virtues of strong postmodern theory is that it forces us to rethink our basic presuppositions, methods, and modes of practice. Indeed, it is precisely the putting into question of modern discourses, the development of novel perspectives, and the rethinking of theory, culture and practices that make the postmodern turn an exciting and challenging one.[505]

It is also evident that phenomenology is the maternity of postmodernism. As the 1960s began in France, the traditional claims of philosophy were represented by phenomenology and the perennial positivistic convictions, challenged by structuralism. After Maurice Merleau-Ponty, the major issue seemed to be that of bringing together the subject-centered standpoint of phenomenology, with the objectivist stance of scientific structuralism. However, the new generation of thinkers, led by Michel Foucauld and Jacques Derrida, took the radical extreme and questioned the ideal of ultimate knowledge that defined not only phenomenology and structuralism but also the very enterprise of philosophy.[506] Consequently, he insists on the priority of difference over the subject, implying that the subject, too, cannot be assumed to be a unitary whole without difference but, rather, must, in turn, itself be deconstructed. In his work, *Of Grammatology*, Derrida makes it clear that his deconstruction of the claims of objectivity goes hand in glove with the deconstruction of

---

[505.] S. BEST and D. KELLNER, *The Postmodern Turn* (New York: Guilford Press, 1997), 25-26.

[506.] Cfr. D. MORAN, ed., *The Routledge Companion to Twentieth Century Philosophy* (London: Routledge Tailor & Francis Group, 2008), 834.

subjectivity because just as claims to objective truth are a narrative that must be dispelled, so, too, is subjectivity a myth.[507]

Following the discussions so far, it is difficult then to decipher, most fundamentally, therefore, what really matters for the postmodern thinkers. No doubt the moral philosopher Alain Finkielkraut satirises the postmodern activists in the following remark: "No transcendent or traditional authority and not even a plain majoritarian one, can shape the preferences of your postmodern man or regulate his behaviour."[508] We can now understand why, as James Richard Mensch observes, because of the hermeneutical or interpretative controversies generated in his works, Nietzsche is considered as the father of postmodernism. "As a spiritual father of postmodernism, his appeal is to our period's discomfort with foundational, 'metaphysical' thinking. He affirms its disquiet with talks of essence."[509] This justifies the assertion that the abandoning of any claim to a foundationalist metaphysics is to cross the line from the modern to the postmodern.[510] Hence, it is inferred that

> If the modern period, beginning with Descartes, sought in the subject a source of certainty, opposite track, rather than taking the self as a foundation, it has taken it as the founded, as dependent on the accident which situates consciousness in the world. The same holds for unity of the subject. Modernity, in its search for a single foundation, held the subject to be an indissoluble unity. Postmodernism takes its lead from Nietzsche who "deconstructs" the subject.[511]

[507.] Cfr. J. DERRIDA, *Of Grammatology* (Maryland: John Hopkins University Press, 1997), 16.

[508.] A. FINKIELKRAUT, *The Undoing of Thought* (London: Claridge Press, 1988), 116.

[509.] J. R. MENSCH, *After Modernity, Husserlian Reflections on a Philosophical Tradition* (New York: State University of New York Press, 1996), 191.

[510.] Cfr. Ibid., 204.

[511.] Ibid., 205.

Putting the self as the founded gives rise to another character-istic of postmodernism which is called secular humanism. It is in this connection that a relationship is seen between Marxism, fascism, nihilism, and postmodernism. Secular humanism strips the human person of all transcendental consciousness, depicting him as the cen-ter of events within which he is the primordial determinant figure. It engulfs "the will to power," moral relativism, relative truth, and the replacement of the traditional religion and moral values. These are fundamental planks of postmodernism.[512]

There is no doubt, however, that ethics comes into play in post-modernism, yet it still remains ethics that is void of an objective transcendental point of reference—ethics based on the consensus of the persons in a particular society as explained by Jürgen Habermas, one of the exponents of postmodern thinking. Habermas calls this communicative action. Communicative action, he intimates, is an action based upon a deliberative process, where two or more individ-uals interact and coordinate their actions based upon agreed upon interpretations of the situation.[513] Such is a kind of a democratic process that goes even to ethics to the extent that every decision to be taken, whether ethical or otherwise, has to ultimately come back to citizens to determine the directions to which they wish to collectively engage themselves.[514]

At the same level of thought with Habermas, Paul Fereyabend sees no relevance of authority over truths and methods. For him, it is mere vote and the ability for one person or a group of persons to

---

[512.] Cfr. B. A. PROCTOR *A Definition and Critique of Postmodernism* (Chicago: Xulon Press, 2012), 57.

[513.] Cfr. J. HABERMAS, *Theory of Communicative Action*, vol. 1, *Reason and the Rationalization of Society*, T. MCCARTHY, trans. (Boston: Boston Beacon Press, 1984), 86.

[514.] Cfr. J. HABERMAS, *L'Ethique de la Discussion et la Question de la Vérité*, P. SAVIDAN, ed. (Paris: Bernars Grasset, 2009), 54.

convince the people at a certain point in time. This can be clearly deduced from his book against method as expressed below:

> It is the *vote* of *everyone concerned* that decides fundamental issues such as the teaching methods used, or the truth of basic beliefs such as the theory of evolution, or the quantum theory, and not the authority of big-shots hiding behind a non-existent methodology. There is no need to fear that such a way of arranging society will lead to undesirable results. Science itself uses the method of ballot, discussion, vote, though without a clear grasp of its mechanism, and in a heavily-biased way. But the rationality of our beliefs will certainly be considerably increased.[515]

Another outstanding characteristic of the postmodernism society is the importance and power of the mass media and popular culture. They both seem to govern and shape other forms of social relationship and the way people define themselves and the world at large. Connected to this is the idea that in the postmodern condition, it is more difficult to distinguish the economy from popular culture because both lay emphasis on style at the expense of substance. It is an era of consumerism, implying that what we buy is not necessarily determined by necessity but is increasingly influenced by popular culture. Therefore, the central role played by culture as such in the society has been neutralized and the very important distinction between culture and society has ceased to exist. This observation is affirmed by Angela McRobbie in the following citation:

> Cultural studies started life as a radical political project, establishing the cultural centrality of everyday life and of popular culture. In a postmodern world where old certainties are under-

---

[515.] P. FEYERABEND, *Against Method* (London: Verso, 1975), 309.

mined and identities fragmented, the way forward for those working with popular culture has
become less clear. In contrast to more pessimistic
readings of the possibilities of postmodernity,
Postmodernism and Popular Culture engage
with postmodernity as a space for social change
and political transformation.[516]

The collapse of the distinction between art and popular culture
is also another way of identifying postmodernism. If deconstruction
is accepted as a postmodern trend of thought, then it follows that,
for postmodernism, anything can be turned into a joke. If the style
takes preference over the content of a work of arts (that is supposed
to have a historical or symbolic value), then it becomes more difficult
to maintain a significant distinction between art and popular culture.
Another way of looking at this is that art becomes progressively integrated into the economy, both because it is used to attract people to
consume through its advertising role and because, in its own right, it
has become a commercial good.

Flowing from the collapse of the distinction between arts and the
popular culture is the concept of the saturated culture which is well
expressed by Jean Baudrillard. In his account, the new postmodern
world is bombarded with information-rich images at every moment
and the consequence is the collapse of any distinction between what
is real and what is not. He is convinced that we now live in a world of
simulacra, and he goes on to define simulacra as "copies of an original
which never existed,"[517] implying that in the world, the image of an
event has replaced direct experience. Therefore, a society apparently
saturated with media messages, information, and meaning implode
into meaningless noise—pure effect without content or meaning.
Thus, according to Baudrillard, entropy is implicated in the very
structure of contemporary culture, which, saturated to the limit, has

516. A. McRobbie, *Postmodernism and Popular Culture* (New York: Taylor & Francis
e-Library, 2005), 1.
517. J. Baudrillard, *Selected Writings*, in M. Poster, ed. (Stanford: Stanford
University Press, 1988), 253.

brought with it the death of art. Accordingly, as Kellner Douglas puts it, citing Baudrillard, "information is directly destructive of meaning and signification, or neutralizes it…information dissolves meaning and the social into a sort of nebulous state, leading not at all to a surfeit of innovation but to the very contrary, to total entropy."[518]

From every consideration, therefore, postmodernism possess a radical challenge to history and culture, especially as implied by Ki-Zerbo and Maritain. Our present endeavor is to systematize these challenges and attempt a way forward.

10.2 Postmodernism: A Venomous Challenge to Joseph Ki-Zerbo and Jacques Maritain

If we have come to talk about postmodernism as a challenge to the concept of history for both Joseph Ki-Zerbo and Jacques Maritain, it is because this system of thought falls within the confines of history and it also has its own outlook of history. The truncated version of postmodernism presented above gives us a vision of the society in which we live today, a society that both Ki-Zerbo and Maritain are addressing and serving with a new version of history that must be rooted in humanism.

Everybody seems to be convinced today that the contemporary society is undergoing tremendous changes, alongside the reality of globalization. We should avoid falling into any inducement of thinking that Maritain and Ki-Zerbo are resistant to change. Rather, they too acknowledge the reality and the inevitability of change, yet they have a perception of change common to both of them and which, at the same time, seems to be confronted by the postmodern thinking. While Maritain proposes that societal changes should move along the lines of Christian humanism, Ki-Zerbo, in the African context, talks of fidelity to history and to traditional African values, which, of course, generally speaking, are concretely on the same lines with what Maritain prescribes as Christian humanism.

[518.] K. Douglas. *Jean Baudrillard: From Marxism to Poststructuralism* (London: Blackwell, 1994), 68.

Ki-Zerbo's recommendation is also expressed by Ben Madu Cisse, who, while affirming that our ancestors had real humanistic and ethical values that must be kept for a healthy society, also advocates for change and adaptation as in the following presentation:

> We must make it clear that changes are through fidelity to our ancestors. Their way of life was in tune with their environment, but today, the environment is different. To be faithful to our ancestors means to adjust to our own environment as they did to theirs, not simply to cling to old ways for no reason.[519]

Notwithstanding the above appeal for the respect of tradition, authority, transcendental, and Christian humanism as implied in the concept of history, postmodernism comes in with a radically different version of reality. To summarize the postmodern thinking already expressed, Bruce A. Proctor draws our attention to the fact that in his book, *Secular Humanism*, Homer Duncan lists five tenets of postmodern secular humanism as given by John Whitehead and John Conlan thus: "(1) the irrelevance of deities, (2) the supremacy of reason, (3) the inevitability of progress, (4) science as the guide to progress, and (5) the autonomy and centrality of man."[520] It is in this connection that we perceive in postmodernism nothing less than a venomous challenge to Maritain and Ki-Zerbo. We shall briefly discuss these challenges on two broad perspectives: history in itself, as a primordial challenge, as well as humanism, considering that the human person is the principal subject of history.

[519.] B. M. CISSE, *Africa: From Independence to Tomorrow* (New York: Atheneum, 1970), 120.

[520.] B. A. PROCTOR, *A Definition and Critique of Postmodernism*, 58.

10.2.1 The Postmodern Conception of History: A Primordial Challenge

This work has been essentially founded on the concept of history, a concept that has all along been projected as an essential pillar on which a real humane society could be constructed—be it a better African society as intimated by Ki-Zerbo or the world at large as Jacques Maritain explains. According to Ki-Zerbo and Jacques Maritain, the world should be educated to imbibe such conceptions of history that recognize the valuable traditional elements in human history and, at the same time, focus on the transcendental values of the human person as being at the very core of history. Yet it becomes provocatively challenging to realize that in the same world, there is a trend of thought that devalues history, shrouding it with relativism and uncertainty to the extent that metanarratives that are very much used in the Bible, in oral tradition, and in other means or transmitting history, is being ridiculed, all in the name of postmodern thinking. While the less radical postmodernists advocate the view that history is what we make of it, the more radical postmodernists see no ultimate purpose in history. Like their spiritual father, Nietzsche, they are instead sponsoring a *nihilist* perspective of history.

Gilles Deleuze and Felix Guattari, for example, are also said to be exemplary representatives of postmodern positions in their thoroughgoing efforts to dismantle modern beliefs in unity, hierarchy, identity, foundations, subjectivity, and representation. Even though Gilles Deleuze does not provide a theory of history, his thought has instead a profound anti-historicist development and we can infer that his strong critical view on historicism requires new concepts suited for subverting historicism and for defining a new philosophy of the historical process, a philosophy of becoming, which projects an ontological opposition between being and becoming. He insists that since the predominant temporality of being is that of the present (with past and future as its deficient modes), the pure becoming—without being means that one should sidestep the present—it never actually occurs; it is "always forthcoming and already past."[521] In his account, therefore, what history grasps in an event is the way it is actualized in particular circumstances; the event's becoming is beyond the scope of history. Becoming is not part of history; history amounts only to the set of preconditions, however recent, that one leaves behind in order to *become*, that is, to create something new.[522]

In the same manner of undermining historicism as a theory of history that centers on every actual happening in the past and the structures built on them, as well as the belief that one can actually learn from the past, is another radical perspective of history propagated by another postmodern thinker, Alun Munslow. Munslow questions the traditional view of history, disputing the idea that truths of history could be objective or authentic as he declares:

> The past is not discovered or found. It is created
> and represented by the historian as a text, which
> in turn is consumed by the reader... The idea of
> the truth being rediscovered in the evidence is a
> nineteenth-century modernist conception and it
> has no place in contemporary writing about the
> past.[523]

Considering his research in 1987, David Cannadine observes that there is a decline at the universities concerning the fidelity that people have for history. Accordingly, he declares that "the belief that history provides an education, that it helps us understand ourselves in time, or even that it explains something of how the present world came into being, has all but vanished."[524] Ten years later, as if to confirm the point posited by David Cannadine that the very concept of

---

[521.] G. DELEUZE, *The Logic of Sense* (New York: Columbia University Press, 1990), 80.

[522.] Cf. G. DELEUZE, *Negotiationi* (New York: Columbia University Press, 1995), 170-171.

[523.] A. MUNSLOW, *Deconstructing History* (London: Routledge, 1997), 178.

[524.] D. CANNADINE, *British History: Past, Present and Future? Past and Present*, vol. 116, 180.

history is under serious challenges, Richard Evans attributed all to the radical postmodern trend of thought, decrying that

> such has been the power and influence of the postmodern critique of history that growing numbers of historians themselves are abandoning the search for truth, the belief in objectivity, and the quest for a scientific approach to the past. No wonder so many historians are worried about the future of their discipline.[525]

This challenge is more severe because once history is threatened, cultural identity in which lies the very identity of a people is also threatened. This again explains why postmodernism negatively reacts to the question of essence and instead introduces cultural complexities, sponsoring a system of cultural fragmentation and the collapse of symbolic hierarchies. It is in this regard that Mike Featherstone conceives of an integral connection between globalization and postmodernism. With the awareness of such a confused atmosphere of cultural intertwines, Featherstone makes it more complex for Ki-Zerbo and Maritain as he sees no middle ground for a common culture. Instead, he recommends that "if there is a global culture it would be better to conceive it not as a common culture, but as a field in which differences, power struggle and cultural prestige contests are played out."[526]

The fact, as Ki-Zerbo perceives, is that in the entire process of globalization or mondialization, Africa stands out as the scapegoat because it is looked upon as a dumping ground. In his observation, globalization is a projection of the extravagances of capitalism which dehumanizes. In the economic sense, it sponsors the drastic shift from the original historical fact that pointed at "the customer as the king." Worse of all, Africa, though it is evolving like every other continent,

---

[525.] R. EVANS, *In Defence of History* (London: Granta, 1997), 4.

[526.] M. FEATHERSTONE, *Undoing Culture, Globalization, Postmodernism and Identity* (London: SAGA Publications Ltd., 2000), 10.

has no significant role in the process of globalization but appears as an innocent or a passive receptor of the Western style, and this, for him, is where the real crisis and challenge to world history and the history and identity of Africa in particular rest.[527] Erroneously, the exponents of globalization take it to be universal civilization whereas for most Africans, it is seen as a threat. Samuel Huntington explains better as we read the following:

> The concept of a universal civilization is a distinctive product of Western civilization... At the end of the twentieth century the concept of universal civilization helps justify Western cultural dominance of other societies to ape Western practices and institutions. Universalism is the ideology of the West for confrontation with the non-Western cultures... The non-West sees as Western what the West sees as universal. What Westerners herald as benign global integration, such as the proliferation of worldwide media, non-Westerners denounce as nefarious western imperialism. To the extent that non-Westerners see the world as one, they see it as a threat.[528]

In the same line of thought, Malcolm Payne takes us another step further, perceiving an interconnection not only between postmodernism and globalization but also between postmodernism, globalization, and post-colonialism, explaining how destructive this combination has been to history and to the current social trends. Malcolm Payne begins by describing globalization as the trend in social changes in economic, political, and cultural relationship between peoples across the world. Then he defines post-colonialism as power relationships in which Western cultural influences dominate other cultures as globalization increases. Finally, he presents post-

---

[527.] Cfr. J. KI-ZERBO, *À Quand L'Afrique?*, 22-25.
[528.] S. P. HUNTINGTON, *The Clash of Civilizations and the Remaking of World Order*, 66.

modernism as the changes in knowledge and understanding about people and societies.[529] With these concepts clarified, Payne does not only discuss their intricacies and their interconnectedness but he also pronounces his observation that they are all leading mankind to the same chaotic direction, as we read the following:

> Globalization, Post-colonialism and Postmodernism offer both conflicting and connected understanding of current social trends. They conflict because an important focus of globalization is the dominance of economic power achieved through industrial, scientific and cultural influence by the western party, through post-colonization. Postmodernism on the other hand, rejects the dominance of rational, technical knowledge in understanding the world which underlies industrial societies. Therefore, it questions the influence of economic and technical form of exploitation... Yet the most important connection between globalization, post-colonialism and postmodernism is that they all represent interlocking social trends in the same direction... Another important aspect that connects these three concepts is the way in which identity is being eroded by social trends, so that people are more insecure and uncertain of themselves.[530]

The common platform of all this is multiculturalism, which implies interculturalism, a reality which cannot be doubted.

The primordial challenge, however, lies in the question as to whether interculturalism has come to pull people away from their

---

[529.] Cfr. M. PAYNE and G. A. ASKELAND, *Globalization and International Social Work, Postmodern Change and Challenge* (Hampshire: Ashgate Publishing Ltd., 2008), 9.

[530.] M. PAYNE and G. A. ASKELAND, *Globalization and International Social Work, Postmodern Change and Challenge*, 9-10.

original culture, to downplay or to outrightly refute the idea of culture as a defined way of life or to propose a new culture. Yet logically speaking, an amalgamation of culture is, by implication, annihilation of culture, and by gambling with culture, we are gambling with history. This is, to a lesser or greater extent, the position of the postmodernists. It is also from this perspective that Wim Van Binsbergen situates the theoretical problems raised by globalization. Making reference to Ram Adhar Mall, the leading intercultural philosopher in Germany and his attempts toward establishing an intercultural hermeneutics, Wim Van Binsbergen confirms our problematic that globalization is not only a central problem in present-day history but it also poses a difficulty in expressing a people's identity and also for a productive intercultural philosophy.[531]

The antennae of postmodernism are manifestly widespread in the world today because of the irresistible reality of globalization. While Maritain, Ki-Zerbo and other personalities with a traditional and classical mind believe that a people's identity, as founded on their culture, irrespective of multiculturalism and the need to integrate with others, is still planted on some fundamental and even metaphysical truths that form a solid part of their identity, postmodern activists like Habermas still insist that history, just like culture, can be radically adjusted and even transformed if it is the people's collective intention. Thus, historical foundations of culture and even ethical truths, for them, are not necessary. This, of course, forms a major challenge to the very concept of history as we have been developing in this work because, in postmodernism, priority seems to be given to the rational over the historical and the ethical.

Habermas, for example, endorses Hegel's dialectic theory though he rejects the Hegelian idea of mechanical causality which, as implied in his philosophy of history, gives the impression that virtue would ultimately be conquered by the way of the world.[532] He appreciates Hegel's idea that the notion of rationality is embedded in the

---

[531.] Cfr. W. V. BINSBERGEN, *Intercultural Encounters: African and Anthropological Lessons towards a Philosophy of Interculturalit*, 38.

[532.] Cfr. G. W. F. HEGEL, *The Phenomenology of the Spirit*, 228-235.

emerging structures of culture, and in this, one could also find better forms of ethical interactions that would ultimately overcome the limits of the past.[533] This implies that culture moves from a traditional base in a consensual collective endeavor to forms which are rationalized by commodification and led by individuals with interests, which are separated from the purposes of the cultural producers. A communicative action for Habermas, therefore, serves to transmit and renew cultural knowledge in a process of achieving mutual understanding. It then coordinates actions toward social integration and solidarity. In this regard, he infers that communicative action is the process through which people form their identities.[534]

A further challenge comes in when we reason from the observation of Habermas that society is integrated socially, both through the actions of its members and systemically by the requirements of the economic/hierarchical/oppressive system, in a way that tends to interpenetrate and overwhelm autonomous action orientations. According to him, such a structuring gives rise to a social theory which is connected to the question of values. He, therefore, insinuates that the theory of values possesses a historic dimension in the sense that it presents an interpretation of the dynamic or the scheme of evolutions of social and cultural modernity. It is within this context that he discusses modernization and the pragmatic theory of language which is implied in communicative rationality.[535] Communicative action, therefore, is an action based upon this deliberative process, where two or more individuals interact and coordinate their actions based upon agreed upon interpretations of the situation.[536]

Due to the above observation, it can be inferred that Habermas fits into the ambient of postmodernism because the members of the postmodern family do not only express conflicting views but are also interested in barely overlapping literature, education matters such as arts, communication media, history, politics, ethics, theology, and

---

[533.] Cfr. J. HABERMAS, *On the Pragmatics of Communication*, M. COOK, ed. (Cambridge: MIT Press, 1998), 248-250.

[534.] Cfr. J. HABERMAS, *Theory of Communicative Action*, vol. 1, 140.

[535.] Cfr. J. HABERMAS, *L'Ethique de la Discussion et la Question de la Vérité*, 43.

[536.] Cfr J. HABERMAS, *Theory of Communicative Action*, vol. 1, 86.

cosmology.[537] As Laurence Choone observes, "it is arguable that postmodernism by itself, needs not lead in any particular political direction. Its usefulness lies in criticizing any established authority."[538]

10.2.2 Postmodern Humanism: A Deviation from Ki-Zerbo and Maritain

The reality of the world today in the midst of the challenging and conflicting *trinitarian* domains of globalization, post-colonialism, and postmodernism, as explained above, gives us the more reason to appreciate Samuel Phillips Huntington's thesis, even from its very title, *The Clash of Civilization and the Remaking of World Order*. Situating history at the very core of the human society which develops in a form commonly known as civilization, Huntington, as if parroting Ki-Zerbo and Maritain, sees the need to make a new order, with due consciousness that the clash in civilization is an inescapable reality. Yet that which is clear to him, under the inspiration of the book, *Civilization Under Stress* by Adda Bozeman, is that

> human history is the history of civilizations. It is impossible to think of the development of humanity in any other terms... Civilization and culture both refer to the overall way of life of a people and a civilization is a culture writ large. They both involve the values, norms, institutions and modes of thinking to which successive generations in a given society have attached primary importance.[539]

Irrespective of the value of history in the human society as stated above, the difficulty in the whole concept of history and civiliza-

---

[537.] Cfr. L. E. CAHOONE, ed., *From Modernism to Postmodernism: An Anthology* (Oxford: Blackwell Publishers, 1999), 1.

[538.] Ibid., 19.

[539.] S. P. HUNTINGTON, *The Clash of Civilization and the Remaking of World Order* (New York: Simon & Schuster Paperbacks, 2003), 41-42.

tion emanates because every school of thought, as seen in this work, seems to be playing the drum of humanism. To be more precise, after going through the humanism of Maritain and that of the Africans and while appreciating the synthesis displayed above in the concept of history and civilization posited by Huntington, it can be evidently conjectured that postmodernism is an unpretentious challenge to the Maritain-Ki-Zerbo's version of humanism.

Heidegger, with his stress on the distinct human person in his concept of the *Da-sein*, seems to give a different direction to humanism. Jacques Derrida, focusing particularly on Heidegger's "Letter," embarks on the special relationship between man and being such that through the capacity for "ek-sistence" man is the distinct shepherd of being.[540] This is a subjective approach to humanism which is without any affinity to the transcendental qualities of the human person and to the transcendental divine being that is implied in such an approach. We already saw Maritain's criticism of this conception which was also described above as secular humanism.

Maritain makes it very clear that both the liberal society, which highlights fundamentally the material well-being of the individual, and totalitarianism, which places at its very core the well-being of the group, have missed the true portrait of the human person. They are, in effect, at the periphery, touching instead only the shadow of personality and failing to address the dignity, that essential aspect which is so unique and which ordains the human person to God. Consequently, by not recognizing the ordination of the human person to God, they erroneously ordain him to the state so that all that is left of the individual is his relationship with the state. This, for Maritain, is where the so-called modern or postmodern concept of development appears as a mirage of what development should actually imply. He, therefore, regrets that the world of today, within our own eyes, in the name of development and civilization, is tending toward barbarianism at an accelerated speed.[541]

[540.] Cfr. B. LETTER and M. ROSEN, eds., *The Oxford Handbook of Contemporary Philosophy* (Oxford: Oxford University Press, 2007), 702-703.
[541.] Cfr. J. MARITAIN, *Scholasticism and Politics*, 11-12.

Moving in the same direction with Maritain, Homer Duncan endorses that secular humanism is basically anti-God and it is a pro-deistic humanism. Looking at the etymological direction, Homer explains that the word *secular* stems from the Latin word *saeculum*, primarily pertaining to this world, the present life, or to temporal things. Accordingly, secular humanism's avowed aim is to replace the theism with humanism, and it is not to be confused with Christian humanism.[542] Marxism also tilts toward this direction and is an unfortunate reality that such Marxist atheistic and materialistic conception of the human person and of history as a whole are still much present in postmodernism.[543] In such a case, one can perceive the difficulties of penetrating the same society with the theocentric and communitarian package embedded in the humanism that is exhibited in the worldview of Maritain and Ki-Zerbo.

Jacques Maritain, we must also indicate, advocates for the autonomy of the secular, that is, a kind of secularization of the human person. Yet his secularism has no resemblance to the postmodern crusade of secularization. Maritain's secular approach is that which is absolutely informed by Christian principles. Thus, he talks of a secular Christianity, implying a Christianity that is lived in the world, thereby using the terminology *secular* not as the opposite but as the inferior complement of the sacred.[544] That the two territories can be antagonistically separated goes without saying, but it will be the work of Christians to ensure their harmonious conjunction. Therefore, Christian philosophy of history must bring the spiritual into the dominion of the temporal.[545] This, of course, cannot be done without enduring the challenges of the postmodern world. What practical proposals can we, thus, present, having reviewed some of the major challenges predicted in a word that is evidently entertaining the postmodern thoughts?

---

[542] Cfr. H. Duncan and B. A. Proctor, *A Definition and Critique of Postmodernism*, 57.

[543] Cfr. Ibid., 62.

[544] Cfr. J. Maritain, *On the Philosophy of History*, 111.

[545] Cfr. J. Maritain, *Integral Humanism*, 291-308.

10.3 What Prospective for the World?

Our undertaking now is to present in a truncated manner what may be considered as our own contribution or recommendations. Irrespective of the distractions posed by the postmodern thinkers, we shall continue to insist on the importance of history. Firstly, we endorse the teleological aspect of history—that history has a certain directionality, moving toward a certain goal. While philosophers in the like of Hegel perceive this goal as the limit which the spirit has set for himself, Senghor, just like Ki-Zerbo and Maritain, identifies God as that omega point in history. This is equally our conviction. Secondly, we invite all to recognize the paramount importance of space and time as the terrain of history. Even the idealist, Hegel, endorses this in his own manner. He considers nature is the display of the idea in space while history is the manifestation of the spirit in time. Thirdly, the importance of the active human person must be acknowledged as the very core of history. Even before postmodern deviation from the sacredness of human values, intellectuals like Hegel had sponsored a kind of fatalism in history that takes away the determination of the person, replacing it with a necessary, influential, and uncontrollable spirit, especially in terms of social progression. According to the Hegelian metaphysics, whatever takes place does so "necessarily, even God necessarily manifests himself."[546] Ben Kimpel sees this as a contradiction to real human situation. In the following words, he seems to satirize Hegel's perspective of history as he inscribes the following:

> This is the same type of contradiction of which the mystic Jeffries was aware. As a monist, he believed that what takes place will take place, irrespective of what men do. Yet, since "good" men do good deeds, in doing so, they "nobly waste

---

[546.] G. W. F. HEGEL, *The Philosophy of History*, 81.

their time." According to Hegel, the process of progressive realization of freedom is inevitable.[547]

Ours, however, under the influence of Joseph Ki-Zerbo and Jacques Maritain, is the appeal for mankind to reinstate the indispensable role of the conscious person in shaping history. William Kluback, in this regard, has this to say:

> We are enamored with the ideas, intellect, the will, and the marvels that abide in creativity. They lift us above the daily course of events. They show us the powers of change, of transfiguration and of transformation. We bring this about in a world which we create in thinking. The marvel of the person fascinates us because it liberates us from the individual. The person is the embodiment, the microcosm of intellectual, moral, and volitional activities which reflect the unique substance of man's place in the universe.[548]

As if to harmonize the concept of humanism in the African and the Christian perspectives, William Klauback, in the last chapter of his book dedicated to the African thinker Léopold Sedar Senghor, and the Christian philosopher Jacques Maritain summarizes the importance of the active human person in history in the following words:

> Man is part of a creation that is not his own. He is subject to the divine powers that have been in him from eternity; he stands under God's laws, as its servant and enunciator. Man's reason... makes him aware of his limits and his possibilities... More often, men forget this distinction

---

[547.] B. KIMPEL, *A Vital Guide to Hegel's Philosophy of History*, 19.
[548.] W. KLUBACK, *Léopold Sédar Senghor, from Politics to Poetry*, 81.

and seek to find in themselves the divinity. They envy God. Philosophic life is the attempt to find the capacities of reason, knowing that there are limits which we do not determine but which are determined for us. In these limits lie the reality of the unknown and unknowable, a reality that we know belongs to all realms of being. We know God in our reason, but we know that this reason is finite, and through this finiteness, God's ways are shown to men.[549]

The above citation posits a challenge to the postmodern thinker who wants to operate without limits. In a more concrete manner, we have two suggestions to propound as a way forward for the world, taking into consideration that globalization and postmodernism are encountered by all even though at various levels and in various intensities.

10.3.1 A Refocus on History and Education with Emphasis on African History

The necessity of educating the people on the importance of history as a discipline that highlights their identity has been well belabored in this work. While focusing on history, we must be aware of the divine imprint in each human person as articulated in the story of creation. The study of history, therefore, is an ideal way for one to understand one's origin, and as it is often said, a person who does not know from where he or she is coming does not know either where he or she is going to. Consequently, if a person does not know where he is heading to, he cannot authentically manage his present situation, including his own very identity amid other creatures (animate and inanimate) in the world. Maritain insists on a very intellectual approach this reality following his conviction that "a time will come when people will give up in practical existence those values

---

[549.] W. KLUBACK, *Léopold Sédar Senghor, From Politics to Poetry*, 97-98.

about which they no longer have any intellectual conviction."[550] This explains why he recommends education as a means of adding value to our lives and our history. We are firmly suggesting, however, that such emphasis on education be geared more to the youths, thanks to the fact that they are the adults or, rather, the society of tomorrow.

With more emphasis on the paramount role of history in restoring an almost broken society, Simon Schama, a historian and a history consultant, reasons in the same direction as we do when he declares that the focus on education today should be more on our children, the youths, as the defenders of societal values of tomorrow. He, therefore, shares our conviction that the only way to secure the world and redeem it from the emptiness and vanities such as those propagated in postmodernism (which are also exhibited in some electronic or internet fantasies that appear more as distractions, moral depravity, or depravations and misappropriation of resources and energy) is to bring our children back to the rich treasures of the ethics of our ancestors as implanted in history. This is the only way that we can perceive the purpose, the sense, and the genuine finality in history and in the totality of life. This is the only way that life can be worth living. Thus, Simon Schama explains with a rhetorical question:

> Who is it that needs history the most? Our children, of course: the generations who will either pass on the memory of our disputatious liberty or be not much bothered about the doings of obscure ancestors and go back to Facebook for an hour or four. Unless they can be won to history, their imagination will be held hostage in the cage of eternal the Now: the flickering instant that's gone as soon as it has arrived. They will thus remain, as Cicero warned, permanent children, forever innocent of whence they have come and

---

[550.] J. MARITAIN, *On the Use of Philosophy: Three Essays* (New York: Atheneum, 1965), 12.

correspondingly unconcerned or, worse, fatalistic about where they might end up.[551]

As we emphasize the point that the education of our children or our youths should be more of a priority for the good of our society, we must also recommend the absolute importance of African history for all, Africans and non-Africans, taking into account that Africa is the foundation of humankind. It was already mentioned in this work that the history of the world from whatever point of view would be handicapped and wanting without a profound knowledge of African history. This fact is again strengthened by the following words of the William Edward Burghardt DuBois:

> Africa is an old and storied continent. It is probable that out of Africa came the first civilization of the world, and certainly, in that continent, the tragedy of the history of mankind has played its greatest part. To the Grecian world, to the Roman Empire, as well as to the American and modern European world, Africa has been of supreme importance, and it is well worthwhile to know something of its peculiar situation, history and meaning.[552]

Real development, we insist, is not merely a matter of machines or technology but, above all, a matter of people's mentality and their heartfelt disposition toward other people; it is, thus, the fundamental attitudes that people have toward life in general, a life that places the terrestrial and transcendental values of the human person at the center focus of every transaction. This is exactly what Thierry Verhelst says in his book, *No Life without Roots, Culture and Development*, as he asserts that "real development is not photogenic, since, above all,

---

[551.] S. SCHAMA, "My Vision for History in Schools" in *Guardian* (2010), of 9 November 2010.

[552.] W. E. B. DuBois, *Africa*, 3.

it takes place in people's hearts and minds."[553] In the case of Africa, therefore, one can perceive, following the tender fraternal and benevolent disposition of the traditional African hearts as evident in the traditional African culture, that theirs was a culture that bore solid grains of development. Such grains of development only needed to have been nurtured, but unfortunately, they were ruptured at some point, and on the contrary, Africa was instead stripped of its identity and later declared underdeveloped till date. It is in this connection that Thierry Verhelst again makes the following declaration:

> When a people is stripped of its identity, it is no longer capable of self-determination. Society, in such a case, disintegrates and is no longer able to function as a society. Such is the ultimate outcome of "underdevelopment," which Vincent Cosmao so aptly describes as "accident caused by one society being in contact with another which is in a dominant position." Underdevelopment is, therefore, the result, rather than the starting point of Third World people's recent history. The real tragedy of "underdevelopment" is that of the gradual destruction of consciousness, by forcing people into dependency. The internalized negotiation of one's self and thus of one's real vitality.[554]

Thierry Verhelst again struggles to convince us that the whole idea of the Western world assisting the Third World in the name of development is nothing but "miss-development" and excessive Eurocentrism and Westernization, a theory which has not only failed but

---

[553.] T. VERHELST, *No Life without Roots, Culture and Development*, B. CUMMING, trans., (London: Zed Books Ltd., 1990), 4.
[554.] T. VERHELST, *No Life without Roots, Culture and Development*, 61.

has equally been destructive to the local people as he explains the following:

> It is unnecessary here to reiterate this theory of development-as-Westernization, which has not only failed to rescue the Third World from poverty, but also dangerously increased the latter's dependence in economic, political and cultural terms and, in certain cases, has accelerated the disturbing depletion of its natural resources and quality of life.[555]

Thierry Verhelst equally proposes education as a kind of solution to this unfortunate reality. To a very great extent, he subscribes to the educational system proposed by Paolo Freire in his book *L'Éducation, Pratique de la liberté* and *Pédagogie de L'opprimé*, which focuses on the consciousness-awareness literacy program. Such a program awakens the awareness of a people who are the principal agents of their liberation.[556]

Historians seem to agree today that Africa was the first continent where the first existing creatures or, more precisely, human beings were traced. It is also proven historically that civilization started in Africa. "The recent archaeological discoveries by the Leakeys in 1959 of Zinjanthropus boisie, the oldest toolmaker, Homo sapiens, has convinced the world that the garden of Eden was in Africa and that Africa was the cradle of human civilization."[557] History testifies that Egypt was an empire before Greece. Most of the ancient Greek thinkers, such as Thales, Homer, and Herodotus, whose influence on world thinking today is often celebrated, either studied in Egypt or had some academic link to Egypt. It is the observation of Innocent Onyewuenyi that "even Aristotle confirmed that the Egyptians were

---

[555] Ibid., 20.
[556] Cfr. Ibid., 20-23.
[557] I. C. ONYEWUENYI, *The African Origin of Greek Philosophy*, 24.

the first people to explain and justify their experiences, thus they created philosophy."[558]

Mansa Musa is confirmed as the richest person that has ever existed in the world. Mansa Musa was an African. He ruled Mali in the early thirteenth century. He equally had superb administrative skills. He was also reputed for his wisdom and military skills. In fact, Mali, at the time, was recognized as a world power, and Mensa was identified as one of the world's most splendid and powerful leaders.[559] It is also indicated that the standard of living in Mali at this time in terms of food and security could be compared to or was even better than in contemporary Europe.[560]

In the annals of history, it is testified that the origin of medical science is Africa. Even Herodotus, who went to Egypt himself, recorded that medicine is practiced among them and there is a compendium of medical writings by the ancient scholars of Egypt and Kush, with real prescriptions and scientific explanations on the concoction of herbs and drugs.[561] It has also been authenticated historically that the first medical practitioner was an African by name Imhotep, yet illogically, all allegiance goes to the European Hippocrates as the father of medicine. With regrets to such a historical paradox, therefore, Innocent Onyewuenyi affirms with further details:

> The first physician of antiquity of any fame was the black Egyptian Imhotep... Imhotep lived two thousand years before the Greek doctor, Hippocrates, who is called the father of medicine. It is an irony of history that African medical doctors are ignorant of the existence and contributions of Imhotep while swearing the oath of

---

[558.] I. C. ONYEWUENYI, *The African Origin of Greek Philosophy*, 35.

[559.] Cfr. J. P. Oliver, *Musa Mensah and the Empire of Mali* (Paperback, 2013), 61.

[560.] Cfr. Ibid., 87.

[561.] Cfr. Y. BEN-JOCHANNAN, *Blackman of the Nile* (Baltimore: Black Classic Press, 1989), 143.

Hippocrates and displaying it in their private offices[562]

The Carlsberg Papyrus 4, as Cheikh Anta Diop discovers, was designed to diagnose sterility in a woman and was copied word for word by Hippocrates, who was taught at the temple of Imhotep at Memphis where the work was well-preserved. It explains how a clove of garlic was used to treat sterility in a woman or to determine whether she would bear children.[563]

Even though Egypt is being highlighted, the fact remains that Egyptian civilization was equally stimulated by her intercultural interactions with Ethiopia, Uganda, and other parts of Africa.[564] Accordingly, no comprehensive history of the world or of any country or subject can be constructed or can be acclaimed as complete without making reference to Africa and to African history. Africa, by necessity, must always be a historical point of departure and a constant point of reference. Coupled with the values embedded in the African traditional system, one may be tempted to think that the Creator's intentions about how the world should be, essentially, is not far from the African notion, especially if we were to examine African interpersonal relationship alongside the version of Christian philosophy of history as Maritain presents.

It is cogent from the above, therefore, that if we were to challenge any dissident approach to history or if we were to search for an authentic approach to reality, we must take not only African history but also the African perception of history as our departure point in one way or another even if we were to eventually spice it with other value-based approaches. Already, we are recommending the Christian viewpoint of Jacques Maritain. Nevertheless, it is regrettable that African history, which is supposed to be the foundation of the history of mankind, is often overlooked and relegated to the background, if not completely distorted to serve some other inter-

---

[562.] I. C. ONYEWUENYI, *The African Origin of Greek Philosophy*, 51.

[563.] Cfr. C. A. DIOP, *Civilization or Barbarianism* (New York: Lawrence Hill Books, 1991), 283.

[564.] Cfr. Ibid., 74-76.

ests. It is even more regrettable that even some African thinkers do not really move out confidently in support and in acclamation of their cultural beliefs under misconceptions and even demolition, valuable as they are. Accordingly, we fully subscribe to the following words of Joseph Ki-Zerbo:

> L'Afrique est le berceau de l'humanité. Tous les savants du monde admettent aujourd'hui que l'être humain a émergé en Afrique. Personne ne le conteste, mais beaucoup de gens l'oublient. Je suis sûr que si Adam et Ève étaient apparus au Texas, on en entendrait parler chaque jour sur CNN. Il est vrai que les africains eux-mêmes n'exploitent pas suffisamment cet 'avantage comparatif' qui consiste en le fait que l'Afrique a été le berceau d'inventions fondamentales, constitutives de l'espèce humaine pendant des centaines de milliers d'années.[565]

The dynamism of culture, African culture inclusive, must be stressed again as we round off this section. Only naivety could make us to glorify the African traditional culture as if it had no flaws. In fact, with cultural integration and Christianity, certain excesses that happened in some areas, such as human sacrifice, the slave trade, and killing of twins, were radically eliminated while some Christian values, such as monogamous marriage, were accepted and amalgamated

---

[565.] (Africa is the cradle of humanity. All the scholars of the world admit today that human beings emerged from Africa. No one disputes it, but many people forget it. I'm sure that if Adam and Eve had appeared in Texas, we would hear about it every day on CNN. It is true that Africans themselves do not sufficiently exploit this "comparative advantage" which consists in the fact that Africa has been the cradle of fundamental inventions, constituting the human species for hundreds of thousands of years.) J. KI-ZERBO, À Quand L'Afrique?, 10.

into the culture. Yet our point remains valid, irrespective of cultural dynamism, that there is no life without roots.[566]

We are also insinuating, with the challenges of postmodernism, post-colonialism, and multicultural realism that the African culture must be studied as embedded in African history. One of the most standard definitions given to the word *culture* is that of Sir Edward Tylor as "that complex whole which includes knowledge, belief, arts, morals, law, custom, and any other capabilities and habits acquired by man as a member of society."[567] Following our adherence to this definition, we must entirely endorse the perception of James Peacock that culture is a social affair, not the property of an individual and that it is learned rather than inherited biologically.[568]

As belabored by Ki-Zerbo, so too is Kenneth Kaunda contending that the Africans must be taught to be aware of and to regain their lost dignity, bearing in mind that colonization emptied Africans of their real value, the value of fraternal consciousness. Africans, Kaunda reminds us, have always been humanistic; they have always concentrated on the human person's intrinsic and extrinsic significance. Thus, he sorted to reenact this system via practical education, not merely by concentrating on men and women in the cities but by improving on the social organizations and the social conditions of the people.[569] To be more practical, we have to visit traditional Africa and discover their system of education, but initially, we must situate the concept of education in the African traditional context.

10.3.1.1 The Concept of Education in the African Perspective

Like many other terminologies and concepts, the term *education* has been assigned a variety of meanings by different scholars

---

[566.] Cfr. A. BOAHEN, ed., *General History of Africa*, vol. VII, *Africa Under Colonial Domination 1880–1935* (Nairobi: Heinemann Educational Books Ltd., 1985), 488.

[567.] S. E. TYLOR, *Primitive Culture*, vol. 1 (New York: J. P. Putnam's Son, 1920), 1.

[568.] Cfr. J. L. PEACOCK, *The Anthropological Lens* (second ed.) (Cambridge: Cambridge University Press, 1997), 3.

[569.] Cfr. M. N. NKEMNKIA, *African Vitalogy*, 63.

and philosophers, and in the end, one finds "no univocal definition of education as the concept has been exposed to different and often contradictory interpretations."[570] Nevertheless, we can better understand the African notion of education if we interpret or study it with the background of the ancient Latin use of the word, that is, the Latin root *educere* which means to "lead out." As Schofield Harry explains, *educare* is also used, and it is most preferable; it means to "form" or "train."[571] Fundamentally, this is how the Africans understand education—to train and to form the young ones especially, assisting them to grow according to the norms of the society, societies that were basically humanistic in their values."

In a broader sense, education in the traditional African perspective is aimed at facilitating the individuals to survive in the society and to nurture good habits, habits that would enable the development of good citizens who are capable of taking care of themselves and of others, who are capable of taking care of their personal values as well as community values. The conception of education, therefore, is its utility in developing skills that can make one to survive morally, economically, and socially, making one an integral part of a larger body—the society.

Though classroom education existed in some other forms, the emphasis was for the community. Therefore, based on the philosophy of communalism, it is the responsibility of the community to ensure that children are raised suitably and that as they develop into adulthood they will provide for the older members of the community. Thus, it is said that character training was central to traditional education. Parents preferred their children to be upright, honest, sociable, courageous, humble, considerate, persevering, daring, truthful, and well-behaved always and would spare no pain to inculcate these qualities into the child. Therefore, childhood is perceived as the foundation which determines the worth of a society. What practical dimension?

[570.] B. O. ABIODUM, "The idea of an 'Educated Person' in Contemporary African Thought," *The Journal of Pan African Studies*, (2008), vol. 2(3), 228.

[571.] Cfr. S. HARRY, *The Philosophy of Education* (London: George Allen & Unwin, 1972), 32.

10.3.1.2. Traditional African Education

In the traditional African society, young children begin to study their physical environment once they learn to play games with the elements that are commonly used in their locality, be it clay, wood, animals, twigs, birds, grass, or water. The games usually replicate real-life experiences. As they grow older, they start getting apprenticeship and learn by doing, either under the guidance of their father or elder brother, or under someone specialized in a particular job or profession in that locality or elsewhere. At the early stage, it is informal and playful, and then it starts getting serious and formal with age and time. The beginning, therefore, is based on informal apprenticeship with kin and early participation in the workforce. Special skills, such as medicine, music, craft, among others, are acquired through more formal apprenticeship with specialized persons. Other special skills, such as tree felling, hunting, and metallurgy, are taught by religious leaders during initiation ceremonies.[572]

Education is also acquired by use of an extensive collection of nonverbal arts, proverbs, myths, or other forms of stories, which help attract people's interest. Children and young people gather in one compound time and again, especially in the evenings, at sunset, to learn these in many practical ways. Again, in all these systems, traditional and societal values were transmitted. Jomo Kenyatta, from the *Gikuyu* experience of Kenya, gives us a good summary of traditional African education in the following words:

> Education begins at the time of birth and ends with death. The child has to pass various stages of age-groupings with a system of education defined for every status in life. They aim at instilling into the children what the Gikuyu call "*otaari wa mocie*" or "*kerera kia mocie*," namely, educating the children in the family and clan tradition.

[572.] Cfr J. R. RAYFIELD, *The Legacy of Colonialism in Education in West Africa*, mimeo paper (Toronto, 1983), 1.

> Apart from the system of schools which has been
> introduced by the Europeans, there is no special
> school building in the *Gikuyu* sense of the word:
> the homestead is the school... This is one of the
> methods by which the history of the people is
> passed from generation to generation.[573]

Sex education was another major theme highlighted in traditional African education, considering the important role of sexuality in human life. In the indigenous classrooms, the physiology of sexual relations, the duty of procreation, and other rules of conduct in married life and the dangers of being promiscuous were taught to the youths with many taboos attached to them so as to guide the people against evils, such as rape, teenage pregnancy, stealing, murder, and other vices, within the community. Many of the taboos were meant to deter the youth from indulging in sexual activities at a tender age and were, therefore, used to complement the teachings through proverbs, folktales, and riddles.

Each child was taught social etiquettes of the community and clan, agricultural methods, and others that ensured the smooth running of the social entity of which he was an integral part. The boys observed and imitated their father's craft and learned practical skills which they performed according to their capacities as they matured into manhood and were now heads of their own households. The education of girls was differentiated from that of boys in accordance to the roles each sex was expected and socialized to play for the remainder of their adult lives.[574]

Inferring from the above, one can trace three main advantages of traditional education: It was effective because children learned practically how to function in the society. It was somehow harsh and severe, yet every child who survived them could "graduate"; the cost of education (e.g., paying masters and religious leaders) was not pro-

---

[573.] J. KENYATTA, *Facing Mount Kenya* (London: Mercury Books, 1961), 99-100.
[574.] Cfr. Ibid., 95-124.

hibitive, and, finally, children were not completely withdrawn from other domestic and societal duties.

Our suggestion, especially for Africa, is that the Western system that is presently being followed, of education, should be adapted to fit into the scheme of the traditional African system of education. In this case, studies become more holistic and relevant to values.

10.3.2 The Need for a Genuine Humanism in Intercultural Studies

Our recombination for a genuine humanism in intercultural studies is as a result of two major realities or conclusions that have already been arrived at in this work. The first is that multiculturalism is a reality in the world today, considering that one cannot do without culture which flows from our very history and from our being part of an existing human society. The second conclusion we have made is that the concept of history cannot be approached from any direction without the human person being the very nucleus. This has generated the concept of humanism which has also been well elaborated in this work. Yet as earlier explained, following the challenges of postmodernism, the very concept of culture is under threat as some cheekily declare that cultures do not exist any longer while others claim that there is no need referring to it, insinuating that even the concept of history is irrelevant, being of no service to humanity.

We have already given our prospective concerning the relevance of the concept of history. We have also recommended the humanistic version of Ki-Zerbo and Jacques Maritain, yet we still have further recommendations to give at this level which would certainly transcend the humanism of Maritain into a more practical ambient. Such humanism must be lived concretely in the inescapable terrain of multiculturalism. Therefore, we talk of a genuine humanism in intercultural studies.

Our proposal of a genuine humanism does not, in any way, diminish our admiration for the humanism of Jacques Maritain or the African valorization of the human person as emphasized by Ki-Zerbo. Our preoccupation, however, is a means of meeting up more convincingly with the challenges of today's society. Accordingly, we have perceived the need to bring humanism much more from the books to reality, from the ivory tower to the grassroots, from literature, stagnation, or theory to practice, and from the offices to the streets and the houses. In this respect, speaking from a solid theological and existential perspective and within the background of the various philosophies of personalism traceable in history, Bernard Häring reminds us:

> Today's personalism is not an abstract philosophy, not a product of thinkers in an ivory tower. Only those philosophers and theologians are heard today who have themselves intently listened to the experience of men, to their problems and questions, their anxieties and hopes and perhaps have shared these in their own suffering and in compassion with their fellow men.[575]

It is this radically practical dimension that inflames our desire to insist on a transition from the Thomistic humanism to that of Karol Wojtyla (who later became Pope John Paul II). The humanism of Karol Wojtyla transcends that of St. Thomas because the former handles and gets involved in more practical life experiences, thereby living personalism and not only proclaiming it. Already as a professor in the University of Lublin, he published *Love and Responsibility* in 1981, inspired by the experiences he had in his relationships with young Catholics in their search for love and a true meaning in life. It is in view of this that Avery Dulles makes concrete comments to a paper presented by Karol Wojtyla himself in 1961 titled *Thomistic Personalism* as follows:

> While enthusiastically affirming the teaching of Thomas Aquinas on most points, Wojtyla took note of one weakness: That St. Thomas paid too

---

[575.] B. Haring, *Morality Is for Persons* (London: Vision Press Ltd., 1972), 6.

little attention to the human person as experienced from within... St. Thomas gives us an excellent view of the objective existence and activity of the person, but it would be difficult to speak in his view of the lived experiences of the person.[576]

The theodicy of Karol Wojtyla takes a more practical and human dimension than that of Thomism. It is observed that at least since the time of Thomas Aquinas, in the domain of natural theology, the standard arguments have been based on the principle of causality, contingency, the degrees of perfection, and the principle of finality. Pope John Paul II does not refute them as such, yet he is curiously silent about them. Alternatively, he takes his point of departure from the longings of the human heart for personal communion with others and with the divine. Making use of the personalist philosophers such as Martin Buber, Nicolas Berdiaeff, and Emmanuel Levinas, the pope insinuates that the authentic path of humanism or personalism instead should pass not so much through being and existence as in Thomism, as through people and their meeting each other in coexistence and dialogue, for through each other, we encounter God as the ultimate Thou.[577] It is from this perspective that he incorporates the principles of phenomenology in his humanism.

Karol Wojtyla, we must remember, grew up at a time when Communism was prominent, especially in his own country, Poland. Communism, like Marxism, goes with atheism. Karl Marx had declared that "religion is the opium of the people." According to the research of Richard Rousseau, John Paul II summarily considered that Communism, like Marxism, is "an unjust and totalitarian system," and he is remarkably known for the very significant role he

---

[576.] A. DULLES, "John Paul II and the Mystery of the Human Person" in *America: The National Catholic Review* (2004), of February 2, 2004.

[577.] Cfr. A. DULLES, "John Paul II and the Mystery of the Human Person" in *America: The National Catholic Review*.

played in bringing about the fall of Communism.[578] He did not stay indifferent to the Nazi oppressive system in the West, and as a pope, on March 12, 2000, he asked for forgiveness for many of the church's past sins, including the unfair treatment of Jews and heretics, as well as for other sins against humanity.

The philosophical trend that was propagated by some existentialists in his days also gave a good foundation for the humanistic philosophy of John Paul II. After endorsing Albert Camus's position that life is an absurdity and under the influence of Nietzsche's pessimistic philosophy of nihilism, for example, Jean Paul Sartre went on to publish *Being and Nothingness*. In this book, he declared that freedom is logically contingent upon the fact that man is nothing and that human reality is its own nothingness. Under this condition, freedom can be nothing other than this nihilism.[579] Therefore, "man is nothing but the pure nihilation of himself."[580] In his book, *Existentialism and Humanism*, he insinuates that there is no plan, order, or essence in nature and that human beings have no essence before their existence because there is no Creator. Hence, his conviction is that existence precedes essence.[581]

The fact that Pope John Paul II based his first encyclical letter, *Redemptor Hominis*, promulgated on March 4, 1979, on the dignity and redemption of the human person, reveals another practical dimension of his humanistic philosophy. The central issue in this document is that from the mystery of the incarnation, God united Himself to the human person and the human person became a partaker of God's life.[582] The Holy Father, therefore, insists that the giant leap in technological development can only become meaningful if it

---

[578.] Cfr. R. ROUSSEAU, "John Paul II: A Catalyst in the Fall of the Berlin Wall and Communism in Europe," in the *Journal of Turkish* Weekly (2009), of Monday, 9 November 2009.

[579.] Cf. J. P. SARTRE, *Being and Nothingness*, in H. BARNES, trans. (London: Methuen & Co Ltd., 1957), 439.

[580.] Ibid., 611.

[581.] Cfr. J. P. SARTRE, *Existence and Humanism* (New Haven: Yale University Press, 1946), 27.

[582.] Cfr. JOHN PAUL II, *Redemptor Hominis*, n. 182.

is done with the recognition of the values embedded in the human person. Thus, he appeals for the recognition of ethics or Christian Personalism amid human progress, particularly technological and social progress as he says the following:

> The development of technology and the development of contemporary civilization, which is marked by the ascendency of technology, demand a proportional development of morals and ethics... But the question keeps coming back with regard to what is most essential—whether in the context of this progress human beings are becoming truly better, that is to say, more mature spiritually, more aware of the dignity of their humanity, more responsible, more open to others, especially the neediest and the weakest, and readier to give and to aid all.[583]

It is also observed that, like John Paul I, John Paul II chose a name which combined the names of the two popes of the Second Vatican Council (1962-65), John XXIII and Paul VI, in order to emphasize that he was committed to the legacy of the council in which he had been an active participant. This commitment is much observed in *Redemptor Hominis*, following the great emphasis that the pope laid on the immense accomplishment of *Gaudium et Spes* and on *Dignitatis Humanae*. These are all documents that are constructed on the fundamental principles of humanism. As if to summarize them, in *Redemptor Hominis* that follows the methodology of *Gaudium et Spes*, John Paul II shares his firm convictions that technological power can lead not only to human progress but also to nuclear war and environmental destruction. It can also widen rather than close the gap between the rich and poor. Hence, there must be "a priority of ethics over technology"[584] so that our technological cre-

---

[583.] JOHN PAUL II, *Redemptor Hominis*, n. 15.
[584.] Ibid., n.16.

ativity is put to the service of human solidarity. He insisted that "the person is the subject of the community; therefore, the community must have an inter-human, interpersonal character."[585]

It is immensely ingrained in the thought of John Paul II that the human person realizes himself in every act. For this reason, he finds the answer to profound personalism in phenomenology. The person is not just a theoretical term but a structure of the praxis, and we must always remember that ethics is a practical philosophy. It is in this regard that while considering the categorical imperatives of Kant as being of a good service to ethics, he still intimates that they are too formal. According to him, Kant did not fully interpret the commandment of love, bearing in mind that the commandment of love is not limited to excluding all behavior that reduces the person to a mere object of pleasure. It requires more; it requires the affirmation of a person as a person.[586] Love implies more of good actions and not merely the evasion of wrongdoings.

As a practical example of his personalism, Wojtyla, in *Love and Responsibility*, passionately appeals that the doctors should be having friendly and hearty-hearty personal relationship with the patients and that people, generally, should handle one another with tenderness, tenderness that "springs from awareness of the inner state of another person...and his situation."[587] This is because "by assuming a human body and sharing in our human nature, Jesus teaches us what it means to be a witness to Love and how to be a witness to Love in and through our bodies."[588]

To this effect, the actual consideration of the human person is not only done in history but in reality, and the human person is considered in all his existential and transcendental qualities, yet it is not only a matter of consideration but also a matter of dealing with, a matter of mutual interaction while recognizing and respecting the

---

[585.] Ibid., n. 243.

[586.] Cfr. JOHN PAUL II, *Crossing the Threshold of Hope*, 201.

[587.] K. WOJTYLA, *Love and Responsibility* (Revised Edition) (London: William Collins and Sons Ltd., 1981), 202.

[588.] JOHN PAUL II, *Man and Woman He Created Them: A Theology of the Body* (Boston: Pauline Books & Media, 2006), 183.

cultures of others, specifically cultures that respect and value the human person. This is the implication of interculturalism. Therefore, while multiculturalism is the acknowledgment of the existence of many cultures, interculturalism goes with the actual participation or active involvement in the various cultural realities.

In advocating for a genuine humanism in intercultural studies, we must acknowledge and challenge the proliferation of the so many counter-humanistic ideas in our multicultural society today. It is not uncommon, for example, for advocates of multiculturalism like Richard Rorty, a humanities professor at the University of Virginia, to propagate the impression that truth is culturally based. Rorty's version of multiculturalism is that which assumes that since multiple descriptions of reality exist, no one view can be true in any decisive sense. Besides, he considers truth as a function of language, insinuating that all language is created by humans, thus concluding also that truth is created by humans.[589] There is no doubt that such an approach is inclined to relativism and skepticism.

Our conviction is that at all levels, truth cannot be relative and the truth about human history and about human values assures each person of his divinely invested dignity. Thus, only the recognition of human dignity in a given culture can supply a noble answer for the recurrent problem in the society today, which borders on how to mitigate the tension between the individual and the community. The problems of interculturality, in living together or in any other human activity, Wim Van Binsbergen explains, are not solved by pretending to assume the other's identity, but by finding ways of negotiating one's own identity *and* the other's in a jointly constructed new situation for which neither of the two identities has fully prepared either of the participants in that new situation; the solution, in other words, lies in creative innovation, negotiating between the various inputs and building them into a new.[590] In the same line of thought, Martin Nkafu explains that intercultural philosophy exists not only as a pas-

---

[589] Cfr. R. RORTY, *Contingency, Irony, and Solidarity* (Cambridge: Cambridge University Press, 1989), 5.

[590] Cfr. W. V. BINSBERGEN, *Intercultural Encounters*, 22

sive mingling between cultures but also as a confrontation that seeks to understand and live with other cultural values at the level of their corresponding history, economics, religious, and artistic convictions as he states thus:

> L'approccio interculturale si ripromette quindi di avviare un confronto tra diverse culture del mondo, nei loro aspetti storici, economici, religiosi, artistici ecc, così da promuovere atteggiamenti di rispetto delle specifiche identità e nel contempo facilitare una crescita comune, globale, di tutti gli appartenenti alla famiglia umana.[591]

Intercultural philosophy, in this regard, would create a certain awareness in each person not only in recognizing and valuing the existence of other cultures but also in tracing the real ingredient in these cultures that can propel authentic growth or development of each person, in himself or herself, as well as toward others and toward God, in any culture. Intercultural existence is a call and an invitation to reprimand the aspects of any culture that stifle genuine personalism or humanism while actually incorporating and practising those that highlight and propel the primary human values that make the human person to be authentically human.

Authentic humanism in intercultural studies rejects the idea of using other human beings as utensils or as a means of achieving some political or economic ends in the name of human rights. We, therefore, appreciate and recommend the ability of the Asian government to resist Western human rights pressure some years ago. This is because they recognized in this *gift* a way of pushing the European and the American socioeconomic and political culture into the East

---

[591.] (The intercultural approach, therefore, intends to start a confrontation among different cultures of the world, in their historical, economic, religious, artistic, etc., aspects so as to promote attitudes of respect for specific identities and, at the same time, facilitate a common, global growth of all the members of the human family.) M. Nkafu, *Aprire la Filosofia all'intercultura* (Bologna: Editrice Missionaria Italiana, 2003), 4.

as American and European businessmen were desperately anxious to expand their trade with their investment in the rapidly growing economy of Asia. The Japanese and other Asian government leaders reminded the United Nations that there are more human right threats in India, in some Latin American countries, Syria, Yemen, Southern Sudan that are of more urgent and practical priorities to be handled.[592]

Homosexuality and same-sex marriage are among other realities which are propagated in the world today, conceived and treated as a kind of culture, stemming from the Western world. Obviously, postmodern thinking conveniently fits such into the general picture of multiculturalism to be lived and adopted as a way of life. Yet within the context of our study of intercultural philosophy, they must be rejected and resisted, considering that objective morality would place them as a manifestation of inhumanity. Reasonably, therefore, and in fidelity to their culture, history, and tradition, most African nations are noted for their radical rejection of such practices, even at the risk of not receiving some foreign aid. Accordingly, in the *African Sun Times Magazine*, Chika Onyeani, in his article "Africa Rejects Homosexuality" states inter alia:

> From east to west and north to south, African countries have enacted laws banning the practice of homosexuality. Their contention is that homosexuality, same-sex marriage and their attributes are western-cultural lifestyle, inimical to the African culture, and any attempt by the western world to impose this kind of lifestyle on Africans in the African continent will be vigorously resisted, even at the cost of sanctions, e.g. withdrawing funding assistance. Currently, about 37 countries in Africa out of the 54 countries have laws that prohibit homosexuality, laws that

---

[592.] Cfr. S. P. HUNTINGTON, *The Clash of Civilization and the Remaking of World Order*, 194-195.

are described as quite harsh, with jail sentences running into many years.[593]

Chika Onyeani also observed that the African population in general has been violent toward the gay as a betrayal of their cultural values. In this regard, many African presidents have refused the pressure from the United Nations to legalize such practices and persistently allowed them as punishable in their penal code. He uses the Republic of Zimbabwe as one of the many examples, saying as follows:

> Since 1995, President Robert Mugabe of Zimbabwe has been employing vitriolic language to describe gays. After shutting down the gay book fair in Harare, he lambasted the gay community by saying, "Homosexuality degrades human dignity. It's unnatural, and there is no question ever of allowing these people to behave worse than dogs and pigs. If dogs and pigs do not do it, why must human beings? We have our own culture, and we must rededicate ourselves to our traditional values that make us human beings. What we are being persuaded to accept is a sub-animal behaviour and we will never allow it here."[594]

It is in accordance with our conviction that intercultural studies must imply the adaptation of cultures that respect humanistic values while radically shunning or rejecting those that propagate the reverse that we abide and subscribe to the idea of Wim Van Binsbergen

---

[593.] C. Onyeani, "Africa Rejects Homosexuality" in the *African Sun Times* (2014), of January 27, 2014.
[594.] Idem.

that intercultural studies must revolve around ethical values as he inscribes the following:

> Intercultural philosophy, therefore, has a prophetic function, not in the derived sense of foretelling the future, but in the original (Greek and biblical) sense of uninvitedly speaking to contemporary society about its ills, predicaments and alternatives, while invoking a transcendent value or being.[595]

It is for the above reason that intercultural philosophy should never be mistaken for postmodern propagation of cultural relativism or the suppression of culture. Ram Adher Mall, following our trend of thought, explains that it is wrong to think that intercultural philosophy is just a trendy expression in the wake of postmodern thinking. "Despite the liberal pluralism common to both intercultural philosophy and postmodern thinking, far from being an outcome of postmodernity, intercultural philosophy exists in its own right, it is beyond mere temporality, historicity and contextuality."[596]

It is within such a clarification that we fit in the theocentric aspect of interculturalism, insisting that the values in each human person must be respected, having concluded with Ki-Zerbo and with Maritain that history started with God creating man, who is the center of history, and man, whose earthly life ends with his accommodation into the spiritual world, ultimately controlled again by God. The beginning and the end of history, ultimately rests in God. Therefore, if man is the center of history, it is because of his divine inheritance. Effectively, therefore, God is the center of history, and by this fact, he should be at the center of events in the world. Focusing on God as the core of history would imply focusing not only on man as he is but also on the sacred in man, that is, his transcendental quali-

---

[595.] W. V. BINSBERGEN, *Intercultural Encounters*, 49.
[596.] R. A. MALL, *Intercultural Philosophy* (Boston: Rowman & Littlefield Publishers Inc., 2000), xii.

ties which distinguish him from any other creatures in the universe. Huntington seems to be reasoning in the same light. He realizes and confirms that from sociology, globalization theory produces a similar conclusion thus:

> In an increasingly globalized world, characterised by historically exceptional degrees of civilization, societal and other modes of interdependence and widespread consciousness thereof, there is an exacerbation of civilizational, societal and ethnic self-consciousness. The global religious revival, "the return to the sacred," is a response to people's perception of the world as "a single place."[597]

The sacred in this case would imply the ethical values which must constitute an integral part of every social structure in the present multicultural world. To this effect, with reference to democracy which seems to be the most highly propagated and assumed form of government today, and as regards values and culture, with concrete reference to Africa and the entire world, we shall finalise this chapter with following pronouncement of Joseph Ki-Zerbo:

> Democracy and development, perceived as nation building, simply cannot be achieved outside the cultural context. Without a culture of democracy, the transition to political democracy is nothing but empty words. Without the cultural foundations for endogenous development, the millions spent on aid are simply poured into a bottomless pit, as the last 30 years have proved. As for the creation of "national" identity, this can come into being only if it is founded on values and a societal model that extend beyond boundaries: even if the common space is not linguistic in the strict

---

[597.] S. P. HUNTINGTON, *The Clash of Civilization and the Remaking of World Order*, 68.

sense of the word, it must allow communication, it must be a space in which everyone is engaged in the same fundamental project. This is where history can intervene, cradling the same memories and awakening a thirst for a shared future. National reality should first be cultural reality, neither solely "racial," nor solely economic, nor solely military or political.[598]

General Conclusion

In the accent of Joseph Ki-Zerbo, we have established the African conception of history with an effort to compare it with other views, focusing of the Western and Thomistic thinker, Jacques Maritain. The central point in this work is that history involves the fundamentals of cultural and traditional practices, and in this regard, whether written or oral, it remains a point of reference and a history of a people. The dynamism of the African culture was well established as it was noticed that there are many cultural practices that no longer exist in Africa as a result of intercultural encounters. One striking issue concerning the African and Eastern conception of history is that, for them, history is sustained in tradition and that which is the traditional is also the religious. Emile Durkhem (1858-1917) considers religion in terms of social interactions or organizations. According to him, human being cannot live without an organized structure.

In his account, therefore, since it is a natural thing to live together, religion is there to bind society together. This, for him, is what makes religion different from private belief.[599] Religion is generally taken to mean a set of beliefs concerning the cause, nature, and purpose of the universe, especially in relation to a superhuman agency or superhuman agencies. It usually involves devotional and ritual observances, and it often contains moral codes governing the

---

598. J. KI-ZERBO, *Which Way, Africa?*, 16.

599. E. DURKHEIM, *The Elementary Forms of Religious Life* (London: George Allen & Unwin, 1915), p. 10.

conduct of human affairs. This is a strong message we have struggled to expound to the postmodern thinkers.

The Thomistic thought, represented by Jacques Maritain, bears the same ideas of personalism or humanism that are expressed in the African philosophy of history as expressed by Joseph Ki-Zerbo. We realized that almost all the theories of personalism or humanism propounded by Maritain are rooted in the traditional African culture. This inference motivated us more to look deeper into the African culture and to recommend Ki-Zerbo's lament for a rediscovery and application of African history, considering that it is rooted in authentic humanistic values. At the same time, we appreciated and recommended the Christian notion of history as presented by Maritain, which also borders on humanism. With the postmodern trend amid multiculturalism and globalization, we realized the difficulty of applying fully the Maritain philosophy of history that verges on humanism, as well as to revitalize the authentic Africa values which are also person- and community-centered, an idea which, as we also noticed, is as well very prominent in Confucianism and other oriental religions.

With the excesses of postmodernism, globalization, and multiculturalism that nurture a kind of moral, political, social, and religious laxity, we saw it as our concern to recommend, as a way forward, a reverberation of true personalistic values not only in Africa but also in the world at large. This, for us, is the pillar on which real development and authentic interculturalism can be built. This explains why our contribution to this work to make Africa and the world a better place to live in, first and foremost, anchored on education, educating the people, especially the youths. Such education, we insist, must begin from the knowledge of history, considering that there must be a foundation for any object or idea to be built, and history stands as the best foundation. We vehemently recommend, for obvious reasons, a special focus, for the world at large, on the study of African history. Considering the complications that have existed in the relationships between the West and the Africans, we find the following words of Edward Hall very relevant not only for the Africans but also for the world at large, especially the policy makers:

> For years, blacks have been regarded as under-developed whites, when in fact black culture is very rich in its own unwritten rules govern-ing behaviour. Recognition of black culture has always been important. Now it is critical... In fact the correct reading of all sensory inputs and their integration into a coherent picture is one of the most important things.[600]

Our second suggestion was to cultivate true humanism in a multifaceted world. This is where we redefined interculturalism, explaining that, in intercultural studies, we are not only copying other cultures and learning to live with them, but most of all, we are also sifting the good aspects of cultures to be copied and the negative aspects to be avoided or rejected. We criticized certain traditional African convictions and strongly recommended others, especially African humanism, as remedies to the challenges posed by postmod-ernism and interculturalism. Accordingly, we are to exercise some caution and stay clear of certain extremes while projecting Africa as a continent of rich historical and cultural values. It is in this respect that Bernard Fonlon makes the following remark:

> It is imperative to steer clear of two extremes: on the one hand, the imperialist arrogance which declared everything African as only fit for the scrap-heap and the dust-bin, and, on the other hand, the overly-enthusiastic and rather naïve ten-dency to laud every aspect of African culture as if it were the quintessence of human achievement.[601]

[600.] E. T. HALL, *Beyond Culture* (New York: Anchor Books, 1989), 82-83.
[601.] B. FONLON, "Idea of Culture II," in *ABBIA: Cameroon Cultural Review* (1967), n.16, 21–22.

BIBLIOGRAPHY

Primary Sources (by Our Main Authors)

Books

Ki-Zerbo, Joseph, *Histoire de l'Afrique Noire*. Paris: Hatier, 1972.

_____. *Storia Dell'Africa Nera, Un Continente fra la Preistoria e il Futuro*. Torino: Guilio Einaudi Editore, 1977.

_____. *L'Afrique Noire ; D'hier à Demain*. Paris: Librairie A. Hatier, 1978.

_____. *General History of Africa*, vol. 1, *Methodology and African Pre-History*. Oxford: James Currey Publishers, 1990.

_____. *La natte des autres (pour un développement endogène en Afrique)*. Paris: CODESRIA/Karthala, 1992.

_____. *À Quand L'Afrique?, Entretien avec René Holenstein*. Lausanne: Editions d'en bas, 2003.

_____. *Which Way, Africa?*. Nairobi: ISGN, 2007.

_____. *Punti Fermi Sull'Africa*. Translated by Marie-Jose Hoyet. EMI, 2011.

Maritain, Jacques, *Some Reflections on Culture and Liberty*. Chicago: Chicago University Press, 1933.

_____. *Les droits de L'homme*. Paris: Maison Française, 1942.

_____. *The Twilight of Civilization*. New York: Sheed & Ward, 1943.

_____. *The Person and the Common Good*. Translated by John J. Fitzgerald. London: Geoffrey Bless, 1948.

_____. *Man and the State*. Chicago: University of Chicago Press, 1951.

_____. *Creative Intuition in Art and Poetry*. New York: Pantheon Books, 1953.

_____. *On the Philosophy of History*. New York: Charles Scribner's and Sons, 1957.

_____. *St. Thomas Aquinas*. Translated by Peter O'Reilly and Evans Joseph. New York: Macmillan, 1958.

_____. *The Responsibility of Artist*. New York: Gordian Press, 1960.

_____. *La persona e il bene comune*. Brescia: Morcelliana Press, 1963.

_____. *On the Use of Philosophy: Three Essays*. New York: Atheneum, 1965.

_____. *L'institution Créatrice dans l'Art et dans la Poésie*. Paris: Desclée de Brouwer, 1966.

_____. *Bergsonian Philosophy and Thomism*. New York: Greenwood Press, 1968.

_____. *The Peasant of the Garonne*. New York: Macmillan, 1969.

_____. *Integral Humanism: Temporal and Spiritual Problems of a New Christendom*. Paris: Notre Dame University Press, 1973.

_____. *Christianity and Democracy and the Right of Man and Natural Law*. San Francisco: Ignatius Press, 1986.

_____. *The Rights of Man and Natural Law*. Translated by Doris Anson. San Francisco: Ignatius Press, 1986.

_____. *Arts and Scholasticism*. Translated by Evans W. Joseph. Oxford: Oxford University Press, 2005.

_____. *Scholasticism and Politics*. Translated by Mortimer J. Adler. Indianapolis: Liberty Funds Inc., 2011.

Articles

Ki-Zerbo Joseph, *United Nations Scientific and Cultural Organization*, UNESCO/EDAF/S/5, Paris (1961).

_____. *UNESCO Courier* (September 1993).

_____. *The Right Livelihood Award* (1997).

_____. *International Bureau of Education*, vol. XXIX, UNESCO (2000).

_____. *Pambazuka News*, n. 256 (2006).

_____. *Dossier* (April 2013).

Internet Material

Ki-Zerbo, Joseph, URL:<*http://www.fondationki-zerbo.org/IMG/ pdf/A_propos_de_culture-Joseph_Ki-Zerbo.pdf*> (accessed March 13, 2014).

Works on Our Main Authors

Dougherty, Jude. P., *Jacques Maritain, an Intellectual Profile.* Washington, DC: Catholic University Press, 1984.

Hudson, Deal. W., and Matthew. J. Mancini. *Understanding Maritain, Philosopher and Friend.* Macon, Georgia: Mercer University Press, 1987.

Secondary Sources

(Books Directly on Our Subject Matter)

Achebe, Chinua. *Hope and Independents.* London: Heinemann, 1988.

_____. *Things Fall Apart.* London: Heinemann Ltd., 1962.

Adorno, Di Theodore. *History and Freedom.* Cambridge: Polity Press, 2006.

Amadi, Elechi. *The Concubine.* London: Heinemann, 1966.

Augustine, St. *De Libero Arbitrio.* Translated by Dom Mark Pontifex. Westminster: Newman Press, 1955.

Augustine, St. *The City of God against the Pagans.* Translated by R. W. Dyson. Cambridge: Cambridge University Press, 1998.

Baradaran, Mehrsa. *The Color of Money: Black Banks and the Racial Wealth.* USA: Gap Har, 2017.

Binsbergen, Wim Van. *Intercultural Encounters (African and Anthropological Lessons towards a Philosophy of Interculturality).* London: New Brunswick, 2003.

Boahen, Adu, ed. *General History of Africa,* vol. VII, *Africa under Colonial Domination 1880–1935.* Nairobi: Heinemann Educational Books Ltd., 1985.

Brezik, Victor B., ed. *One Hundred Years of Thomism*. Houston, css, 1981.

Brown, Lee M., ed. *African Philosophy—New and Traditional Perspectives*. Oxford: Oxford University Press, 2004.

Clarke, John Henrick. *African World Revolution*. New Jersey: African World Press, 1996.

Cooper, David E., ed. *World Philosophies: An Historical Introduction*. Oxford: Blackwell, 1999.

Cooper, John Wesley. *The Theology of Freedom: The Legacy of Jacques Maritain and Reinhold Niebuhr*. Mercer: Mercer University Press, 1985.

Dawson, Christopher. *Dynamics of World History*. Edited by John J. Mulloy. Wilmington: Del.: ISI Books, 2002.

Diop, Cheikh, Anta. *Civilization or Barbarianism*. New York: Lawrence Hill Books, 1991.

DuBois, William Edward Burghardt. *Africa, Its Geography, People and Products*. New York: Kto Press, 1977.

Duignan Pete, and Lewis H. Gann, eds. *Colonialism in Africa 1870-1960*, vol. IV. New York: Cambridge University Press, 1975.

El Fasi, Mohammed M., and Ivan Hrbek, eds. *General History of Africa, Volume III, Africa From the Seventh to the Eleventh Century*. California: University of California Press, 1988.

Ela, Jean-Marc. *Innovations Sociales et Renaissance de L'Afrique: Défis du monde d'enbas*. Paris : L'Harmattan, 1998.

Ezeh, E. Chukwudi, ed. *African Philosophy, an Anthology*. Oxford: Blackwell Publishers, 1998.

Fingarette, Herbert. *Confucius—The Secular as Sacred*. New York: Harper and Row, 1972.

Gates, H. L., and S. O. Anozie. *Black Literary Theory*. New York: Routledge, 1990.

Gregory of Nyssa, St. *De beatitudinibus*, 1:PG 44, 1200D.

Hall, Edward T. *Beyond Culture*. New York: Anchor Books, 1989.

Hapgood, David. *Africa: From Independence to Tomorrow*. New York: Atheneum, 1970.

Haring, Bernard. *Morality Is for Persons*. London: Vision Press Ltd., 1972.

_____. *Shalom: Peace.* New York: Image Books, 1989.

Hume, Robert E. *The World's Living Religions.* New York: Charles Scribner's Sons, 1959.

Huntington, Samuel Phillips. *The Clash of Civilization and the Remaking of World Order.* New York: Simon & Schuster Paperbacks, 2003.

Hunziker, Peter, ed. *The Story of Africa.* London: K Gygax, 2005.

Kenyatta, Jomo. *Facing Mount Kenya.* London: Mercury Books, 1961.

Klunack, William. *Léopold Sédar Senghor, from Politics to Poetry.* New York: Peter Lang Publishers, 1997.

Legge, James. *The Four Books.* New York: Paragon Book Reprint, 1966.

Letter, Brian and Michael Rosen, eds. *The Oxford Handbook of Contemporary Philosophy.* Oxford: Oxford University Press, 2007.

Madu, Okere R. *African Symbols, Proverbs and Myths: The Hermeneutics of Destiny.* New York: Peter Lang, 1992.

Malinavaud, Edmond, and Mary Ann Glendon, eds. *Conceptualization of the Person in Social Science.* Vatican City: Pontifical Academy of Social Science, 2002.

Mall, Ram Adhar. *Intercultural Philosophy.* Boston: Rowman & Littlefield Publishers Inc., 2000.

Markovitz, Irving Leonard. *Léopold Sédar Senghor and the Politics of Négritude.* New York: Atheneum, 1969.

Masolo, Damis A. *African Philosophy in Search of Identity.* Nairobi: East African Educational Publishing, 1895.

Mazrui, Ali Al' Amin. *The African Condition (The Reith Lectures).* London: Heinemann, 1980.

_____. ed. *Julius Nyerere K, Africa's Titan on a Global Stage (Perspectives from Arusha to Obama).* Durham: Carolina Academic Press, 2013.

Mbae, Justus, ed. *Research and Documents (Property and Work in the Perspective of Inculturation).* Nairobi: Opus Matriae-Focolare, 1997.

MBITI, John Samuel. *African Religions and Philosophy*. London: Heinemann, 1969.

Michelet, Jules. *Introduction à l'histoire Universelle*. Paris : Librairie Plon, 1836.

Moila, Moeahabo Phillip. *Challenging Issues in African Christianity*. Pretoria: CB Powell Bible Centre, 2002.

Mondin, Battista. *Philosophical Anthropology*. Rome: Urbania University Press, 2005.

_____. *Uomini nel Mondo (Personal, Cultura e Valori nella Societa Globalizzata)*. Bologna : Editioni Studio Domenicano, 2005.

Mueller, Max, ed. *Sacred Books of the East*. Vol. 3. Ahmadabad : Krishna Press, 1910.

Ngal, Mpaang. *Aimé Césaire: Un homme à la Recherche d'une patrie*. Abidjan: Les Nouvelles Editions Africaine, 1975.

Niane, Djibril Tamsir, and Joseph Ki-Zerbo. *General History of Africa*, vol. IV, *Africa from the Twelfth to the Sixteenth Century*. California: University of California Press, 1984.

Nkemnkia, Martin Nkafu. *African Vitalogy (A Step Forward in African Thinking)*. Nairobi: Pauline's Publications Africa, 1999.

_____. *Aprire la Filosofia all'intercultura*. Bologna: Editrice Missionaria Italiana, 2003.

_____. *Dove Un Giorno Regnava la Foresta*. Milano: Paoline Editoriale Libri, 2014.

Nkrumah, Kwame. *Towards Colonial Freedom*. Edinburgh: Thomas Nelson and Sons Ltd., 1957.

_____. *Consciencism*. London: Heinemann, 1964.

Nyambura, Njoroge, and Musa W. Dube, eds. *Talitha Cum! Theology of African Women*. Pietermaritzburg: Cluster Publications, 2001.

Nyerere, Julius K. *Ujamaa: Essays on Socialism*. Nairobi: Oxford University Press, 1968.

Oduyoye, Mercy A. *Introducing African Women's Theology*. Sheffield: Sheffield Academic Press, 2001.

Ogot, Bethwell A. *Reintroducing Man into the African World*. Nairobi: Bookwise, 1987.

_____. *General History of Africa*, vol. 5. Berkeley: University of California Press, 1992.

_____. *My Footprints on the Sands of Time: An Autobiography*. Victoria: Trafford, 2003,

Olikenyi, George I. *African Hospitality*. Steylerverlag: Nettetal, 2001.

Olupona, Jacob K., ed. *African Spirituality, Forms, Meanings and Expressions*. New York: Crossroad Publishing Company, 2000.

Onwubiko, Oliver. *African Thought, Religion and Culture*, vol. I. Enegu: SNAAP Press, 1991.

Onyewuenyi, Innocent C. *The African Origin of Greek Philosophy*. Enegu: SNAAP Press Ltd., 1994.

Oruka, Henry Odera. *Sage Philosophy: Indigenous Thinkers and Modern Debate on African Philosophy*. Leiden: Brill E. J., 1990.

_____. *Sage Philosophy*. Nairobi: Acts Press, 1991.

Oxtoby, Willard G., ed. *A Concise Introduction to World Religions*. New York: Barnes and Nobles, 1997.

Parker, John, and Richard Rathbone. *African History, a Very Short Introduction*. Oxford: Oxford University Press, 2007.

Parrinder, Geoffrey. *Religion in Africa*. England: Penguin African Books Ltd., 1969.

Pavan, Antonio, and Emanuela Magno, eds. *Antropogenesi*. Milano: Società Editrice il Mulino, 2010.

Rainero, Romain. *Storia Dell'Africa; Dall'epoca Coloniale ad Oggi*. Italiana, Torino: Eri-Edizioni Rai Radiotelevisione, 1966.

Reader, John. *Africa: A Biography of the Continente*. New York: Vintage Books, 1999.

Reader, John, and M. Nicola, trans. *Africa, Biografia di un Continent*. Milano: Oscar Mondadori, 2003.

Rilley, Dorothy Winbush. *The Complete Kwanza, Celebrating our Cultural Harvest*. New York: Harper Collins, 1995

Rodney, Walter. *How Europe Underdeveloped Africa*. Nairobi: East Africa Education Publishers, 2005.

Rosalie, David. *The Ancient Egyptians: Religious Beliefs and Practices*. London: Routledge & Kegan Paul, 1982.

Ruch, Ernest A., and Kemafor C. Anyanwu. *African Philosophy, an Introduction to the Main Philosophical Trends in Contemporary Africa*. Rome: Catholic Book Agency, 1984.

Sartre, Jean Paul. *Black Orpheus*. Translated by S. W. Allen. Paris: Présence Africaine, 1976.

Senghor, Léopold Sédar. *Pierre Teilhard de Chardin et la Politique Africaine*, vol. 3. Paris: Editions du Seuil, 1962.

____. *On African Socialism*. New York, Praeger, 1964.

Smart, Ninian. *The World's Religions*. Cambridge University Press, 2002.

Smith, Huston. *The Religions of Man*. New York: Harper and Row, 1965.

Taliaferro, C., ed. *The Cambridge Companion to Christian Philosophical Theology*. Cambridge: Cambridge University Press, 2010.

Trapani, John. *Poetry, Beauty and Contemplation: The Complete Aesthetics of Jacques Maritain*. Washington, DC: Catholic University of America Press, 2011.

Tutu, Naomi. *The Words of Desmond Tutu*. London: Hodder and Stoughton, 1989.

Tylor, Sir Edward. *Primitive Culture*, vol. 1. New York: J. P. Putnam's Son, 1920.

Vaillant, John G. *Black, French, and African, a Life of Léopold Sédar Senghor*. London: Harvard University Press, 1990.

Viotto, Piero. *Jacques Maritain: Dizionario delle Opere*. Roma: Città Nuova Editrice, 2003.

Ware, James R., trans. *The Sayings of Confucius*. New York: New American Library, 1955.

Willett, Frank. *African Art*. Singapore: Thomas and Hudson Inc., 1993

Wiredu, Kwasi. *Cultural Universals and Particulars: An African Perspective*. Indianapolis: Indiana University Press, 1996.

Other Sources

Aquinas, Thomas. *Summa Theologica*, 1a. q. 89, a 8.

Asmal, Kader, ed. *Nelson Mandela, from Freedom to the Future*. Johannesburg: Jonathan Ball Publishers, 2003.

Augustine, St. *The City of God*, book 14, section 28.

Aylesworth, Gary. *Continental Philosophy IV, Gadamer and Hermeneutics.* London: Routledge, 1991.

Basti, Gianfranco. *Filosofia Dell'Uomo.* Bologna: PDUL Edizioni Studio Domenicano, 1995.

Barnett, Stuart, ed. *Hegel after Derrida.* London: Routledge, 1998.

Baudrillard, Jean. *Selected Writings.* Edited by M. Poster. Stanford: Stanford University Press, 1988.

_____. *Hegel.* London: Routledge, 2005.

ben-Jochannan, Yosef. *Black Man of the Nile.* Baltimore: Black Classic Press, 1989.

Benoist, Luc. *Signes, Symboles et Mythes.* Paris: PUF, 1975.

Bergson, Henri. *An Introduction to Metaphysics.* Translated by Thomas Ernest Hulme. New York: Putman's and Sons, 1912.

Best, Stephen, and Douglas Kellner. *The Postmodern Turn.* New York: Guilford Press, 1997.

Browne, Anthony. *The Retreat of Reason.* London: Hartington Litho Ltd., 2006.

Brdar, Mario. et al., eds., *Space and Time in Language.* Frankfurt: Peter Lang, 2011.

Buell, Raymond Leslie. *The Native Problem in Africa,* vol. II. New York: Atheneum, 1928.

Burnyeat, Myles. *The Theaetetus of Plato.* Translated by M. J. Levett. Cambridge: Hackett Publishing Co. Inc., 1990.

Cahoone, Laurence E., ed. *From Modernism to Postmodernism: An Anthology.* Oxford: Blackwell Publishers, 1999.

Cartey, Wilfred, and Martin. Kilson, eds. *The African Reader.* New York: Atheneum, 1970.

Cassirer, Ernst. *The Myth of the State.* New Haven: Yale University Press, 1946.

Charles, de Montesquieu. *De l'esprit des lois.* Garnier Frères, 1952.

Chinweizu, Ibekwe. *The West and the Rest of Us.* New York: Vintage Books, 1975.

Collingwood, Robin George. *Autobiography.* Oxford: Oxford University Press, 1993.

Constant, Isabelle, and Kahiudi C. Mabana, eds. *Négritude: Legacy and Present Relevance*. Cambridge: Cambridge Scholar Publishing, 2009.

Cooper, John Wesley. *The Theology of Freedom: The Legacy of Jacques Maritain and Reinhold Niebuhr*. Mercer: Mercer University Press, 1985.

Copleston, Frederick. *A History of Philosophy*, vol. VI. New York: Image Books, 1994.

Dawson, Christopher and Forsyth Thomas, eds. *Essays in Order*. New York: Sheed & Ward, 1940.

De Saussure, Ferdinand. *Cours de linguistique générale*. Paris: Payot, 1998.

Deleuze, Gilles. *The Logic of Sensei*. New York: Columbia University Press, 1990.

____. *Negotiations*. New York: Columbia University Press, 1995.

Derrida, Jacques. *Of Grammatology*. Maryland: John Hopkins University Press, 1997.

Dieng, Amady Aly. *Hegel et L'Afrique Noire; Hegel était-il raciste?*. Dakar: Imprimerie Graph Plus, 2006.

Donna, Oorange M. *Emotional Understanding*. Oxford: Oxford University Press, 1994.

D'Souza, Dinesh. *The End of Racism: Principles for a Multiracial Society*. New York: Free Press, 1995.

Douglas, Kellner. *Jean Baudrillard: From Marxism to Poststructuralism*. London: Blackwell, 1994.

Evans Richard. *In Defence of History*. London: Granta, 1997.

Featherstone, Mike. *Undoing Culture, Globalization, Postmodernism and Identity*. London: SAGA Publications Ltd., 2000.

Feyerabend, Paul. *Against Method*. London: Verso, 1975.

Findlay, John Niemeye. *HEGEL, a Re-Examination*. New York: Humanities Press Inc., 1970.

Finkielkraut, Alain. *The Undoing of Thought*. London: Claridge Press, 1988.

Fischer, Kuno. *Hegel's Leban, Werke und Lehre*. Heidelberg, 1911.

Fouda, Juléat B. *Philosophie Negro-Africaine de L'Existence*. Lille, 1967.

Gales, Henry Louis, and Sunday O. Anozie. *Black Literary Theory*. New York: Routledge, 1990.

Gadamer, Hans-Georg. *Truth and Method*. London: Sheed & Ward, 1975.

_____. *Philosophical Hermeneutics*. California: University of California Press, 1976.

Gerald, Bonner. *God's Decree and Man's Destiny*. London: Variorum Reprints, 1987.

Gillespie, Michael Allen. *Hegel, Heidegger, and the Ground of History*. Chicago: University of Chicago Press, 1984.

Glenn, Paul John. *An Introduction to Philosophy*. London: B. Harder Books Co., 1952.

Habermas, Jürgen. *Theory of Communicative Action, Vol. 1: Reason and the Rationalization of Society*. Translated by Thomas mccarth. Boston: Boston Beacon Press, 1984.

_____. *On the Pragmatics of Communication*. Edited by M. Cook. Cambridge: MIT Press, 1998.

_____. *L'Ethique de la Discussion et la Question de la Vérité*. Edited by Patric Savidan. Paris: Bernars Grasset, 2009.

Hammermeister, Kai. *The German Aesthetic Tradition*. Cambridge: Cambridge University Press, 2002.

Haring, Bernard. *Morality Is for Persons*. London: Vision Press Ltd., 1972.

Harry, Schofield. *The Philosophy of Education*. London: George Allen & Unwin, 1972.

Hegel, Georg Wilhelm Friedrich. *Lectures on the History of Philosophy, Vol. 1*. Translated by E. S Haldane. New York: Humanities Press, 1963.

_____. *Hegel's Aesthetics: Lectures on Fine Arts*, vol. 1. Translated by T. M. Knox. Oxford: Oxford University Press, 1975.

_____. *Lectures on the Philosophy of World History: Introduction*. Translated by H. B., Nisbet. Cambridge: Cambridge University Press, 1975.

_____. *Phenomenology of Spirit*. Translated by A. V. Miller. Oxford: Oxford University Press, 1977.

_____. *Reason in History*. Translated by R. S. Hartman. New Jersey: Prentice-Hall Inc., 1997.

_____. *The Philosophy of History*. Translated by J. Sibree. New York: Cosmo Classics, 2007.

Heidegger, Martin. *Being and Time*. Translated by J. Macquarie and E. Robinson. New York: Harper & Row, 1996.

Husserl, Edmund. *Logical Investigations*. Translated by J. N. Findlay. London: Routledge & Kegan Paul, 1970.

John Paul II (Pope). *Crossing the Threshold of Hope*. New York: Alfred Knopf Inc., 1995.

_____. *Man and Woman, He Created Them: A Theology of the Body*. Boston: Pauline Books & Media, 2006.

Kant, Immanuel. *Critique of Practical Reason*. Translated by W. Lewis. Cambridge: Cambridge University Press, 1956.

Kimpel, Ben. *A Vital Guide to Hegel's Philosophy of History*. Boston: Student's Online Company, 1963.

Lauer, Quentin. *Hegel's Idea of Philosophy*. New York: Fordham University Press, 1974.

Layman, Charles Stephen. *The Power of Logic*. New York: MaGraw Hill, 2005.

Lowith, Karl. *Meaning in History*. Chicago: University of Chicago Press, 1962.

Luper, Steven. *Existing, an Introduction to Existential Thoughts*. London: Mayfield Publishing Co., 2000.

Lyotard, Jean Francois. *Il Postmoderno Spiegato ai Bambini*. Milano: Giangiacomo Feltrinelli Editore, 1987.

_____. *La Condition Postmoderne, Collection Critique*. Paris: Les Editions de Minuit, 1979.

McRobbie, Angela. *Postmodernism and Popular Culture*. New York: Taylor & Francis e-Library, 2005.

Melady, Thomas Patrick P. *Profiles of African Leaders*. New York: MacMillan Company, 1962.

Mensch, James Richard. *After Modernity, Husserlian Reflections on a Philosophical Tradition*. New York: State University of New York Press, 1996.

Meseguer, Pedro. *The Secret of Dreams*. West Minster: Newman Press, 1961.

Messinese, Leodardo. *The Problem of God in Modern Philosophy*. Translated by Philip Larrey. Rome: Lateran University Press, 2001.

Moran, Dermot, ed. *The Routledge Companion to Twentieth Century Philosophy*. London: Routledge Tailor & Francis Group, 2008.

Munslow, Alun. *Deconstructing History*. London: Routledge, 1997.

Payne, Malcolm, and Gurid Aga. Askeland. *Globalization and International Social Work, Postmodern Change and Challenge*. Hampshire: Ashgate Publishing Ltd., 2008.

Peacock, James L. *The Anthropological Lens*, second ed. Cambridge: Cambridge University Press, 1997.

Peter, Green. *Alexander the Great*. London: Weidenfeld & Nicolson, 1970.

Piligliucci, Massimo. *Nonsense on Stilts, How to Tell Science from Bunk*. Chicago: University of Chicago Press, 2010.

Plamenatz, John Petrov. *Man and Society: From Montesquieu to the Early Socialists*, vol. II. New York: McGraw Hill, 1963.

Proctor, Bruce A. *A Definition and Critique of Postmodernism*. Chicago: Xulon Press, 2012.

Rayfield, John R. *The Legacy of Colonialism in Education in West Africa*. Mimeo paper. Toronto, 1983.

Ricoeur, Paul. *Finitude et Culpabilité II*. Paris: Aubier, 1960.

Rorty, Richard. *Contingency, Irony, and Solidarity*. Cambridge: Cambridge University Press, 1989.

Schilpp, Paul Author, ed. *The Philosophy of Bertrand Russell*. New York: Library of Living Publishers, 1951.

Stenger, Fritz., ed. *Africa Is Not a Dark Continent*. Nairobi: Pauline Publications Africa, 2005.

Stern, Alfred. *Philosophy of History and the Problem of Values*. The Hague: Mouton & Co. Publishers, 1962.

Stern, Robert. *Hegel and the Phenomenology of the Spirit*. London: Routledge, 2004.

Sweet, William. *The Philosophy of History, a Re-Examination*. Hampshire: Ashgate Publishing Limited, 2004.

Toynbee, Arnold. *A Study of History*, vol. 3. Oxford: Oxford University Press, 1947.

Tweyman, Stanley., ed. *René Descartes Meditation on First Philosophy in Focus*. New York: Routledge Taylor and Francis Group, 1993.

Verhelst, Thierry. *No Life without Roots, Culture and Development*. Translated by Bob Cumming. London: Zed Books Ltd., 1990.

Walsh, Martin J. *A History* of *Philosophy*. London: Cassell Ltd., 1985.

Weinert, Friedel. *Kant, Idea for a Universal History: A Running Commentary*. Bradford: Bradford University, 1784.

Wojtyla, Karol. *Love and Responsibility* (revised edition). London: William Collins and Sons Ltd., 1981.

Dictionaries And Encyclopaediae

Akyeampong, Emmanuel et al., eds., *Dictionary of African Biography*. Oxford: Oxford University Press, 2012

Audi, Robert, ed. *Cambridge Dictionary of Philosophy*. Cambridge: Cambridge University Press, 1999.

Benton, William, ed. *Encyclopedia Britannica*, vol. 7. London: Encyclopedia Britannica Inc., 1973.

Hill, McGraw. *The New Catholic Encyclopedia*. Washington, DC: CUA Press, 1967.

Inwood, Michael, ed. *A Hegel Dictionary*. Oxford: Blackwell Publishers Ltd., 2002.

Ladrière, Jean. *Encyclopédie Philosophique Universelle*, vol. 2. Paris: Press Universitaires de France, 1998.

Lenzerini. Federico. *The Culturalization of Human Rights Law*. Oxford: Oxford University Press, 2004.

Levinson, David, and Melvin Ember, eds. *Encyclopedia of Cultural Anthropology*, vol. 2. New York: Henry Holt and Company, 1996.

Macey, Samuel L., ed. *Encyclopaedia of Time*, vol. 810. Garland: Garland Reference Library, 1994.

Neilson, William Allan, ed. *Webster's New International Dictionary*, vol. 2. London: G. Bell & Sons Ltd., 1934.

Sills, David, L., ed. *International Encyclopedia of the Social Science.* Vol. 1. London: Collier-Macmillan, 1972.

Preece, Warren Eversleigh, ed. *Encyclopaedia Britannica,* vol. 17. London: William Benton Publishing, 1974.

Procter, Paul, ed. *Longman Dictionary of Contemporary English.* London: Longman Group Ltd., 1984.

Taylor, Victor E., and Charles E. Winquist. *Encyclopedia of Postmodernism.* London: Routledge Taylor and Francis Group, 2001.

Webster, Merriam. *Webster New Collegiate Dictionary.* New York: G & C. Merriam Co., 1956.

Unpublished Works

Odera, Oruka Henry. "The Philosophical Roots of Culture in Kenya." Government of Kenya, 1976.

Mbuy, Tatah Humphrey. "The Faith of Our Ancestors," (unpublished work). Rome, 2012.

Newspapers and Magazines

Brennan, Robert. *The Thomist,* vol. 5 (1943).

Cannadine, David. *Past and Present,* vol. 116, n. 987.

Collier, Paul, and Jan Willem Gunning. *Journal of Economic Perspectives,* n. 13 (1999).

Decalo, Samuel. *African Affairs,* vol. 91, n. 362 (1992).

Dulles, Avery. *America: The National Catholic Review* (February 2, 2004).

Fonlon, Bernard. *ABBIA: Cameroon Cultural Review,* n. 16 (1967).

Fowler, John. *Faith and Learning Seminar.* University of Eastern Africa, Baraton, Kenya (1998).

Imani, Nikitah Okembe-Ra. *The Journal of Pan African Studies,* vol. 5, n. 4 (June 2012).

Jenkins, Orville Boyd. *Focus on Communication Effectiveness* (1998).

Lessing, Doris. *The New York Review of Books* (2003), New York, of June 2000 and April 2003.

Lobkowicz, Nicholas. *Review of Politics*, vol. 53/2, spring (1991).

Maxwell, Owusu. *The Journal of Modern African Studies*, v. 30, n. 3, 1991.

Nkemnkia, Martine Nkafu. *Aquinas*, vol. 10/LIII (1999) 2-3.

Sanderson, Stephen. *International Journal of Comparative Sociology*, no. 46 (March 2005).

Schama, Simon. *Guardian*, (9 November 2010).

Senghor, Léopold Sédar. *Présence Africaine*, nn. 24-25 (1959).

_____. *Présence Africaine*, n. 78 (1971).

_____. *Discours à l'Assemblé National* (April 1963).

Tymieniecka, Teresa, ed. *Analytica Husserliana, the Yearbook of Phenomenological Research*, vol. LIX. Kluwer Academic Publications, London (1999).

Whitehead, William. *Journal of Education*, vol. XIV.

Zigliara, Tommaso Maria. *Summa Philosophica*, vol. 3, Paris (1889).

Internet Sources

Ayleworth, Gary. *Stanford Encyclopaedia of Philosophy*. Accessed on June 23, 2014. http://plato.stanford.edu/entries/post modernism.

Arne, Eide. *Disability and Poeverty: A Global Challenge*. Accessed on December 28, 2014. http: //books.google.it/books.

Daniel, Little. *Philosophy of History*. Accessed on June 20, 2014. http://plato.stanford.edu/entries/history>.

Feser, Edward. "The Thomistic Tradition," part 1. Accessed on April 14, 2015. edwardfeser.blogspot.it/2009/10/thomistic-tradi-tion-part-i.html? m-1.

Grills, Chery. Accessed on June 14, 2020. https://abc7.com/george-floyd-protests-los-angeles-downtown-la-dr-cheryl-grills/6222321/.

Jeffrey, Robinson. Accessed on June 14, 2020. https://www.mic.com/articles/184042/the-aclu-defends-the-free-speech-of-white-su-premacists-but-now-wants-confederate-monuments-removed.

Joshua, Zeitz, https://www.politico.com/magazine/story/2017/08/20/why-there-are-no-nazi-statues-in-germany-215510

Sharpton, Alin. Accessed on June 14, 2020. https://www.rev.com/blog/transcripts/reverend-al-sharpton-eulogy-transcript-at-george-floyd-memorial-service.

ABOUT THE AUTHOR

BASILE SEDE NOUJIO was born on December 28, 1970, in Fiango, Kumba, Cameroon. He did his secondary and high school studies in St. Francis College Fiango and Bishop Rogan College, Soppo, respectively. He then proceeded to St. Thomas Aquinas Major Seminary, Bambui, Cameroon, where he studied philosophy and theology for seven years while undergoing his priestly formation. He was ordained a Catholic priest on April 16, 1998.

After working in some parishes and institution in the Diocese of Buea, Cameroon, Basile was admitted into the Université Catholique D'Afrique Central, Yaoundé, where he obtained a master's degree in philosophy. He was appointed executive vice president of the Catholic University Institute of Buea (CUIB), Cameroon. In 2012, he enrolled into the Pontifical Lateran University, Rome, and obtained a PhD in philosophy in February 2016, specializing in philosophy of history and comparative studies.

While studying in Rome, he also enrolled into the Sophia University, Florence, where he took some courses in management sciences and economy of communion.

He has two books in his credit: *Catholic Religious Studies* and *Hegel's Philosophy of History, a Challenge to the African Thinker.*

Fr. Basile Sede now serves in the Diocese of Charlotte, North Carolina, and he is presently the pastor of Our Lady of Consolation Catholic Church.

CPSIA information can be obtained
at www.ICGtesting.com
Printed in the USA
BVHW072247240721
612192BV00003B/4